LEARNING TO LEAD
A Handbook for
Postsecondary Administrators

James R. Davis

AMERICAN COUNCIL ON EDUCATION
PRAEGER
Series on Higher Education

Library of Congress Cataloging-in-Publication Data

Davis, James R., 1936–
    Learning to lead : a handbook for postsecondary administrators / James R. Davis.
       p. cm.—(ACE/Praeger series on higher education)
    Includes bibliographical references and index.
    ISBN 1–57356–497–4 (alk. paper)
    I. Title. II. Series.
  LB2341.D35 2003
  378.1'11—dc21   2002029866

Formerly ACE/Oryx Press Series on Higher Education

British Library Cataloguing in Publication Data is available.

Library of Congress Catalog Card Number: 2002029866
ISBN: 1–57356–497–4

First published in 2003

Praeger Publishers, 88 Post Road West, Westport, CT 06881
An imprint of Greenwood Publishing Group, Inc.
www.praeger.com

Printed in the United States of America

∞™

The paper used in this book complies with the
Permanent Paper Standard issued by the National
Information Standards Organization (Z39.48–1984).

10 9 8 7 6 5 4 3 2 1

CONTENTS

PREFACE

Learning to Lead is designed for people in postsecondary institutions—community colleges, four-year colleges, universities, and proprietary schools—who shoulder and carry out administrative responsibilities. This surely includes presidents, provosts, deans, and department chairs, but also those in the myriad of professional and staff positions engaged in administrative functions across the campus. These include, to name a few, those who work in student affairs, athletics, finance, admissions, institutional research, development, and alumni relations. The audience also includes faculty, who often take on quasi-administrative functions in the development of centers, the administration of grants, or the development of programs. This book is for administrators, broadly defined, but it is primarily about leadership.

Leadership is a tricky concept, one that is not easy to pin down, and is often juxtaposed to administration, although most leaders know that effective leadership is balanced by able administration. The term *leadership* has often carried with it a connotation of elitism, that it is something exercised by a few people who reside somewhere near the top of the organization in positions of power and prestige. This is the traditional idea of leadership and seems to have great staying power, perhaps because it satisfies certain needs people have to let someone else be in charge. Formal leadership is still important, but more recently leadership has been recognized as an activity that can bubble up in various places in the organization and need not be associated only with formal leadership roles.

Leadership has been the object of vigorous formal study over the last half of the last century, and practical concepts of leadership have evolved over the years as the result of an emerging body of leadership theory.[1] In some respects, however, the study of leadership has left us more confused about leadership, even raising the question of whether leadership is actually possible.

This book is based on the following assumptions:

- *Leadership is possible.* Although a case can be made for the intractability of organizations and their stubborn resistance to change, leadership is more than symbolic.

- *Leadership is necessary.* Organizations seldom manage themselves, they usually resist change and they require sound and committed leadership to move ahead.

- *Leadership is both formal and diffuse.* Leadership comes from the few at the top as well as the many scattered in the far corners of the institution.

- *Leadership can be learned.* Although the context of leadership is important, certain basic leadership skills can be identified, learned, and transferred from one setting to another.

This book provides a broad overview of leadership and administration and a chapter-by-chapter presentation of the skills needed to be an effective leader. Although the book is designed for practicing administrators, or those who have at least some previous experience, it may also be used for leadership workshops, mentoring, or courses on leadership and administration in the formal study of higher education.

Colleges and universities are in many respects unique institutions but they are also organizations, and there is much to be learned about leadership from the broader literature on organizations. Books and articles on organizational structure, teamwork, conflict resolution, communication, work environments, quality, and change, now prominent in the business literature, often remain beyond the purview of college and university administrators. This literature is often drawn into the discussion in this book, with appropriate reservation about the unique context of higher education, to provide a broader perspective on leadership and administration than often occurs within academe. The more traditional literature on higher education, of course, has also been included.

The book is divided into ten chapters and is written in a style that accommodates the busy reader by providing a continuing case (about Mary) presented at the outset of each chapter, bulleted lists, **main points in bold**, and a list of lessons learned under the heading "Mary's Mentor" at the end of each chapter. Indented sections with the heading "Reflection" are included to provide the reader with opportunities to apply concepts to practical situations and take perspective on what is being described. A conscious decision was made not to seek out and provide illustrations from actual institutions because these are often limited by context, they quickly become outdated, and they run the risk of misrepresentation. Instead, the continuing case and the sections marked "Reflection" are designed to help readers generate their own illustrations drawn from personal experience in institutions where they work or have worked previously. This is not only a book to read, but one that invites interaction. It is designed to teach, in the best sense of the word, by providing enough information for the reader to make up his or her own mind about how to lead.

At the end of the book in the Appendix is a directory of selected key resources for continuing one's learning about postsecondary education, including information on higher education associations, key journals, magazines and newspapers, and key Web sites. The best source for further reading is the notes at the end of each chapter which contain the works cited, almost all of which deserve further study.

Having begun my career as the academic dean at a struggling, historically-black college during the turbulent times of the civil rights movement, I remember clearly my desperate need to learn everything I could about leadership and administration as fast as possible, and my complete lack of time to read or study. Fortunately our president, the late Rembert Stokes, became my mentor, providing day-by-day short courses in administration, race relations, and understanding human nature. Had I only known then what I know now! This book, therefore, is written partly to and for my former self, that novice administrator scrambling for the key to effectiveness, but also for the more seasoned, but still perplexed leader (which I became years later) who still has not read as widely or reflected as systematically on the field of higher education as might be advisable for greater success. Those readers who find they know most of what is presented here, probably will not have much trouble finding a colleague who does not, and can serve the cause of enlightened leadership by making the book available to them, perhaps even by reading it together with them as mentor and protégé.

Although this book has been designed for busy administrators, a sincere effort has been made to provide a scholarly discussion of each topic and to acquaint the reader with essential concepts drawn selectively from the best writing in the field. Concepts and theories are the lenses that help leaders see what they need to see to be effective. As the old adage states: If you don't know how to look, you will never see. The overall goal has been to provide a readable and useful book, but one of substance. The strategy has been to survey the literature, select the best ideas, organize and synthesize them, and provide useful insights and interpretations. The most useful literature for this project was found in books, handbooks, and summaries of research rather than in articles or on Web sites.

The scope of this book is broad, making it difficult for one author to be an expert on each chapter. In an age that emphasizes disciplinary subspecialization, few are bold enough to undertake a book like this, even when the need is great. Colleagues have provided their encouragement and readers have provided their specialized insights for each chapter. Even so, a book like this always feels like an unending work in progress. At some point in time, however, the text must be typeset. Comments from readers can be sent to: jdavis@du.edu.

NOTE

1. Estella M. Bensimon, Anna Newman, and Robert Birnbaum, *Making Sense of Administrative Leadership: The "L" Word in Higher Education* (ASHE-ERIC Higher Education Report No. 1) (Washington, DC: School of Education and Human Development, The George Washington University, 1989). See also the classic summary of research on leadership: Bernard M. Bass, *Bass and Stogdill's Handbook of Leadership: Theory, Research and Managerial Applications*, 3rd ed. (New York: Free Press, 1990).

ACKNOWLEDGMENTS

There are many people whose help with this work I want to acknowledge. I especially want to thank Mandy Anderson, who served as part-time research assistant to this project while carrying out her duties as project manager at the Center for Public Policy and Contemporary Issues at the University of Denver. A graduate of the master's program in Higher Education and Adult Studies, Mandy brought useful skills and energy to the task of literature search and to the compilation of the Directory of Resources. She led me to the right books and used her Internet search skills to track down the very detailed information for the Directory.

Credit for typing the manuscript through many drafts and revisions goes to my program assistant, Michelle Kruse-Crocker. Michelle is a Ph.D. candidate in Higher Education and Adult Studies and brought keen insights and valuable criticism to the text as well as patience and tireless persistence in putting ten handwritten manuscript chapters onto one small diskette. Thanks also to Sharon Irwin and Beverly Kohl for typing early drafts of initial chapters as well as the proposal to the publisher. Thanks also go to James Murray III at the American Council on Education, Susan Slesinger at Greenwood Publishing Group for seeing potential in the work, John Wagner for adding value to it through his expert editing, and to Rebecca Homiski for her work as production editor.

Colleagues at the University of Denver have read selected chapters where I felt I needed guidance or "double-checking." These include Michele Bloom, Dean of the Women's College and University College;

Richard Gartrell, Director of Human Resources; Fred Gibson, Director of the Pioneer Leadership Program; Alton Barbour, Professor of Human Communication Studies; Dean Saitta, Associate Professor of Anthropology; Virginia Maloney, Dean of the College of Education; Julie Nice, Professor of Law; Janet Allis, former Associate Provost for Budget and Planning; and Margaret Henry, Controller and Assistant Treasurer; Bruce Hutton, Professor of Marketing and former Dean of the Daniels College of Business; Doug Allen, Professor of Management; Catherine Alter, Dean of the Graduate School of Social Work; and James Griesmer, Dean of the Daniels College of Business. I also want to thank my immediate colleagues in Higher Education and Adult Studies, Cheryl Lovell and Les Goodchild for occasional advice on sources. Sharon Gabel, Assistant Director of Human Resources, welcomed me to her "Workplace Law Seminar" and led me to resources on time and information management. Thanks also go to Christine Zamastill, another doctoral student for her legal research in support of chapter six.

More generally, I want to thank the many friends who have been my administrative colleagues through the years, particularly William Zaranka, the former Provost, and Elinor Katz, the former Dean of the College of Education. Working for and with Ellie and serving Bill on the Provost's staff stimulated my thinking about leadership, as did many class discussions with my students in "Leadership and Administration." It is a pleasure to work at the University of Denver, where leadership is encouraged in so many different ways and where the wheels of administration run smoothly while others write books about it.

INTRODUCTION
The Need for
Institution-Wide Leadership

Administrators in colleges and universities across the United States and around the world face a broad range of challenges generated by life in a new era. It is not so much the new century that is important but the new era—the high-technology global information age that impacts daily our lives and now our education systems.

At the end of the nineteenth century, colleges and universities were witnessing the emergence of the disciplinary structure and the professions; the introduction of majors, minors, and general education; and the widespread development of departments, professional associations, and graduate study.[1] At the time, it was also a new era. The changes that were put in place at the end of the nineteenth century and beginning of the twentieth established a structure for higher education that lasted nearly a century. Now once again, higher education is faced with the prospect of major change in response to the influences of a new era. Just how radical the transformation will be—serious adjustments in the existing model or a radical new paradigm—remains to be seen. In any case, the implications for individual institutions and for whole systems of institutions with regard to mission, delivery, organization, personnel, instruction, and finance are likely to be enormous.

THE LEADERSHIP CHALLENGE

Serving as an administrator in a college or university today is no picnic. It has never been an easy job, but it has perhaps been made more difficult recently by a deluge of new technologies, merciless public scrutiny, critical consumers, intrusive government regulations, a decline in civil discourse, a growing sense of normlessness, and a creeping suspicion that the whole enterprise is no longer manageable. The list of current issues facing higher education is truly daunting: governance, finance, access, diversity, federal and state relations, planning, content, delivery, assessment, technology, and relationships with schools and schooling.[2] Most of these issues suggest change, sometimes major change, for many campuses. How will institutions respond to these challenges? What will their leaders do? And who are their leaders?

Unfortunately, leadership itself is in crisis. Few people agree on exactly what leadership is, how it should be exerted, who should lead, or whether leadership is even possible. Studies of leadership and the growing complexity of leadership theory only seem to make leaders more confused about leadership. Is leadership situational? Is it only symbolic? Is a good leader primarily a good mediator—a person highly skilled in negotiating power and interests—or are leaders expected to have vision? Should they try to discern the common good or seek uncommon achievement? Are leaders found chiefly at the top of the organization chart, or might they reside throughout the institution, even in unlikely places?

INSTITUTION-WIDE LEADERSHIP

An important discussion of the need for leadership in higher education is found in Alexander Astin and Helen Astin's *Leadership Reconsidered: Engaging Higher Education in Social Change*, a work produced for and published by the W.K. Kellogg Foundation.[3] The authors define leadership as a "process that is ultimately concerned with fostering change."[4] Leaders are viewed as change-agents who intentionally undertake value-based transformation. Because leadership takes place in a social context, leaders must work with and rely on other leaders. "Leaders, thus are not necessarily those who merely hold formal 'leadership' positions, on the contrary, all people," the authors argue, "are potential leaders."[5] "A leader, in other words, can be anyone—regardless of formal position—who serves as an effective social change agent."[6] The Astins call particular attention in this study to the leadership roles of students, faculty, student affairs professionals, and presidents.

Perhaps the greatest leadership challenge facing higher education today is to create an environment that values leadership at all levels of the institution. Sometimes this challenge is referred to as "creating a culture of leadership" that "empowers all members of the institution."[7] A culture of leadership draws on the combined efforts of those in designated positions of leadership and persons in various roles scattered across the institution who might be leaders if they only thought of themselves in that way and were prepared to lead. Fortunately, many creative programs for developing promising postsecondary leaders already exist at the national level,[8] in campus-based institutes, academies, and workshops,[9] and in leadership programs sponsored by multicampus systems, consortia, networks, and regional associations.[10]

An important challenge for colleges and universities today is the cultivation of leadership itself in all corners of the organization, so that collectively the resources of the institution can be marshalled to address the issues spawned by the new era. Today there is no such thing as too many leaders. Many people will need to get involved in learning to lead.

INFORMED AND SKILLED LEADERS

Leadership is expected from a provost, dean, or department chair, but leadership opportunities also emerge in less obvious places, sometimes in remote outposts of the institution. Leadership is more likely to occur and to be effective when the people who attempt to provide it have a clear concept of what leadership is and possess the well-developed skills, abilities, and appropriate attitudes associated with it. Some people want to be leaders for the wrong reasons—for the status that goes with the title, the perceived power, or the opportunity to impose their own ideas and values on the institution. They are usually spotted and weeded out in postsecondary institutions. There are also some people who "just like to do their job" and actually have no leadership aspirations. Usually they make valuable contributions in keeping the organization running smoothly. There are also some people who aspire to leadership, who truly want to improve the organization and build the collective dream, but alas—one might say of them a little unkindly—they are filled with enthusiasm but unhampered by knowledge or skill. Effective leaders have not only appropriate attitudes but essential knowledge and a useful set of generic skills and abilities.

What do postsecondary leaders need to know? As defined for discussion in this book, the knowledge, skills, abilities, and attitudes deemed necessary for effective postsecondary leadership are as follows:

- Knowledge of what leadership is, how it has been distinguished from administration, and the ability to develop a practical and personally useful definition of leadership.

- Appropriate attitudes about leaders and followers and the ability to serve as a courageous follower as well as a skillful leader.

- Knowledge of basic organizational theory and the ability to describe accurately the organization one serves, including mission, history, and current developments.

- Knowledge of the key administrative offices at the institution, including staff and line functions, reporting relationships, and awareness of the opportunities and limitations of one's own niche.

- Ability to collaborate in program planning, including the skill to expand on ideas, keep plans realistic, use institutional goals as criteria, and build in usable assessment.

- Awareness of what learning is and why it must be guarded as the fundamental purpose of the institution.

- Knowledge of rational models used for problem solving and decision making, and the ability to consider legal and ethical implications.

- Skill at collaboration, including serving on and working with task forces, committees, and administrative units to help them function as high-performance teams.

- Ability to communicate effectively in a variety of forms.

- Knowledge of basic conflict resolution models and the ability to employ them effectively.

- Knowledge of basic financial planning and accounting methods and the ability to use them for budget development and control.

- Knowledge of change theories and skill in responding to, initiating, and managing change.

- Awareness of what constitutes a positive work environment and the ability to work with others in creating such an environment.

- Positive attitudes about personal renewal and the ability to engage in perpetual learning to become more effective as a postsecondary leader.

One might call these *leadership competencies* because they are derived from what leaders actually do. Unlike most sets of competencies, however, they are more than a formulaic list of behaviors. They involve a complex integration of knowledge, skill, ability, and attitude, sometimes referred to as *professional judgment*.

REFLECTION

As you review the bulleted list of competencies, which are the areas in which you feel better prepared, and which are the areas you regard as underdeveloped? Based on your present work, are some of your competencies in more urgent need of development than others?

> Have you noticed that the list of competencies corresponds roughly to the topics addressed in the individual chapters of this book?

To be an effective leader, one must know certain things, be able to apply this knowledge, cultivate specific skills and abilities, and maintain appropriate attitudes. There is no magic formula for doing this. It is learned as part of one's profession over the years, just as a doctor or an attorney learns through practice. Leadership is learned through formal study, or by reading about it, engaging in it, and reflecting on experience systematically. Leaders who are able to do this effectively are eventually recognized as "seasoned," are sometimes held in high esteem, and may even be regarded as wise.

NOTES

1. Burton Clark, *The Academic Life: Small Worlds, Different Worlds* (Princeton, NJ: The Carnegie Foundation for the Advancement of Teaching, 1997).

2. There are many lists of current issues in the literature. See especially Association of Governing Boards, "Ten Public Policy Issues for Higher Education in 1999 and 2000" (AGB, Public Policy Paper Series Number 99-1, 1999); Joseph Losco and Brian L. Fife, *Higher Education in Transition: The Challenges of the New Millennium* (Westport, CT: Bergin & Garvey, 2000); Werner Z. Hirsh and Luc E. Weber, *Challenges Facing Higher Education at the Millennium* (Phoenix: The American Council on Education and The Oryx Press, 1999); and Lester Goodchild, Cheryl Lovell, Edward Hines, and Judith Gill, *Public Policy and Higher Education* (Needham, MA: Simon & Schuster Custom Publishing, ASHE Reader Series, 1997). See Part II where articles on public policy issues appear concerning access, affordability, performance, reform and restructuring, collaboration among sectors, governance, distance education, curriculum, and research. Also see an older set of predictions in Richard I. Miller, *American Higher Education: Issues and Challenges in the 21st Century* (London and Philadelphia: Jessica Kingsley, 1988).

3. Alexander W. Astin and Helen S. Astin, *Leadership Reconsidered: Engaging Higher Education in Social Change* (Battle Creek, MI: W.K. Kellogg Foundation, 2000).

4. Ibid., p. 8.

5. Ibid.

6. Ibid., p. 2.

7. Sharon McDade and Phyllis Lewis, *Developing Administrative Excellence: Creating a Culture of Leadership* (New Directions in Higher Education Series, 87, Fall) (San Francisco: Jossey-Bass, 1994), p. 5.

8. Phyllis Lewis, "Creating a Culture of Leadership," in McDade and Lewis, *Developing Administrative Excellence.*

9. Phyllis Lewis, Laura Fino, Julie Hungar, William Wallace, Jr., and Richard Welch, "Campus-Based Academies, Institutes, and Seminars or Workshop Series," in McDade and Lewis, *Developing Administrative Excellence*.

10. Phyllis Lewis, Kenneth Anderson, Frances White, and Maria Santos, "Programs Sponsored by Multicampus Systems, Consortia, Networks, and Associations," in McDade and Lewis, *Developing Administrative Excellence*.

PART I

Understanding the Context for Leadership

The two chapters in this section are designed to provide intellectual tools for understanding the phenomena of leadership and the context where leadership is practiced. Gaining this understanding is a pre-requisite for effective leadership. No matter what skills one may have, the actual practice of leadership is always performed in some specific context, and understanding that context is an essential foundation for effectiveness. Leaders know what they believe about leadership and they know how to look at an institution to discern the terrain that at once restrains and challenges them.

CHAPTER 1

Leadership and Administration: Building Practical Definitions

At eight o'clock sharp, on the warm, sunny morning of August 1st, Mary Williams enters the office suite of the dean of the college of arts and sciences. She arrives at her new position, having been drawn there from another institution after a national search. She knows that she was selected from a long list of candidates primarily because the search committee expressed confidence in her "leadership ability." A momentary ripple of self-doubt sends a shiver up her spine as she steps into her spacious office. Leadership? What, after all, is leadership? She was a successful administrator in her previous position as associate dean, as her letters of reference attest, but leadership? Does she have the right qualities? Is this the right situation for her? Will she really be able to play a role in helping to transform this institution? And what about her colleagues—Fred Newton, the associate dean in the adjoining office, and Dolores Ortiz, the bright new intern from the doctoral program in higher education—should she think of them as leaders, too, or as followers? She knows that she needs to build consensus with the faculty and report their wishes to the provost, but she is also obliged to express convincingly to the faculty the intentions of the provost and the president. How can she avoid just being a messenger? She wanted this job badly. Now she's not so sure. She recognizes that although she has many strengths and some good administrative experience, she still has many things to learn about leadership. Why, on her very first day, is she feeling the need for a mentor?

Jacques Barzun, for twelve years the provost of Columbia University, once offered this classic, if ironic, view of administration: "Administration is seeing to it that the chalk is there."[1] Barzun points out that education, the main job of the institution, "also requires that courses be scheduled and catalogues printed, students registered, classrooms and offices be assigned, heated, and lighted, and so on down a long list of services, useless if not provided regularly and on time. Offhand, such management does not seem suited to the tastes and talents of part-time elected improvisers, which faculty members would necessarily be."[2]

DEFINITIONS AND DISTINCTIONS

Although faculty may long for a community of scholars devoid of administrators, certain things must be done to make sure that an institution runs well. As Rudolph Weingartner notes: "Administrators manage. . . . [M]anagers are needed to sequence and coordinate their operations, to ensure that required work is done properly, to correct errors, and to cope with unforeseen incursions. Some people who are called *managers* in the secular world are called *administrators* on a campus."[3] The focus of administration is on enabling the organization to carry out its established mission in an effective way. In general, the term *administration* has been reserved for the implementation of policies and procedures rather than establishing new directions—seeing that the chalk is there!

Some people are not very good at administration. They tend not to excel at setting priorities, delegating tasks, controlling expenditures, and getting things done on time. They enjoy concepts and ideas or their interactions with people, and they often detest details and numbers. Administrators who are aware of these custodial deficiencies often surround themselves with people who are good at what they, as administrators, are not.

The term *leadership*, on the other hand, implies movement, taking the organization or some part of it in a new direction, solving problems, being creative, initiating new programs, building organizational structures, and improving quality. It is the antithesis of carrying out established policies. It involves asking profound questions, such as: Is chalk really necessary in the classroom of the future?

Classic views of leadership relate it to power and position. Rosabeth Moss Kanter refers to leadership as "the existence of people with power to mobilize others and set constraints."[4] Phillip Selznick calls it "the art of institution building, the reworking of human and technological materials to fashion an organism that embodies new and enduring values."[5] Michael Hammer and James Champy, authors of the best-selling *Reengineering the Corporation*, offer this definition of leadership:

> We define a leader not as someone who makes other people *do* what he or she wants, but as someone who makes them *want* what he or

she wants. A leader doesn't coerce people into change they resist. A leader articulates a vision and persuades people that they want to become part of it, so that they willingly, even enthusiastically, accept the distress that accompanies its realization.[6]

Perhaps the best guidance for defining leadership comes from Joseph C. Rost, who has devoted several chapters of his book, *Leadership for the Twenty-First Century*, to the problems of making a satisfactory definition of the word *leadership*. Rost wants the definition to suggest that leadership is essentially a "relationship of influence" that is "multidirectional and noncoercive"; that "active followers" are an important part of that relationship; that leaders and followers develop "mutual purposes"; and they "intend" to make (even if they do not always actually make) "real changes" and "substantive transformations."[7] The strength of this definition is that it de-emphasizes the notion of hierarchy and subordination, it diminishes the importance of formal position, and it stresses the idea of transformation, thus distinguishing leadership from management and administration.

Another way to approach the problem of defining leadership is to ask what leaders actually do. What behavior do they exhibit? James Kouzes and Barry Posner, the authors of the well-known study *The Leadership Challenge*, have identified the following behaviors of leaders when they are at their personal best:[8]

- *Challenging the Process.* Leaders "venture out." They "seek and accept challenge." and "change from the status quo." "Leaders are pioneers . . . willing to take risks."

- *Inspiring a Shared Vision.* Leaders have "visions and dreams" that become "the force that invents the future." They are "confident in their ability to make extraordinary things happen." They "ignite the flame of passion in others" through their "enthusiasm" and their "vivid language and expressive style."

- *Enabling Others to Act.* Leaders "enlist the support and assistance" of "all those who have a stake in the vision." They "create a sense of ownership" by "making people feel strong, capable, informed, and connected." They use their power by "giving it away."

- *Modeling the Way.* "Leaders model the way through personal example and dedicated execution." They have "beliefs to stand for," and they create "action adventure stories."

- *Encouraging the Heart.* When "people become exhausted, frustrated, and disenchanted," leaders "encourage the hearts of their constituents to carry on." Leaders must also encourage themselves.

These five practices support the more traditional idea of a leader as one who is set apart and who inspires followers to bring about change. Estela Bensimon and Anna Neumann, like Rost, criticize the classic discourse on leadership with its emphasis on bureaucracy and hierarchy and "one person set apart from the rest of the organization."[9] Margaret Wheatley, for example, suggests that effective leadership involves communicating "simple governing principles: guiding visions, strong values, organizational beliefs . . ." to "allow individuals in the system their random sometimes chaotic-looking meanderings."[10] Thus definitions of leadership may range from those that assume a hierarchical position-based role to those that stress a context of influence involving collaboration with followers.

Although people differ sharply in their views of leadership, when leadership is compared to administration, it appears to be distinguished by its association with change, with moving the organization and its people forward in some positive way.

Some people are not very good at leadership. They may be excellent at the work described above as administration, but they may lack, initially at least, the conceptual understanding and the skills and abilities needed for leadership. They, too, if they are aware of these deficiencies, can draw on people around them in the organization who are good at what they are not. Or they can learn to lead.

REFLECTION

> As you think of your natural propensities, do you tend to be somewhat better at administration or at leadership? What feedback do you get about your abilities as leader and administrator? Can you identify people around you in the organization who are clearly stronger in one area than the other? Do you know people who are already outstanding at both? How would you define leadership?

Although it may be useful to distinguish administration and leadership conceptually and as a matter of emphasis, in the day-to-day work of most campuses leadership and administration are inextricably intertwined. Looking back over a single day's activity, one will find some of each. It is important, therefore, to recognize the significance of both and to balance them appropriately.

In the midst of administration there are opportunities for leadership. The most creative leadership ideas when put into practice become administration.

EXAMPLES OF LEADERSHIP

Although leadership is hard to define, most people can describe examples of it. Consider these two rather different examples of leadership drawn from the world of business. What can be learned from these contrasting illustrations?

Motorola

In 1979 Robert Galvin, the CEO and president of Motorola had proposed to his board of directors that "the firm make an extraordinary commitment to training its workers—from executives to shop floor workers." As a leading manufacturer of electronic equipment and components, Motorola at the time had $2.7 billion in sales, but Galvin believed that the future of the company depended on learning—a commonplace idea today, but a somewhat radical concept for the time. Unfortunately, the eleven other directors voted against Galvin's proposal. They simply did not see the need for so much emphasis on training in a company that was already doing so well. After serious consideration, Galvin decided to move ahead with his ideas anyway, to link learning to quality improvement, and to persuade those who would follow him toward his vision to make Motorola a learning organization. Within the next ten years Motorola was investing three percent of its payroll on education (compared to one percent in other American companies), claiming a $30–33 return on every dollar invested in learning, and was in the midst of establishing Motorola University, the huge international umbrella for coordinating its learning activities.[11] By that time top management "had stopped seeing education as a cost and had begun to accept it as an indispensable investment."[12]

Three important lessons can be learned from this example:

- Leadership at the top is necessary and essential.
- Leadership sometimes involves taking people where they are reluctant to go.
- Leadership often involves communicating a vision and getting others to support it and be enthusiastic about it.

British Airways

Alan G. Robinson and Sam Stern, the authors of *Corporate Creativity*,[13] recount how a baggage handler for British Airways noticed that first-class passengers were often the last to receive their luggage, standing at the carousel long after other passengers were gone. The system unintentionally gave priority to standby passengers. The

baggage handler thought about how the luggage was loaded and unloaded and realized that the first-class luggage was among the first
to be loaded but last to be unloaded. He suggested to his supervisors
that first-class luggage be loose loaded separately, like that of standby
passengers, so that it could be unloaded first. He wrote up the idea
and it was implemented. He eventually won the Chairman's Customer Service Award of the Year (about $18,000) and two round-
trip Concorde tickets to the United States.

Three important lessons come from this example:

- Leadership can come from unexpected places.
- Organizations need to be open to leadership.
- Leadership needs to be valued and rewarded.

Although these are strikingly different examples of leadership, most
people would agree that in some sense leadership was involved, though
coming from different places in the organization and in different forms.
This means we need to have a broad definition of leadership.

REFLECTION

Examine your niche in the institution. What are the formal aspects
of your leadership position? How are you expected to provide leadership? If you are not a formal leader, what unexpected leadership
opportunities sometimes appear around you? To what extent are new
ideas welcome at your institution? Are they rewarded? What factors
support or inhibit institution-wide leadership?

LEADERSHIP THEORIES

Leadership was the object of intense study during the last half of the twentieth century and there is now an immense body of research and theory
on the subject. The classic work is *Bass and Stogdill's Handbook of Leadership*, but an excellent application of this research to higher education can
be found in the work of Estela M. Bensimon, Anna Neumann, and Robert Birnbaum entitled *Making Sense of Administration Leadership: The "L"
Word in Higher Education*. They categorize theories and models of leadership into six groups: trait theories, power and influence theories, behavioral theories, contingency theories, cultural and symbolic theories, and
cognitive theories.[14]

The earliest efforts to study leadership focused on the traits of leaders
such as assertiveness, self-confidence, or decisiveness. *Trait* theories set
forth the hypothesis that effective leaders share common traits. At first
there was support for this hypothesis, but as studies accumulated, the list

of traits grew longer and longer and the evidence suggested that "possession of certain traits does not guarantee effectivness, nor does their absence proscribe it."[15]

Other studies focused on *power and influence*—the way leaders use their formal and informal power to influence followers. Some studies suggested that this influence was reciprocal and dynamic, involving interactions and productive exchanges between leaders and followers, a kind of *quid pro quo*. These theories are called *transactional*. Other studies suggested that leaders sometimes are able to go beyond meeting basic expectations and needs, and can inspire additional effort, confidence, and involvement in changing the organization. This leadership is sometimes called *transformational*.[16]

Other studies examined what leaders actually do. They focused on the balance of autocratic and democratic styles, degree of task orientation and people orientation, and the various roles that leaders take on. These are called *behavioral* theories.

Other researchers began to recognize that a leader's effectiveness depends to a great extent on context. Some leaders who are effective in one situation may not be effective in another. Furthermore, different situations make different demands on leaders and require different talents and actions. These studies stress that effective leadership depends on the situation and are referred to as *contingency* theories.[17]

Cultural and symbolic theories stress the role of leaders in creating shared meanings for the organization through ceremonies, rituals, and public communications. The key role of the leader is the "management of meaning."[18] Because there is no agreement that an institution's culture can in fact be managed, the leader's role may be more a matter of reflecting the institution's culture. These theories downplay what leaders actually can do to change an organization, that is, to lead in the traditional sense.

Cognitive theories go a step further. The whole idea of leadership, they suggest, appears to arise from the social cognition of organizations and involves "constructions of meanings that help participants to believe in the effectiveness of individual control."[19] These theories tend to "deconstruct" the explicit activities of leaders, rendering the so-called leadership of leaders suspect. "Leaders, then, are people believed to have caused events."[20] Leadership is reduced to a subjective act existing only in the mind of the beholder.

REFLECTION

To what extent are these theories useful for viewing the activities of leaders in your institution? Are these valuable lenses? Is there any way to organize or coordinate these theories?

A PRACTICAL INTERPRETATION

Just as there is no unified theory of the universe in physics (for now at least), there is currently no unified theory of leadership. Although proponents of a particular theory or set of theories will be inclined to attack efforts at synthesis—largely because the theories are contradictory and conclude strikingly different things about the nature of leadership—it is useful to attempt a modest interpretation of this research and draw some practical, if not theoretical, conclusions.

Positive leadership traits may not help us to distinguish leaders from nonleaders, but certain negative traits such as arrogance, lack of imagination, extreme disorganization, and overt pomposity may serve as predictive criteria, especially when combined in a single individual. We may not know what traits effective leaders possess, but we have all had our experience with individuals destined for failure. Furthermore, if leadership is situational, certain positive traits will be more useful in some situations than in others. In some settings, only certain traits that appear on the long list of leadership traits may be necessary. Likewise, certain behaviors (autocratic or participatory, task or process orientation) will also be more appropriate in some settings than others. Contingency theories hold forth the promise that varied contexts will produce appropriate leaders and that leadership ability may be more broadly distributed than is often assumed. Although certain minimal levels of satisfaction must be established through the transactions of leaders and followers for a leader to be effective (the *quid pro quo*), leadership that is only transactional seldom achieves much. For leadership to produce any significant impact on the organization, it must be to some degree transformational. Although some leadership is primarily cultural and symbolic, and is important for those reasons, leadership that is only symbolic has little effect on the institution. Likewise, if leadership is only in the mind of the beholder after the fact, how is it that organizations change, and why should the significant contributions of individuals instrumental in that process be discounted as illusory? When individuals in a variety of contexts exert influence and work collaboratively with followers, they can make a difference in transforming an institution in various ways, and when that occurs, we use the term *leadership* to describe that process.

REFLECTION

Consider once again the two examples of leadership from Motorola and British Airways provided earlier. What traits do you think each leader (Robert Galvin and the baggage handler) probably possessed?

What behaviors did they display? To what extent was their leadership contingent? Can you identify transactional elements? Was the organization transformed in an important way? Was their leadership also symbolic and cultural? To what extent was their leadership only in the mind of the beholder as a perception? How do leadership theories help us to see things we might otherwise miss?

An old-fashioned, common sense view of leadership asserts that at various levels of the organization, sometimes in established leadership roles but also in unexpected places, individuals with varying talents can make positive contributions that actually transform the institution in large or small ways. Collectively, these contributions add up, so that institutions that are able to nurture informed and skilled leadership at many levels simultaneously are in a better position to make continuous advancements than institutions that reserve leadership for a select few at the top or regard leadership as a mere illusion of the unsophisticated.

LEADERS AND FOLLOWERS

The concept of leadership is clarified further by thinking more carefully about the role of followers. Sometimes the term *follower* carries negative connotations. The traditional meaning has often implied someone who is subordinate or even subservient. A more current view, spelled out clearly in the stimulating work of Ira Chaleff entitled *The Courageous Follower: Standing Up to and for Our Leaders* suggests that "any organization is a triad consisting of leaders and followers joined in a common purpose. . . . Followers and leaders both orbit around purpose; followers do not orbit around the leader."[21] This puts leadership and followership in a new perspective. Leaders and followers may take on certain formal roles in the organization. What differentiates them is their roles. What unites them is the organization's purpose.

Chaleff identifies five types of courage a follower should have:

- the courage to assume responsibility
- the courage to serve
- the courage to challenge
- the courage to participate in transformation
- the courage to leave.[22]

The picture of follower that emerges is hardly that of subordinate. The courageous follower takes on responsibilities of value to the organization and steps into the hard work ready to serve. The follower stands up for the leader when support is warranted, but is not afraid to challenge the leader who strays from the institution's purposes. Sometimes, when the leader's behavior jeopardizes common purposes, the follower seeks to transform the leader, and if this fails, the follower must be prepared to leave.[23]

Some followers may wince at these suggestions, protesting that the leaders they follow are not willing to share their power or admit shortcomings, let alone be open to transformation. Suggesting that the leader needs to change is far too risky; besides, these followers say, they need their jobs. Keep in mind, however, that Chaleff is speaking of *courageous* followers, who have the purposes of the organization as their primary focus.

Although *The Courageous Follower* provides strong advice for followers, it also lays down a challenge to formal leaders to provide a context where followers can afford to be courageous. Leadership, when viewed in this way, is not so much about using power as it is working side-by-side with followers to achieve a common purpose. Seen in this way, the hierarchical space between leaders and followers is definitely diminished.

The traditional distinction between leaders and followers almost disappears when we stop to think that in most cases leaders simultaneously play the role of follower and leader. Department chairs are the leaders of their departments, but as followers they report to a dean. The dean is their leader, but as a follower reports to the provost, and so forth. Even the president reports to a board of trustees, and to a certain extent is a follower in that role. Most administrators wear both hats—follower and leader.

REFLECTION

> In your own work, whatever your niche in the organization, how do you sometimes play the role of leader while at other times playing the role of follower? Do traditional ideas about leaders and followers need to be reconsidered? Are you more of a leader or a follower? Is that even a meaningful question?

CHARISMATIC LEADERSHIP

Traditional views of leadership bring to mind charismatic individuals in formal roles near the top of the organization who have extraordinary vision and are able to enlist large numbers of loyal followers. Jay Conger's recent study of charismatic leaders, *The Charismatic Leader: Behind the Mystique of Exceptional Leadership*, suggests that they are charismatic partly because of what they do but also as a result of the way they are perceived by their followers. The term *charismatic* has roots in "an ancient Greek word meaning gift, in particular a gift from the gods. Powers that could not be explained by ordinary means were called *charismata*."[24] The German sociologist Max Weber introduced the concept to the study of leadership in the early twentieth century. Charismatic leaders, when compared with generally effective leaders who are not considered charismatic, tend to be especially good at seeing the big picture, communicating their ideas, laying out a vision, and modeling it.[25] They are also energetic expressive, self-confident, self-determined, eloquent, and surprisingly lacking in internal conflict.[26]

Because most postsecondary institutions have at least some tradition of shared governance or participatory processes for decision making, a charismatic leader is often viewed with suspicion. Academics are quick to discount flashy leaders who have a declared vision. Consequently, presidents, provosts, deans, and department chairs often pursue a policy of "leadership by consensus." They are diligent in setting forth the collective will of the unit, sometimes suppressing their own good instincts and creative ideas in deference to the will of the majority. There are three problems with this view. First, the collective will, often arrived at after long and acrimonious debate, may consist only of the least common denominator and is hardly ever a bold and creative new departure. Second, a new vision, by definition, is not simply the majority view, but an unthinkable dream that almost no one else in the organization has been able to imagine. Third, leadership by consensus is useful for maintaining the status quo or making incremental changes, but it will hardly ever produce institutional transformation of significant magnitude. One may wonder if leadership by consensus is actually leadership at all.

REFLECTION

Can you provide examples of charismatic leadership in your institution or other campuses where you have worked or studied? What are your reservations about charismatic leadership? Do you also have reservations about leadership by consensus?

Academics are probably right in being suspicious of charismatic leaders. In a final chapter entitled "The Dark Side of Charismatic Leadership," Conger notes potential problems with charismatic leadership. The vision can be flawed, perceptions can be exaggerated, communications can be manipulative, and the management of change can be dysfunctional.[27] As Conger concludes, "charismatic leaders present a paradox for organizations: Their very strengths are also their potential weaknesses."[28]

Charismatic leadership may be vastly overrated. A better concept is *inspirational leadership,* through which "followers are drawn to the goals and purposes of the leader, but not the leader as such."[29] Inspiring leaders are able to bring out the best in others by working with them to achieve elevating goals. They can be inspiring yet humble.

SERVANT-LEADERSHIP

Although the concept of *servant-leadership* appears to be relatively new and is usually associated with the posthumous publication of books by Robert Greenleaf after 1996, the original expression of the concept by Greenleaf goes back to an essay he wrote in 1970 entitled "The Servant as Leader."[30] In that essay Greenleaf cites Hermann Hesse's *Journey to the East*[31] as one of the inspirations for his concept of servant-leadership. In this story, a band of men on a mythical journey is accompanied by the servant Leo who "does their menial chores" and "sustains them with his spirit and song." All is going well until Leo disappears and the group falls into disarray. The narrator, after years of searching finally locates Leo, whom he had first known as the servant. Leo is actually the great and noble leader of an official order.[32] Greenleaf develops the idea that effective leaders appear first as servants, and that the essence of leadership is service. (One might also note that this is an old idea found in the Judeo-Christian and other religious traditions.) In its modern garb, servant-leadership suggests first taking care of the needs of those whom the organization serves. Greenleaf asks these searching questions: "Do those served grow as persons? Do they, while being served, become healthier, wiser, freer, more autonomous, more likely themselves to become servants? And what is the effect on the least privileged in society; will they benefit, or, at least, not be further deprived?"[33]

Although academics may scoff at these ideas as hopelessly naïve when seen against the backdrop of the often-cynical scramble for resources in a college or university, there are two implications here that leaders may find valuable. The first is the suggestion that leaders are most effective when they are reminded frequently of the purpose and the people the institution serves. The second is the idea introduced earlier that leadership may come from unexpected places. Elsewhere this idea has been described as "a new grassroots model of leadership," so named because it is rooted in behaviors that can be performed by anyone regardless of position."[34]

Leadership is sometimes manifest in charismatic or inspirational efforts but also appears as servant-leadership.

REFLECTION

What are your own beliefs about leadership? Can you craft a practical definition? What components of such a definition are you certain you do not want to omit? Will your ideas about leadership work better in some settings than in others? Have you observed convincing examples of leadership?

The concept of leadership has evolved as it has been studied over the years. Although leadership means different things to different people in different places and the debates among those who study it will not be easily resolved, having a practical definition and defensible concept of leadership is indispensable for those who would lead. Although institutional setting and assigned role may limit or expand opportunities for leadership, wise leaders know when and how to lead.

MARY'S MENTOR

Mary's mentor wants her to remember these things about leadership and administration:

- Administration emphasizes implementation; leadership focuses on transformation.
- An examination of leadership behavior suggests that leaders challenge the process, inspire a shared vision, enable others to act, model the way, and encourage the heart.
- Leadership and administration are conceptually distinct but intertwined in practice, and it is useful to learn how to be good at both.
- Ideas about leadership have changed as a result of continuing research.
- Leadership theories can be classified as trait, power and influence, behavioral, contingency, cultural and symbolic, and cognitive theories.
- Leaders and followers are joined by a common purpose. Followers follow the purpose; they do not orbit around the leader.
- Followers need the courage to assume responsibility, to serve, to challenge, to participate in transformation, and to leave.
- Effective leaders create environments in which followers can speak up.
- Most people serve in dual roles as both leaders and followers simultaneously.
- Some leaders are inspirational and are able to exert the visible influence normally associated with their formal office.
- Sometimes leadership comes from people who serve in humble ways in unexpected places.
- Effective leaders can articulate their views of leadership.

NOTES

1. Jacques Barzun, *The American University: How It Runs, Where It Is Going* (New York: Harper & Row, 1968), p. 96.

2. Ibid., pp. 96–97.

3. Rudolph Weingartner, *Fitting Form to Function: A Primer on the Organization of Academic Institutions* (Phoenix: American Council on Education and The Oryx Press, 1996), p. xii

4. Rosabeth Moss Kanter, *The Change Masters: Innovation and Entrepreneurship in the American Corporation* (New York: Simon & Schuster, 1983), p. 249.

5. Phillip Selznick, *Leadership in Administration: A Sociological Interpretation* (New York: Harper & Row, 1957), p. 152.

6. Michael Hammer and James Champy, *Reengineering the Corporation: A Manifesto for Business Revolution* (New York: HarperCollins Publishers, 1993), p. 105.

7. Joseph C. Rost, *Leadership for the Twenty-First Century* (Westport, CT: Praeger, 1993), pp. 102–103.

8. James M. Kouzes and Barry Z. Pousnev, *The Leadership Challenge: How to Get Extraordinary Things Done in Organizations* (San Francisco: Jossey-Bass, 1987). The quotations are taken from pages 1–6. See also a booklet that summarizes their ideas, *Five Practices of Exemplary Leadership* (San Francisco: Jossey-Bass, 2000).

9. Estela Bensimon and Anna Neumann, *Redesigning Collegiate Leadership: Teams and Teamwork in Higher Education* (Baltimore: Johns Hopkins University Press, 1993), p. 10.

10. Margaret Wheatley, *Leadership and the New Science: Learning about Organization from an Orderly Universe* (San Francisco: Jossey-Bass, 1994), p. 133.

11. Matt Keleman, "*Motorola A*" and "*Motorola B*": *The Business Enterprise Trust* (Boston: Harvard Business School Publishing, 1997). These case studies were developed from research by Stephanie Weiss under the supervision of Kathleen Meyer.

12. William Wiggenhorn, "Motorola A: When Training Becomes Education," *Harvard Business Review* (July–August 1990), p. 78.

13. Alan G. Robinson and Sam Stern, *Corporate Creativity: How Innovation and Improvement Actually Happen* (San Francisco: Berrett-Koehler, 1997), pp. 9–10.

14. Estela Bensimon, Anna Neumann, and Robert Birnbaum, *Making Sense of Administrative Leadership: The "L" Word in Higher Education* (ASHE-ERIC Higher Education Report No. 1) (Washington, DC: School of Education and Human Development, The George Washington University, 1989), pp. 7–26. A more technical authoritative review of leadership theory can be found in "An Introduction to Theories and Models of Leadership," Chapter 3 in Bernard M. Bass, *Bass and Stogdill's Handbook of Leadership: Theory, Research, and Managerial Applications*, 3rd ed. (New York: The Free Press, 1990), pp. 37–55.

15. Ibid., p. 8.

16. Ibid., pp. 9–10.

17. Ibid., pp. 14–15.

18. Ibid., p. 21.

19. Ibid., p. 23.

20. Ibid., p. 24.

21. Ira Chaleff, *The Courageous Follower: Standing Up to and for Our Leaders* (San Francisco: Berrett-Koehler, 1995), p. 11.

22. Ibid., pp. 6–7.

23. Ibid., pp. 6–8.

24. Jay Conger, *The Charismatic Leader: Behind the Mystique of Exceptional Leadership* (San Francisco: Jossey-Bass, 1989), p. 22.

25. Ibid., pp. 26–36.

26. Bernard Bass "Charismatic, Charismalike, and Inspirational Leadership," Chapter 12 in *Bass and Stogdill's Handbook of Leadership Theory*, pp. 190–192.

27. Conger, *The Charismatic Leader*.

28. Ibid., p. 159.

29. Bass "Charismatic, Charismalike, and Inspirational Leadership," p. 206.

30. Robert Greenleaf, "The Servant as Leader" (Indianapolis, IN: The Robert Greenleaf Center, 1970).

31. Herman Hesse, *Journey to the East* (New York: Nooday Press/Farrar Straus and Giroux, 1956).

32. Larry C. Spears, *Insights on Leadership: Service, Stewardship, Spirit, and Servant-Leadership* (New York: John Wiley & Sons, 1996), p. 19. The essay by Greenleaf cited above appears in this work along with other writings on this theme.

33. Ibid.

34. Horst Bergman, Kathleen Hurson, and Darlene Russ-Eft, *Everyone as a Leader: A Grassroots Model for the New Workplace* (New York: John Wiley & Sons, 1999), pp. 13–14.

CHAPTER

Institutional Structure and Mission: Knowing Your Place in Time and Space

Admiring the bright fall colors of the stately oak trees, Mary Williams starts out across the campus to find the office of Professor Kennedy, former chair of the history department, who is reputed to know more about the institution than anyone on campus—partly because of his own long career, but also through his formal role as campus archivist. Since her arrival in August, the new dean has made it a point to spend a few hours each week getting acquainted with key figures on campus within and outside her college, and reading everything she can find to gain some sense of the history and present scope of the institution. She is struck by how different this campus appears to be from any with which she has been associated previously. Control, size, configuration of colleges and schools, sources of funding, attitudes about teaching and research—all seem to be quite foreign. The culture strikes her as a little odd, but she can't quite put her finger on it. People don't appear to be very open; competition among the various units for resources is fierce, yet an atmosphere of superficial congeniality appears to predominate. She is not quite sure whom to trust and feels a little lost. She would like to gain a better understanding of the institution to know how some of her new ideas will be received; that is, to anticipate the boundaries of her actions and to know her niche as a leader.

"Well, it's our new dean," Professor Kennedy greets her warmly. "How nice of you to visit. How can I help?"

"I want to find out where I am in time and space," Dean Williams replies with a wry smile.

Professor Kennedy laughs. "You've come to the right place. None of your five predecessors—all of short duration, I might add—bothered to find out. They simply started deaning without a thought to how this place came to be, what it is, or how it operates."

E dward Gross and Amitai Etzioni in their 1971 book *Organizations in Society* point out that "[w]e are born in organizations, educated by organizations, and most of us spend much of our lives working in organizations."[1] One would think that through our immersion in the activity of organizations we would know intuitively what organizations are. As with the term *leadership*, the concept, *organization* is slippery. During the last century many scholars produced useful intellectual tools for understanding the life of differing types of organizations and the behavior that takes place within organizations. The scholarship began in sociology, with the work of Weber and Merton, but the study of organizations is now a broad and impressive interdisciplinary field of research.[2]

UNDERSTANDING ORGANIZATIONS

Gross and Etzioni provide a classical definition of *organization* that has weathered the test of years: "Organizations are social units (or human groupings) deliberately constructed and reconstructed to seek specific goals."[3] The authors also note that organizations are characterized by deliberately planned divisions of labor, one or more power centers to control their efforts, and interchangeability (removal and replacement) of personnel.[4] Although recent theory about organizations suggests that they may be less rational and goal-driven and more subject to outside influence (as open systems) than we may have thought earlier, the classical definition of Gross and Etzioni fits postsecondary institutions fairly well— they are social structures designed to support learning.

W. Richard Scott suggests a useful way of thinking about the elements that make up an organization. Most organizations have these five basic components:

- *social structures*—"the patterned or regularized aspects of the relationships existing in an organization"
- *participants*—"those individuals who, in return for a variety of inducements, make contributions to the organization"
- *goals*—"conceptions of desired ends . . . that participants attempt to achieve through their performance of task activities"
- *technology*—the means used (equipment, technical knowledge, skills) to get the work of the organization done
- *environment*—"the specific physical, technological, cultural, and social environment to which it must adapt."[5]

Organizations are complex social structures set up and perpetuated to accomplish specific goals. They exist in a context and their partici-

pants develop and use a "technology" to accomplish goals. Organizations are not, however, simply goal-oriented. The behavior within organizations is more complex than that.

TYPES OF ORGANIZATIONS

Organizations can be divided into three categories by fundamental purpose: business, government, and not-for-profit.[6] Postsecondary educational institutions can fall into any of these categories, and noting where they fit is one of the first steps in understanding them as organizations.

- *Business organizations* are entrepreneurial, and their purpose, even their responsibility, is to make a profit. Although profit shapes the bottom line, most of their activity focuses on the services or products to be consumed. Independent colleges and schools, sometimes called proprietary or trade schools, fall into this category. They are often family-owned businesses, but may also be large corporate entities operating across state lines, or even internationally, with many local campuses.

- *Government organizations* do not make a profit, but they are held accountable both for funding and outcomes by the sponsoring unit of government. They are often called *public* to reflect their dependence on public funds and the agencies that administer them. State colleges and universities (often organized into state systems), district- and state-supported community colleges, and federally supported service academies as well as armed service colleges fall into this category.

- *Not-for-profit organizations* are set up not to make money and they are called *not-for-profit*, as opposed to *nonprofit*, because it is not their purpose to make a profit. (A business that is nonprofit eventually goes bankrupt.) Not-for-profit postsecondary institutions are usually referred to as *private*, and include universities, most liberal arts colleges, and some junior colleges. They receive little or no direct tax funds, but may receive state support indirectly through the funding of students as well as federal funds for research or student aid.

Although the sharp distinctions among these three categories of postsecondary institutions are blurring somewhat today—public institutions, for example, now rely more on student tuition and fundraising, the hallmarks of private institutions—the differences remain significant and shape the character and preoccupations of the institution in important ways.

REFLECTION

Which category of postsecondary institution do you serve—proprietary, public, or private? Can you identify ways that fundamental purposes affect such things as program planning, budgeting, admission of students, fundraising, campus building projects, and student services?

Another dimension in which organizations vary is size. How big is the organization? Is it a small business or a huge multinational conglomerate? Is it a local municipality or a unit of the federal government? Postsecondary institutions may be as small as a few hundred students, may have a campus of several thousand students, or may be part of a statewide system coordinating education for over 100,000 students. Leadership and administration will take on a very different character at a small liberal arts college, as compared with a huge public multiversity, although many of the same functions will need to be addressed. As size increases, so does complexity, and many aspects of the institution are affected, including the focus of the mission, patterns of communication, and systems for budget generation and control.

REFLECTION

How big is the institution you serve and what difference does that make in your role in the institution, your challenges in administration, and your opportunities for leadership?

Organizations also vary by type, and certain concepts, metaphors, and images have been generated to describe and categorize them in this way. Sociologists J. Eugene Hass and Thomas Drabek classify organizations into the following categories:

- *Rational*—scientific in their pursuit of specified goals, usually bureaucratic in their management
- *Classical*—preoccupied with efficiency and formal structures to achieve desired results
- *Human relational*—composed of human beings who are social creatures who work best together as their needs are met
- *Conflict oriented*—driven by internal conflict, which is seen as natural and essential, and concerned with maintaining equilibrium through balances of power
- *Interactional*—characterized by simple trades or complex interactions, in which exchange, reciprocity, and mutual dependence are important
- *Technological*—structured by the technologies used to shape raw material into a product or deliver a service
- *Holistic*—operating as systems within systems to be seen not as parts but as one open system, fluid within and open to its larger environment.[7]

A more recent scheme developed by Gareth Morgan in *Images of Organization* categorizes organizations as machines, organisms, brains, cultures, political systems, psychic prisons, flux and transformation, and instruments of domination.[8] These images begin to suggest how organizations affect their participants, not always for the better.

Using images for examining organizations can be valuable, and although the tendency is to conclude that *all* of the descriptions fit, usually every organization has one or two dominant ways of focusing its efforts so that one image is more accurate and illuminating than another. For example, using the categories developed by Hass and Drabek, one can think of certain technological institutes or service academies that fit the categories of "rational" or "technological," certain liberal arts colleges that are primarily "human relational," and certain community colleges that are mainly "interactional." Using the images developed by Morgan one may think of certain cloistered institutions (where faculty work in their own specialized worlds) as "psychic prisons," whereas on occasion one may even encounter a postsecondary institution with such strict rules for students and faculty that it may qualify as an "instrument of domination."

REFLECTION

> Using the descriptors presented above, or by creating some of your own, what image do you think best describes the postsecondary institution you are currently serving? Are alternative images needed to describe other institutions you know or have known? As you employ these images to describe the institution you serve, what difference does it make to you as an administrator and leader to think of the institution in this way?

Institutions vary according to fundamental purpose, size, and image. Classifying the institution, that is, locating it by type and image, provides a valuable framework for thinking about why certain things happen at the institution, why problems take the shape they do, and which solutions are likely to be acceptable and unacceptable.

ORGANIZATIONAL BEHAVIOR

Lee Bolman and Terrence Deal, in their book *Reframing Organizations*, note that "because organizations are complex, surprising, and deceptive, they are often ambiguous."[9] Anyone who has worked in a postsecondary institution for a while is able to note certain behavior that appears to be unclear and open to multiple interpretations—odd practices that appear to be highly ambiguous. Why, for example, do some units—a college of law, a school of education, an athletic department—appear to live in their own small world, offering cynical criticisms of the administration while contributing grudgingly to the overall financial welfare of the institution? Why does a student affairs division develop programming that is criticized by a faculty member in the student newspaper as "antithetical to the purposes of education." Why do some faculty members work long hours to employ new technologies in their teaching, while others view the campus as a stopping-off place between professional meetings and consulting ventures? Sometimes it seems like "anything goes." Does the behavior within organizations have any rational consistency? Does it make any sense?

Theories about the internal workings of organizations provide useful insights into the way people behave in organizational contexts. W. Richard Scott, in his valuable work on organizational theory, *Organizations: Rational, Natural, and Open Systems*, suggests that there are three lenses that can be used in trying to understand behavior within organizations. These include viewing organizations as

- *rational systems*—"collectivities oriented to the pursuit of relatively specific goals and exhibiting relatively high formalized social structure"
- *natural systems*—"collectivities whose participants are pursuing multiple interests, both disparate and common, but recognize the value of perpetuating the organization as an important resource"
- *open systems*—organizations that "are systems of interdependent activities linking shifting coalitions of participants."[10]

Postsecondary institutions ought to be, in the normative sense, quintessential rational systems, composed of rational people, using their rationality to discover new knowledge, while teaching others to become rational like themselves. And at one level of analysis these institutions are: They set rational goals about how to structure learning, they pursue those goals systematically, and they attempt to be efficient and effective in using time and resources. The key question when looking at an organization through this lens is: How does the organization make arrangements to meet its goals? But this is only one lens for viewing organizations. What happens when the others are used?

The scholar of organizations casts a critical eye at the institution and asks: What is really going on inside? How do people actually behave? They form groups, they have diverse goals, and they focus on their own survival in their own particular circumstances. Organizations actually function to meet the diverse needs of participants, who want to see the organization survive so that their own goals can be protected and achieved.[11] People bring to the institution their own ideas about what is to be valued, which don't always fit with institutional goals and prescribed norms. The key question when looking at an organization through this lens becomes: How does the organization actually function for the participants?

When viewed as open systems, organizations appear to be an assemblage of various interdependent parts, varying from simple to complex. The relations among the parts and their relationships to entities outside the organization are loosely coupled (weakly connected) and changing. Seen as a cybernetic system, organizations are open and complex, subject to outside influences, but also capable of self-regulating actions. Organizations have boundaries, but they are connected to the world outside and influenced by it.[12] The key question, when looking at an organization through this lens is: What are the important parts and connections and how are they being regulated?

Seen in this light, some of the behavior manifest in postsecondary institutions may not appear to be so ambiguous after all, but quite natural, even expected. The three lenses provide an opportunity for taking perspective; that is, for trying to understand the behavior before judging it. Using the three lenses, one might gain a better understanding, for example, of why a dean is so preoccupied with strategic planning and goal setting, why a department chair is so excited about a recently developed connection with a local company, and why a newly appointed assistant professor can't wait to go on leave to work with a colleague on a funded research project in New Zealand. Is it not natural that the three people described here would be as ships passing in the night, each participating in the organization in a separate way and for different reasons, each thinking the other a little strange?

REFLECTION

Select one or two instances of what seem to you to be puzzling or ambiguous behavior in your institution. Complete the sentence: "I don't understand why . . ." and then try to explain the behavior by using one or more of the organizational perspectives: rational, natural, and open systems.

Some of the odd behavior in organizations also relates to dominant patterns of governance. Postsecondary institutions are governed in very different ways, and some useful insights about organizational behavior can be gained from the literature on academic governance. The most valuable volume in this respect is the work by Robert Birnbaum, *How Colleges Work: The Cybernetics of Academic Organization and Leadership*. Birnbaum develops five "models of organization functioning" as follows:

- *The Collegial Institution.* The emphasis is on consensus, shared power, and consultation. A strong community is held together by shared values, and civil discourse is used to resolve disagreements. Leaders come from the group and are the agents for the faculty.

- *The Bureaucratic Institution.* A clear and hierarchical organization chart establishes chain of command through job descriptions and rules and regulations. The emphasis is on effective and efficient operation, and tradition or charisma legitimates leaders.

- *The Political Institution.* Conflict is regarded as inevitable and the allocation of resources is vigorously contested. Decision making is political, diffuse, and decentralized. Leadership is by persuasion, diplomacy, and mediation.

- *The Anarchical Institution.* Participants do almost as they wish in a semiorganized anarchy, characterized by minimal coordination and control. Goals are ambiguous and there is no clear educational philosophy. People move in and out of the governance process, participating only when they have interest. Issues are clouded by additional "garbage" thrown into the system. Leadership is an illusion, or at best symbolic with low influence.

- *The Cybernetic Institution.* A reasonable degree of stability is brought to a complex system through organizational thermostats working as self-correcting monitors. Multiple decision makers work in subsystems to provide structural controls. Leaders engage in squeaky-wheel administration, paying attention mostly to what is wrong, and offering short-term solutions.[13]

The tendency is to see some of each type of governance model in the various decision-making processes at a single institution—a reasonable response—but the greater likelihood is that one or at most two of these models is the *predominant* pattern. These global patterns of governance provide the framework and set the tone for human relations at most postsecondary institutions—the way colleagues relate, the formality and informality of communication, and even the degree to which people like each other. One major task in learning to lead is to characterize accurately the governance process at the institution being served and to spell out specifically how that process affects the behavior of individuals within the organization.

REFLECTION

Recall one or two recent decisions at your institution. Do they il-
lustrate or at least suggest a dominant governance model that may
be operative for the institution? How do decision-making processes
affect the way individuals behave toward each other at your institution? What are the implications for leadership; that is, given this
dominant governance model, how might you contribute most as a
leader?

**In addition to understanding the type of institution being served, it
is also important to think about the various kinds of behavior that take
place within the organization. In seeking explanations for behavior that
may at first appear to be puzzling or ambiguous, it is useful to examine the institution through the lenses of rational, natural, and open
systems, and to try to identify the predominant governance model as
collegial, bureaucratic, political, anarchic, or cybernetic. An effective
leader understands organizational behavior.**

MISSION, HISTORY, AND CULTURE

Postsecondary institutions also have a mission. Sometimes this mission
is focused and explicit, and sometimes it is diffuse and ill-expressed; but
all institutions to some degree conceptualize their purposes as mission or
as multiple missions. Usually a formal mission statement has been developed; one way to get better acquainted with an institution is to find and
read its mission statement.

George Keller, well known for his work in helping colleges and universities focus their missions, wrote a classic work on planning entitled
Academic Strategy: The Management Revolution in Higher Education. In it
he notes:

> As with individuals in desperate straits who are forced to ask them-
> selves who they really are and what they value most, campuses across
> the land are being pressed to inquire What business are we really in?
> and What is most central to us? And How shall we proceed? [14]

Although some academics may cringe at the word *business*—taken in its
broader meaning of *enterprise* or *activity*—asking "What business are we
really in?" is precisely the question of mission. Knowing the mission provides what Keller calls "self-consciousness for the organization."[15]

Institutional mission has been especially important in American higher
education because there are so many different types of institutions springing

from unique historical origins—small liberal arts colleges, land-grant universities, church-related colleges, historically black colleges, Native American tribal colleges, and community colleges, to name a few.[16] American higher education prides itself in this diversity. All the more reason for an institution to know its mission and for the individuals who serve it to know the mission of the institution where they are working.

To understand this institutional diversity better and to bring some conceptual order to it for scholars and researchers, the Carnegie Foundation, under the guidance of Clark Kerr in 1970, developed a classification system for institutions "according to their mission."[17] As Ernest Boyer notes in the foreword to the 1994 edition of the report, "Over the years, we have modified the definitions somewhat to improve the groupings." The most recent report, for the year 2000, includes a major redefinition of categories and significant regrouping as shown in Figure 2.1. The latter categories are for institutions that award most of their degrees in a single discipline. The criteria for the classifications involve numbers and types of higher degrees awarded, research volume in dollars, and disciplinary focus. The report contains the names of over 4,000 individual institutions, making it possible to look up one's own institution to gain a better perception of its classification by mission.

Figure 2.1
Carnegie Classification System, 2000

DR Ext	Doctoral/research universities—extensive
DR Int	Doctoral/research universities—intensive
MA I	Master's (comprehensive) colleges and universities I
MA II	Master's (comprehensive) colleges and universities II
BA LA	Baccalaureate colleges—liberal arts
BA Gen	Baccalaureate colleges—general
BA AA	Baccalaureate/associate's colleges
AA	Associate's colleges
Faith	Theological seminaries and other specialized faith-based institutions
Med	Medical schools and medical centers
Health	Other separate health-profession schools
Engr	Schools of engineering and technology
Bus	Schools of business and management
Art	Schools of art, music, and design
Law	Schools of law
Teach	Teachers colleges
Other	Other specialized institutions
Tribal	Tribal colleges

An institution's self-concept as expressed in its mission begins with its Carnegie classification but includes many other facets that grow out of its history and form its culture. Some institutions have a long history and many traditions, and even a newly founded one has at least some history. It is not the amount of history that is important, of course, but the substance of that history—the purposes, values, and norms that are expressed in that history.

Many institutions develop what Burton Clark has referred to as an *organizational saga*, a "collective understanding of unique accomplishment." Drawing on the medieval Icelandic or Norse concept of *saga*, "a narrative of heroic exploits," Clark suggests that colleges and universities often generate a self-told story that is "intrinsically historical but embellished through retelling and rewriting." The saga contains "publicly expressed beliefs" that are "rooted in history," claim "unique accomplishment," and are "held with sentiment by the group." Sagas vary in their fragility, but those with high durability usually have a strong initiator (perhaps founder or reformer), distinctive programs, and strong believers (usually senior faculty, alumni, and students). The saga is expressed in a "set of communal symbols and rituals invested with meaning," and is communicated through ceremonies and written histories, that convey a certain "air about the place."[18]

One might think of institutional saga as a snowball gathering size as it rolls downhill through time. Because the saga is invested with belief in heroic accomplishments and is prone to exaggeration with retelling, one can never be quite sure about the veracity of the story, but as with myths and legends, the power is not in historical accuracy, but in the perception of meaning ascribed to the players—the explanation and celebration of sustained communal purpose.

Organizations also have cultures, and this is true for postsecondary institutions as well. Terrence Deal and A.A. Kennedy popularized the idea of culture in *Corporate Culture*[19] and Thomas Peters and Robert Waterman made *organizational culture* a key concept in their book *In Search of Excellence*.[20] The term *culture* comes originally from anthropology and sociology, where it was applied to the customs and traditions of whole societies, but now the concept is used to shed light on behavior within organizations. Rosabeth Moss Kanter describes the culture of an organization as follows:

> Out of the design and structure of the organization arises a set of patterns of behavior and cultural expectations that guide what people in the system consider appropriate modes of operating. . . . Such expectations or cultural "norms" guide behavior in a holistic sense.[21]

In their book *Collegiate Culture and Leadership Strategies*, Ellen Chaffee and William Tierey point out

> The culture of an organization is grounded in the shared assumptions of individuals participating in the organization. Often taken for granted by the actors themselves, these assumptions can be identified through stories, special language, norms, institutional ideology, and artifacts that emerge from individual and organizational behavior.[22]

In postsecondary settings this includes such things as "the governance pattern, philosophy of education, perspectives on teaching/learning, the nature of an educational or academic community, and the commitment to a clientele."[23] The culture of an institution is manifest in "the deeply embedded patterns of organizational behavior and the shared values, assumptions, beliefs, or ideologies that members have about their organization and its work."[24]

Organizational cultures can be strong or weak. "A strongly articulated culture tells employees what is expected of them and how to behave under a given set of circumstances. . . . In colleges with stronger cultures there is a greater coherence among beliefs, language, ritual and myth. Weak cultures lack this coherence."[25] One hopes that strong cultures will also be positive, because, as Kanter points out, cultures can be strong and also negative and dysfunctional; in fact, organizations can have "strong cultures of mediocrity."[26] Cultures can also be called *distinctive*, marking them off sharply from those of other institutions, and cultures also can vary with regard to *clarity* and *congruity* across many units of the institution, and by *consensus* or degree of agreement about the culture.[27]

Why is it important to understand the institution's culture and what can be done to learn about it? Effective leaders want to know the cultural norms and to take them into account in decision making and in designing change. They also realize that going against the culture has its perils and is often a key source of conflict. A leader's actions, and the activities of followers, take on symbolic significance in expressing or changing the culture.

To find out about an institution's culture, one can interview key players, pay close attention to ceremonies such as convocation or graduation, read formal statements such as brochures and catalogs, listen to often-told stories, and try to identify heroes. Even "the language people use when they talk about an organization reveals its culture."[28] Above all, one should ask questions about what is seen and heard—about the environment, the mission, the process of socialization, the way information is held and disseminated, the strategies used in decision making, and the way people conceptualize leadership. Effective leaders ask these questions about the organization's culture:[29]

- "What holds this place together?
- How does this place run?
- What does it expect from its leaders?
- How are things done around here?"

Besides having a dominant culture, institutions also have subcultures. It is common to speak of subcultures within the academic disciplines and to identify subcultures within student bodies. William Bergquist, in his book *The Four Cultures of the Academy: Insights and Strategies for Improving Leadership in Collegiate Organizations*, identifies four cultures, one of which may be dominant, but all of which can exist side by side simultaneously within an institution:

- *collegial culture*—values the "disciplines," "faculty research and scholarship," "the generation, interpretation and dissemination of knowledge," and building "qualities of character" in "future leaders."
- *managerial culture*—finds meaning in "the organization, implementation, and evaluation of the work" of the institution and values "fiscal responsibility" and "supervisory skills."
- *developmental culture*—"finds meaning in the creation of programs and activities" that benefit the "personal and professional growth of all members of the collegiate community," and encourages "cognitive, affective, and behavioral maturation among students, faculty, administrators, and staff."
- *negotiating culture*—values "equitable and egalitarian distribution of resources and benefits," "confrontation and fair bargaining among constituencies" with opposite interests, and the development of "more liberating social attitudes and structures."[30]

These cultures or subcultures have their distinct memberships and interact in important ways. Leaders, particularly when they are involved in change, must take them into account.

Because leaders become embedded in an institution's culture, it is sometimes difficult for them to disengage sufficiently to discover the salient aspects of the culture or various subcultures. Some people who cannot identify their institution's culture or who have come to believe either that the institution does not have a culture or that the culture doesn't matter will have a rude awakening when they have unknowingly broken an important cultural or subcultural norm.

Clifford Geertz, the renowned sociologist, sums up the discussion in this way: "Man is an animal suspended in webs of significance he himself has spun. I take culture to be those webs, and the analysis of it to be therefore not an experimental science in search of law, but an interpretive one in search of meaning."[31]

REFLECTION

What is the mission of the institution you serve? How is it expressed? What is your institution's Carnegie classification? What is its organizational saga? How would you characterize your institution's culture? Is it a strong or weak culture? Is it positive or negative? Is it distinctive, clear, and congruent, and is there consensus about it? What are the subcultures? To which one do you belong? Have you ever broken cultural norms at your institution? What "webs of insignificance" have been spun there? How do the answers to these questions help you to become a more effective leader?

Postsecondary institutions have a mission, an organizational saga, and various manifestations of culture and subculture. Effective leaders are diligent in finding out about the nature of the institution they serve, and they search systematically for the webs of meaning that have been woven at the institution to explain its purposes and norms. They ask three important questions about the institution: What business are we in? What story do we tell? What is the cultural glue that holds the place together?

ADMINISTRATIVE ROLES

Gross and Etzioni, in their definition of *organization* cited earlier, stressed division of labor and interchangeability (removal and replacement) of personnel.[32] All organizations develop ways to structure their work into jobs, and the roles of participants in the organization are usually formally designated. Sometimes these roles are precise and tightly bounded; at other times they are open and intentionally ill-defined.

Companies have presidents, vice-presidents, managers, and directors. Armed service personnel are structured in ranks with precise job assignments. Postsecondary institutions have typical ways of designating administrative roles, and commonly used terms are found at most institutions. Administrators need to know what the work of other administrators is at their institution, how key roles are defined and filled, and how various positions are related. This is not always easy because a position at one institution—dean, for example—may mean something rather different at another institution, and reporting structures may vary widely from one setting to another. Another way to get acquainted with the institution one serves is to know the roles of key players and how they relate to each other.

Colleges and universities, with all their variety in mission, history, and culture, have four basic types of work they must get done: the academic functions of research, teaching, and service; the provision of services to students; the management of finances and business operations; and the cultivation of resources, including public relations and interactions with alumni and parents. The administrative structure of most institutions grows out of these functions and is established through the creation of offices and positions designated by titles such as president or chancellor, provost or vice president, dean, director, or department chair. Useful literature on each of these offices is available to those who wish to pursue it.[33] Other administrative officers include a chief financial officer or treasurer who manages the business affairs of the enterprise; a vice president or director of advancement, including fundraising, legislative relations, alumni programming, and sometimes public relations; a chief student affairs officer, under whom departments of residence and student life are included; numerous managers of services sometimes called directors, as with athletics or computing services; and certain specialized functions such as the head of the library (often called dean), the registrar, and directors of such units as admissions, financial aid, and institutional research. The important point to understand about these various offices is that the administrators who perform these functions play roles, and these roles—in the sense that sociologists refer to social roles—determine to a large extent the way people behave in these offices and the way they perceive the rest of the organization.

REFLECTION

Can you identify the key administrative offices in your institution and the names of the people who occupy these offices? Do you know what they do and what they believe about their work? How do their roles affect the way they see the organization?

REPORTING LINES

All of the administrative units of an organization need to be coordinated in some way. The army, for example, creates arrangements in which smaller units are incorporated into progressively larger units, such as team, squad, platoon, troop, squadron, and corps. Businesses develop command

and control reporting lines, although in recent years there has been widespread experimentation with arrangements that are flatter, decentralized, nonhierarchical, and fluid, and in which much of the work is done by cross-functional teams. Most postsecondary institutions are organized in traditional patterns, with a president (or chancellor) who reports to a board of trustees, a provost or vice president (chief academic officer) who reports to the president, deans who report to the provost, and chairpersons reporting to deans. Beyond this, the arrangements among various other vice presidents or "senior staff," and the various service functions of the administration take on considerable variation across institutions. Some institutions have more than one campus or become part of larger state systems of institutions (not unlike corporate conglomerates), which also affects internal organizational arrangements.

The important point to note is that certain arrangements may be more functional than others *for that particular institution*. Much has to do with the "span of control" (the number of people reporting to a single individual), the arrangements for communication across reporting lines, and the placement of various functions with line (reporting) and staff (supporting) functions to manage the work flow. The best single-volume resource for gaining understanding about administrative offices and organization charts is Rudolph Weingartner's *Fitting Form to Function: A Primer on the Organization of Academic Institutions*.[34] Weingartner does not suggest that there is one best way to draw the organization chart, but he does imply that there are better ways and worse ways to do so, and that the intelligent clustering of similar functions in manageable groupings makes a difference in performance. Knowing one's niche—the precise fit, the reporting relationship, and the rules about relating to other offices—is extremely important.

REFLECTION

> Do you know how your institution is organized? What do you note when you study its organization chart? Is the form well fitted to function? Can you foresee potential problem areas? Do you know where you fit?

All institutions organize work into offices and roles. Understanding these roles and who serves in them is important. Having an overview of how they are arranged provides additional insight into the institution as an organization. Sometimes leaders need to redefine roles and change the arrangements among them.

Effective leaders make significant efforts to understand the institution they serve. In particular, they avoid treating the institution as if it were their own undergraduate or graduate institution, or some romanticized ideal institution of their dreams. They also know where they fit in the larger structure of the institution and are realistic about what that niche is. An institution is what it is, and anyone who hopes to make it a little better in some way as a leader needs to begin with the givens. Taking time to get acquainted helps leaders avoid blunders, work efficiently, and conserve effort.

MARY'S MENTOR

Mary's mentor wants her to remember these things about institutional structure and mission:

- Intuitive knowledge of organizations can be supplemented by studying them systematically.
- Organizations have social structure, participants, goals, and various technologies, and they exist within environments.
- Organizations can be classified as business, government, or not-for-profit and they vary greatly in size.
- Organizations develop distinctive characteristics and images that enable them to be classified by type.
- Organizations can be seen as rational, natural, or open systems and these lenses help explain how people in organizations behave.
- Postsecondary institutions have distinctive patterns of governance (collegial, bureaucratic, political, anarchic, and cybernetic) that influence human interactions within them.
- Institutions have a mission that expresses what business they are in.
- Postsecondary institutions often have an organizational saga that sets forth accomplishments and creates meaning for participants.
- Institutions generate cultures and subcultures that establish common practices and norms for behavior.
- The work of an institution is divided into typical roles and offices, such as president, provost, dean, and department chair, and these roles shape the behavior and outlook of those who act in them.
- The relationship between the roles and offices is expressed in an organization chart that attempts to relate form to function.
- An effective leader explores the territory before undertaking pioneering ventures.

NOTES

1. Edward Gross and Amitai Etzioni, *Organizations in Society* (Englewood Cliffs, NJ: Prentice-Hall, 1985), pp. 5–6.

2. Richard W. Scott, *Organizations: Rational, Natural, and Open Systems* (Upper Saddle River, NJ: Prentice-Hall, 1998), p. 9.

3. Gross and Etzioni, *Organizations in Society*, p. 11.

4. Ibid.

5. Scott, *Organizations*, pp. 17–21.

6. James R. Davis and Adelaide B. Davis, *Effective Training Strategies: A Comprehensive Guide to Maximizing Learning in Organizations* (San Francisco: Barrett-Koehler, 1998), p. 58.

7. J. Eugene Hass and Thomas Drabek, *Complex Organizations: A Sociological Perspective* (New York: Macmillan, 1973), pp. 23–93.

8. Gareth Morgan, *Images of Organizations* (Newbury Park, CA: Sage Publications, 1986).

9. Lee Bolman and Terrence Deal, *Reframing Organizations: Artistry, Choice, and Leadership* (San Francisco: Jossey-Bass, 1991), p. 26.

10. Scott, *Organizations*, pp. 26–28.

11. Ibid., pp. 57–58.

12. Ibid., pp. 83–89.

13. Robert Birnbaum, *How Colleges Work: The Cybernetics of Academic Organization and Leadership* (San Francisco: Jossey-Bass, 1989). The models are described on pages 86–103, 107–124, 130–148, 153–167, and 179–199, respectively.

14. George Keller, *Academic Strategy: The Management Revolution in Higher Education* (Baltimore: The Johns Hopkins University Press, 1983), p. 72.

15. Ibid., p. 75.

16. Christopher Jenks and David Riesman, *The Academic Revolution* (Garden City, NY: Doubleday, 1968).

17. Carnegie Foundation for the Advancement of Teaching, *A Classification of Institutions of Higher Education*—Technical Report (Princeton, NJ: The Carnegie Foundation for the Advancement of Teaching, 1994). Foreword by Ernest Boyer. Quotation is from p. vii.

18. Burton Clark, "The Organizational Saga in Higher Education," in Marvin Peterson, ed., *Organization and Governance in Higher Education*, 4th ed. (ASHE Reader Series) (Needham, MA: Simon & Schuster Custom Publishing, 1991). The quoted phrases are from pp. 46–51. See also Burton Clark, *The Distinctive College* (Chicago: Aldine Publishing, 1970).

19. Terrence Deal and A. A. Kennedy, *Corporate Culture: The Rites and Rituals of Corporate Life* (Reading, MA: Addison-Wesley, 1982).

20. Thomas Peters and Robert Waterman, *In Search of Excellence* (New York: Harper & Row, 1982).

21. Rosabeth Moss Kanter, *The Change Masters* (New York: Simon & Schuster, 1991), p. 178.

22. Ellen Chaffee and William Tierney, *Collegiate Culture and Leadership Strategies* (New York: American Council on Education and Macmillan, 1988), p. 7.

23. Marvin Peterson and Melinda Spencer, "Understanding Academic Culture and Climate," in Peterson, *Organization and Governance in Higher Education*, p. 144.

24. Ibid., p. 142.

25. Andrew Masland, "Organizational Culture in the Study of Higher Education," in Peterson, *Organization and Governance in Higher Education*, pp. 118, 119.

26. Kanter, *The Change Masters*, p. 193.

27. Peterson and Spencer, "Understanding Academic Culture and Climate," p. 144.

28. Masland, "Organizational Culture in the Study of Higher Education," p. 121.

29. William Tierney, "Organizational Culture in Higher Education: Defining the Essentials," in Peterson, *Organization and Governance in Higher Education*, pp. 130, 126.

30. William Berquist, *The Four Cultures of the Academy: Insights and Strategies for Improving Leadership in Collegiate Organizations* (San Francisco: Jossey-Bass, 1992), pp. 4–5.

31. Clifford Geertz, *The Interpretation of Cultures* (New York: Basic Books, 1973), p. 5.

32. Gross and Etzioni, *Organization in Society*, p. 11.

33. For an overview of major administrative positions in colleges and universities see Rudolph Weingartner, *Fitting Form to Function: A Primer on the Organization of Academic Institutions* (Phoenix: American Council on Education and The Oryx Press, 1996), p. 1. For presidency see Clark Kerr, *The Uses of the University* (New York: Harper & Row, 1963), and Clark Kerr and Marian Gade, *The Many Lives of Academic Presidents* (Washington, DC: The Association of Governing Boards of Universities and Colleges, 1986). The provost's work is described in Weingartner's *Fitting Form to Function*. The dean's role is presented in Allan Tucker and Robert Bryan, *The Academic Dean: Dove, Dragon and Diplomat* (New York: American Council on Education and Macmillan, 1988); in Henry Rosovsky, *The University: An Owner's Manual* (New York: W.W. Norton & Company, 1990), and in Mimi Wolverton, Walter H. Gmelch, Joni Montez, and Charles T. Nies, *The Changing Nature of the Academic Deanship* (ASHE-ERIC Higher Education Report Volume 28, No. 1) (San Francisco: Jossey-Bass, 2001). The role of the department chair is well described in Allan Tucker, *Chairing the Academic Department* (Phoenix: American Council on Education and The Oryx Press, 1992); in Alan Seagran, John W. Creswell, and Daniel Wheeler, *The*

Department Chair: New Roles Responsibilities and Challenges (ASHE-ERIC Higher Education Report No. 1) (Washington, DC: The George Washington University School of Education and Human Development, 1993); and in the older work John Bennett, *Managing the Academic Department* (New York: American Council on Education and Macmillan, 1983). This is just a sample of the many books available on academic administrative officers.

34. Weingartner, *Fitting Form to Function.*

PART II

Building the Skills for Leadership

Leadership is always expressed in a specific context, but certain generic skills can be transported from one setting to another. Without these skills leaders will flounder in any setting, and although having them does not ensure success it increases the probability of effectiveness and satisfaction. The seven chapters in this section are designed to provide an understanding of the most commonly used skills of leaders in postsecondary settings. Leaders know that learning to lead involves a continuous process of building these basic skills, practicing them, and reflecting on their use.

CHAPTER

Program Planning and Review: Exerting Influence and Maintaining Accountability

Dean Williams hears the friendly greetings of her colleagues gathering for the ten o'clock meeting in the conference room next to her office. She checks her daily schedule to remind herself of the participants. Bruce Olson from anthropology and Beth Kime from art are the authors of the proposal that arrived on her desk, but she learned from Professor Kennedy that his new colleague from history, Jody Goodchild, was the person who first suggested the idea; she is still interested, so she was invited also. Fred Newton, the associate dean usually attends these meetings, and he most often takes a cautious approach to any new programming. At some point in the meeting he can be counted on to say, if nothing else, "I think we need to be careful about overextending ourselves." The intern, Dolores Ortiz, on the other hand will offer her enthusiastic endorsement to almost anything that appears innovative. Which raises the question for Dean Williams: Exactly what is her own role and how might she best provide leadership for program planning?

After four months on the job, she is beginning to receive a flood of creative proposals—as if the faculty has just been waiting for a little encouragement from her office. She is wondering now how to decide among the many good suggestions coming forth, and what criteria to use in selecting them for funding as new initiatives. At the last institution at which she served, programs were added, then dropped, only to return again, rising like a phoenix from the ashes of their failure. In retrospect, she would call that institution opportunistic, entering whatever new market that promised sufficient enrollments.

Mary is noticing that some ideas that come to her office are not very well developed, and need to be expanded or connected to other good proposals; while other ideas are a bit grandiose, and need to be chopped down to a realistic size. Some proposals appear to be very complete, as if the planners had used a checklist, but she often discovers that the ideas have not had very wide discussion and exist primarily in the minds of two or three people who believe in them. At other times, the ideas have had broad consideration, but have not been written up in a comprehensive and convincing manner. Then, of course, there is always the assessment question: How is one to know if the proposed program has achieved its good intentions?

The interesting challenge, Dean Williams believes, in reviewing all of these proposals, is to discover what the authors mean by learning. She is not at all convinced that the proposals she receives are based on what is now known about learning, or take into account sufficiently the changed environment for learning produced by the information age.

Perhaps her role as leader, Dean Williams reflects, is to ask a lot of questions about all of these matters. She catches herself lost in reverie as a sharp knock startles her and Dolores pokes her head around the opening door. "We're waiting for you, Dean Williams."

Leaders become involved in program planning in many ways. Those who occupy formal offices with explicit leadership roles are often the recipients of program proposals from units that report to them. Often they must help shape these proposals, pass judgment on them, or seek funding for them. Sometimes leaders, whatever their niche, are the ones who initiate proposals. Their leadership takes the form of generating the creative ideas that others will shape, fund, and implement. At other times leadership is expressed from the vantage point of a member of a task force or committee where program ideas are being proposed, examined, or reviewed. In all of these situations, it is useful to understand the process of program planning and reflect on what leaders do to enhance that process.

Programs come in various shapes and sizes and have many different purposes. Academic programs usually involve curriculum planning or proposals for research or training, and these often reside in academic departments; although at other times academic program planning is interdisciplinary, cutting across many units, often residing in a division, center, or institute. Program development also takes place in student affairs and may affect residence life, student activities, orientation, and a host of service units such as health services, counseling and career services, academic support services, and so forth. Other units of the institution, such as the library, athletics, alumni and parent relations, personnel, safety, and day care services also engage in program planning; although the activities and outcomes are somewhat different from academic programs, the issues, principles, and planning processes are essentially the same.

Postsecondary institutions are in essence service organizations, and their central activity is program planning and delivery. For the purposes of this chapter, a *program* is defined as any planned and structured activity regularly using the space, personnel, and financial resources of the institution to provide services to a designated group of constituents.

USING INSTITUTIONAL CRITERIA

The key problem that leaders face in program planning is the surplus of good ideas and the scarcity of resources. This situation necessitates choice, so that even before a program idea is elaborated or developed, someone must begin to raise questions about whether this program is appropriate for the institution or some unit of the institution to undertake. Even well-endowed, prestigious institutions make public pronouncements about the agony of hard choices, noting their inability to be "all things to all people." Choices can be impulsive, emotional, and opportunistic, of course, but they can also be rational, which involves using criteria, evidence of need, and carefully selected strategies and techniques for measuring results.

The first place to look for institutional criteria for decision making is in the mission of the institution. As noted in Chapter 2, most postsecondary institutions have a mission statement. In recent years, most institutions have engaged in some form of planning, a process that may include a vision statement as well as statements of mission, core values, and long-range and annual goals. Over the last half century, the focus of planning has moved from *long-range planning* to *strategic planning*, and more recently to *contextual planning*, a more proactive approach that suggests not only how an institution might respond to its environment but also how to shape that environment in creative ways that benefit the whole higher education enterprise.[1] Although some administrators see planning as a time-consuming public relations exercise, effective leaders recognize that a well-articulated mission and specific goals provide useful guidelines for "identifying the appropriate scale and scope of an institution, as well as articulating the community values by which an institution determines programs that are academically and economically viable."[2] Although mission statements are best thought of as guidelines and are subject to revisions that give the institution room to capitalize on unforeseen opportunity, having a well-articulated set of goals provides program planners with at least the initial criteria needed for deciding whether new ideas are worthy of consideration at all. Program planners in colleges and universities can look at the mission statement, as people in the business world do, as a definition of *core competency*. It defines what the institution is here to do, what it does uniquely, and what it often does better than others can do. A mission statement keeps an institution from being "everything in general and nothing in particular."[3]

Institutions with clear missions have found it valuable to identify additional *strategic choice criteria* for making decisions about adding and eliminating programs. A study of major institutions (including public institutions in the midwest as well as private universities on the east and west coasts) revealed these common, if not universally adopted, criteria:

- *quality*—the ability of the institution to produce a program of genuine high quality
- *centrality*—the importance of the program to the central mission of the institution
- *demand*—the need and identified market for the program
- *cost-effectiveness*—the probability that the program will be financially viable within the context of institutional guidelines
- *comparative advantage*—the extent to which having the program gives the institution advantage over competitors as opposed to duplication of effort.[4]

These criteria can be elaborated and adapted to the needs of a particular institution. Quality, for example, may be elaborated as how well a particular need is met for students or an important demand is served for the community. Cost-effectiveness may be defined to include not only anticipated revenue and expense, but the opportunity cost of having chosen to do one program instead of another. Although not all institutions will have official planning policy statements or clearly articulated strategic choice criteria, effective leaders look for and use them when they are available and raise questions when they are missing.

REFLECTION

Bring to mind a recently established new program or a proposed program at your institution. Does the program fit the institution's mission and goals? How would the program be ranked when strategic choice criteria of quality, centrality, demand, cost-effectiveness, and comparative advantage are used?

Leaders ask if an existing or proposed program fulfills the mission and meets institutional criteria for decision making. Institutions that

know what business they are in are not afraid to ask of new programs: Is this really our business?

EMPLOYING RATIONAL PLANNING MODELS

When program planners begin to address the specifics of planning, they often follow *rational planning models*. These sometimes take the form of linear models that employ stepwise progressions, or they may take the shape of flexible checklists of important elements to consider in planning. The oldest and most famous of these has come to be known as *the classical viewpoint*, or more informally as *Tyler's four questions*:

- What educational purposes should the school seek to attain?
- What educational experiences can be provided that are likely to attain these purposes?
- How can the educational experiences be effectively organized?[5]
- How can we assess whether the purposes are being attained?

The questions contain an inner logic that has helped them stand the test of time—note the familiar ring in many accreditation standards—and for almost any program these are still good questions to ask. The classic viewpoint suggests steps—things to be done first, second, third, and so forth.

Over the years, the classical viewpoint has been elaborated with engineering principles and ideas from behavioral psychology to produce a type of linear planning model called *instructional design*. Growing out of a set of fields that already employ design (architecture, industrial design, and various types of engineering), instructional design is used to "engineer solutions to performance problems."[6] The emphasis is on "front-end analysis" of desired outcomes and systematic interventions that have been carefully designed to address these outcomes. Effectiveness and efficiency are key values, as instructional designers spell out selected elements and organizing principles to use in achieving specified learning outcomes.[7] Although some planners in postsecondary institutions may find instructional design too rigid and linear, the scientific mentality behind its engineering approach provides a useful framework for addressing the fuzzy thinking and awesome vagueness often found in ill-conceived program proposals. Instructional designers ask program planners to identify needs, operationalize outcomes, and be specific about interventions that will produce learning.

For those who regard instructional design as too confining, a more flexible approach can be found in Rosemary Caffarella's "An Interactive

Model of Program Planning."[8] Caffarella offers the model "as a guide, not a blueprint" and as a viable alternative to the "linear, step-by-step process."[9] She provides a simple but valuable list of key tasks to consider, not all of which may need to be addressed for each program, but which can be used flexibly within each new planning situation. Planners will usually need to consider (in no particular order) most of the following:

- Establishing a basis for the planning process
- Identifying program ideas
- Sorting and prioritizing program ideas
- Developing program objectives
- Preparing for transfer of learning
- Formulating evaluation plans
- Determining formats, schedules, and staff needs
- Preparing budgets and marketing plans
- Designing instructional plans
- Coordinating facilities and onsite events
- Communicating the value of the program.[10]

The value in this model is both its flexibility and adaptability to a wide range of program types.

REFLECTION

Consider some program planning you have been involved in recently. Were rational planning models used? In what ways do rational models help? What happens when they are not used? Does something bother you about rational planning models?

Rational planning models require systematic thinking about program planning. They assume that planners can articulate what they want to achieve and that general agreement exists about outcomes.

EXPANDING AND CONTAINING GOOD IDEAS

Usually the people who generate program ideas are specialists. Faculty contribute to the life of the institution through their disciplinary specialties and subspecialties, and many midlevel administrators work in a defined niche, drawing on their specialized professional skills as accountants, computer scientists, security officers, counselors, and so forth. Their ideas for new programs are often very specific, such as: Let's develop a floor in the residence hall for students interested in environmental studies. Although these are usually ideas that appear to have initial merit, they are often very narrowly focused on a particular activity for a specific population and stand in isolation. Those who propose them are not always oriented to the so-called "big picture" and seldom engage in what Peter Senge calls the fifth discipline of *systems thinking*.[11] This is not necessarily the fault of the person, but rather a natural outcome of defined roles in organizations. An effective leader helps people expand their good ideas by asking "what-if questions," such as: What if we consider turning that residence hall into a living-learning center with several defined areas of student interests? In addition to expanding the initiator's thinking, the effective leader connects people with good ideas to other people with good ideas. Gradually, working together, they are able to let a small idea grow into a bigger and better one.

On the other hand, some ideas that come forth may have the opposite tendency of being grandiose and unrealistic. When some people generate good ideas they are often initially unmanageable, such as: holding backyard barbecues in twenty major cities for incoming students and their parents. Although this may also be an idea with initial merit, the overall scope of the proposal is worrisome and overlap may occur with programs already in existence, for example, the orientation of new students. A skilled leader still asks "what-if questions," but of a different order, such as: What if we try this in our own city first for students from our area? In addition to containing the initiator's thinking, the effective leader connects people with big ideas to others who will be helpful in a positive way in cutting ideas down to a manageable size. Working together, they may discover that there is no need for the proposed program or they may find that a more targeted and economical effort may work just as well.

REFLECTION

> What examples can you provide of program ideas that have needed to be expanded or contained? What do leaders need to consider when they work with program planners in expanding and containing good ideas? How can program planning be used as a communication tool?

To address in a systematic way the need to expand or contain program ideas, leaders can use a series of questions and concepts that have grown out of the field of curriculum planning, but that are just as useful as another checklist for the more general task of program planning. They are adapted here as follows:

- *Need*. What population is served? What is the market need and is there a demand for the program?

- *Scope.* Where does the program begin and end? What are the general boundaries?

- *Breadth.* How much is to be covered in this program in the allotted time?

- *Depth.* How deeply are certain areas to be pursued and in what detail?

- *Centrality and balance.* Of the many things that could be covered, which ones are most important and deserve the most emphasis?

- *Flexibility.* To what extent should participants be given choices within the program?

- *Sequence.* In what order should activities take place and does it matter? Are some things prerequisite to others?

- *Gap.* What things are being left out? Are the gaps unconscious or intentional?

- *Intention.* What is intended and what actually takes place? Do some outcomes occur unwittingly?[12]

In facing key questions about the components of a program, planners are forced to make and justify choices that augment or diminish the program as appropriate and identify its essence.

NEGOTIATING POWER AND INTERESTS

Some program planners who have attempted to use rational planning models, checklists, and key questions complain that they find them inadequate for what they call *the real world of planning.* Program planning, they insist, seldom proceeds in a logical way; in fact, more often than not, some of the best program ideas are "shot down" by superiors, shredded by committees, or sabotaged by the very participants who might profit from them. What goes wrong with the best-laid plans of planners?

Insight into this problem is provided in a valuable book by Ronald Cervero and Arthur Wilson entitled *Planning Responsibly for Adult Education: A Guide to Negotiating Power and Interests.*[13] Although the authors' audience consists primarily of those who provide programs for adult learners, their thesis is broadly applicable to all forms of program planning. Their point is that program planning is essentially a political process, involving the negotiation of power and interests.[14] Because plans eventually require commitment from various constituencies—for example, faculty, administrators, participants, and employers—"the crucial first step is to move planning out of the minds of individual planners and into the social relations among people working in institutional settings."[15] It is natural that different constituencies want different things from a proposed program, and it is necessary to negotiate these interests, recognizing that those who enter the negotiating process bring varying levels of power to the table. Program planners, therefore, need to employ and manage a democratic (participatory and inclusive) process, and in fact, the authors argue, this democratic process is the ethical approach to program planning. This does not mean that the role of planner is reduced to negotiator; "planners both act in and act on their settings through negotiating."[16] Planners still have ideas, they still exercise creativity, but they put their proposals through a process that enlists support, invites criticism, and anticipates problems, so that in the end the program will have broad ownership and will ultimately be more successful.

REFLECTION

> Identify two programs, one in which a democratic process was used and one in which it was not used. What difference do you observe? Does the negotiation of power and interests generally make programs weaker or stronger?

Rational approaches to program planning are useful for generating and shaping program ideas, but attempts to plan programs without negotiating the legitimate interests of those affected, painful as this process may be at times, are doomed to failure or at least major disappointment. Obvious as this advice may seem, no program will succeed if the person who has the power to approve it won't support it, or the targeted audience won't attend or participate enthusiastically. Programs planned in a vacuum are still subject to the laws of gravity and can fall flat quickly.

ASSESSING PROGRAM OUTCOMES

Teachers have always corrected tests and graded papers to give students feedback about their achievement. More recently the same idea (providing evaluative feedback) has been applied to entire programs, such as a departmental major or residence life program, and to the programmatic efforts of an entire institution. What was once called *program evaluation* is now called *assessment*, a somewhat broader process that not only includes gathering data about program outcomes, but also actually using the data as a basis for modifying programs to improve quality.

Although reviewing an institution's quality has long been a concern of regional and specialized accrediting bodies, that concern was given new urgency by the federal Department of Education by the establishment of new criteria for recognizing accrediting bodies and requiring them to include assessment ("a focus on educational effectiveness") in their accreditation processes.[17] During the 1990s many accrediting agencies began to examine assessment processes at institutions more carefully, require institutional plans for assessment, and assist institutions in learning about assessment. The American Association for Higher Education (AAHE) also sponsored national conferences on assessment, providing (and continuing to provide) valuable forums for discussing assessment and sharing successful techniques.

As with many movements that affect postsecondary institutions, assessment has been part of a larger effort within many different types of organizations to establish and meet quality standards, sometimes referred to as Total Quality Management.[18] The central purpose of assessment in higher education is the documentation of quality through evidence. The key questions for institutions are the same as those faced by any program planner: "How do we know we have quality? Where is the evidence?"[19]

What are some useful models for assessment? The following models are interesting because they focus on different levels of assessment. At the most fundamental level, assessment should take place in the classroom, providing immediate feedback to teachers and students about learning. Thomas Angelo and K. Patricia Cross provide a valuable collection of fifty classroom assessment techniques that employ simple yet creative ways to find out what students are or are not learning, such as "empty outlines," "minute papers," "muddiest point," "concept maps," "student-generated test questions," and so forth.[20]

At the program level, a useful model is Alexander Astin's I-E-O model, sometimes known as the talent development model.[21] To assess any program within an institution or the impact of an entire degree program, one might ask the following:

Inputs: What characteristics do students have as they enter a program? What are they already able to do?

Outputs: What outputs describe the students at the end of the program? What do they know now and what are they now able to do?

Environment: What experiences in the educational environment have contributed to the outputs? To what experiences can talent development be attributed?

Various types of quantitative and qualitative assessment data can be gathered to address these questions, including tests, questionnaires, observations, and interview data; the challenge is to document measurable or perceived development and to link that growth to the experiences that are facilitating it. To what experiences do the learners and those who observe them attribute their development?

At the institution level, the North Central Association (NCA), a regional accrediting body, has provided a model for assessment that lists the key characteristics of an effective assessment program:

1. *Flows from the institution's mission.* Assessment flows from the way each individual institution defines its purposes and methods of educating its students.

2. *Has a conceptual framework.* The institution employs a framework for examining systematically the relationship of curriculum design, teaching, learning, and assessment.

3. *Has faculty ownership/responsibility.* Judging the academic attainment of students is taken on as a central role of faculty because the goal of assessment is the improvement of student learning.

4. *Has institution-wide support.* Leaders provide support and financial resources across the institution so that assessment becomes a routine way of life.

5. *Uses multiple measures.* The institution uses a variety of measures to capture a full description of student achievement at various stages.

6. *Provides feedback to students and the institution.* Useful assessment data provides feedback to students as well as programs.

7. *Is cost-effective.* The goal is to obtain the most useful data for the expenditure of time and money.

8. *Does not restrict or inhibit goals of access, equity, and diversity established by the institution.* Assessment should be matched to the distinctive institutional character and student body.

9. *Leads to improvement.* Assessment is not an end itself but a means of improving educational programs and practices.

10. *Includes a process for evaluating the assessment program.* The assessment program itself needs to be evaluated to see if the characteristics described above are present and working.[22]

Although this list of characteristics is provided by NCA to guide institutions in developing institution-wide assessment planning, the principles are useful, with minor adaptation, for program planners generally.

One of the weaknesses in many assessment plans is the limited attention paid to the assessment of graduates. In addition to the impetus provided to assessment by accreditation agencies, federal law, specifically Public Law 101-542, The Student Right-to-Know and Campus Security Act of 1990, requires institutions to provide information about enrollments, graduation rates, and information about what happens to graduates, including data about what they know and can do.[23] Help can be gained in this area from an assessment model used by human resource professionals who work in training and development in business organizations. They have developed models for assessing how learning is applied, such as the model set forth in Donald Kirkpatrick's *Evaluating Training Programs: The Four Levels.*[24] The four levels are:

- *Reaction*—the degree to which participants enjoyed the program
- *Learning*—measured changes in knowledge, skills, and attitudes.
- *Behavior*—actual change of behavior in the work setting.
- *Results*—long-term impact on the organization.

This model is especially interesting because it suggests the need to move beyond expressions of satisfaction and measures of learning to actual behavioral and organizational outcomes. In most postsecondary settings assessment efforts have focused on learning, with some interest also in satisfaction, but because students graduate and are often difficult to reach, follow-up assessment on their professional behavior with employers or their impact on the organization where they work, is usually very weak. In certain types of programs conducted by postsecondary institutions, such as customized training in community colleges or certain student life programs designed to influence student drug use or drinking habits, assessment at levels three and four is essential. As demands for public accountability of all sectors of higher education increase, institutions will no doubt search for better methods to follow up on how graduates perform in organizational settings.

Effective leaders not only encourage assessment and require assessment plans for new programs, they also establish regular reviews of existing programs. These are often conducted on a rotating basis of a set number of months or years and where appropriate are linked to accreditation or certification processes. The purpose of such reviews is to help the personnel who direct and carry out the program refocus their goals, plan for the future, initiate modifications, and project resource needs. Regular review also helps to hold programs accountable for their use of resources and for the educational development of their students. At times a review will lead to a decision to close a program that no longer serves its original purposes, meets standards of high quality, or maintains financial viability. To the extent that program reviews are based on actual data, including extensive assessment data, they are more valuable and are more likely to be undertaken with a positive attitude.

REFLECTION

In what ways have you been involved in efforts to assess program effectiveness? What conditions appear to be necessary to make assessment and program review a positive experience? Should closing old programs be a condition for opening new ones?

Program assessment is a means of documenting quality. The desired outcome of assessment is an improved service characterized by more appropriate, efficient, and effective learning. Leaders are concerned about program quality and accountability.

THE LITMUS TEST OF LEARNING

Although individual institutions have their unique mission in the diverse, decentralized, non-system of American higher education, one may surely conclude that all are engaged, one way or another, in the general enterprise of facilitating learning. Many new approaches to learning have come before postsecondary educators recently—including a few that some would regard as fads—and the array of options now includes, in addition to the standard choice of lecture and discussion, learning in groups and teams (sometimes called cooperative learning), learning through cases, problem-based learning, computer-assisted learning, experience-based learning (service learning, overseas travel, cooperative education), distance learning, and numerous other formats.

One test—perhaps the ultimate test—of any program sponsored by a postsecondary institution is whether and in what ways the program enhances learning. This is true also of programs developed by areas generally referred to as support services. What concept of learning is expressed in the proposal? What assumptions about learning are not expressed? In the last half of the twentieth century researchers investigated many aspects of learning; as a result, our general understanding of learning has increased greatly. Today any useful definition of learning needs to be broad enough to accommodate many types of learning activities. Consider the following definition of learning:

> Learning is that varied set of processes whereby individuals and groups of individuals acquire knowledge or skill, change attitudes, become better informed about something familiar, or discover, inquire about, or become more aware of something new.[25]

Many kinds of learning are implied in this definition. One can identify (at least) seven distinct ways of learning as follows:

1. *Learning New Skills: Behavioral Learning.* Does this learning involve a skill? Is this something concrete and observable? Is it a routine (though not necessarily easy) set of mental or physical operations that can be tested or observed? Is this a task that you can learn to do or learn to do better?

2. *Learning from Presentations: Cognitive Learning.* Does this learning involve information? Does it involve new ideas, new terminology, or useful theories? Does it require understanding of how something works or functions? Is this information that might be presented through an explanation? Is it possible to identify key concepts, main ideas, or points to be understood and remembered?

3. *Learning to Think: Inquiry Learning.* Does this learning focus on thinking? Does it involve criticizing information, evaluating arguments and evidence, or reasoning to conclusions? Does this learning involve creative thinking—actually producing unusual but relevant new ideas? Does it involve appreciating how other people think?

4. *Learning to Solve Problems and Make Decisions: Using Mental Models for Learning.* Does this involve learning how to find and define problems, how to generate solutions, and how to evaluate and choose among solutions? Does this learning require that you deal with issues where you need to make choices, weigh the value of different options, and predict outcomes as probabilities?

5. *Learning in Groups: Collaborative Learning.* Does this learning involve changing opinions, attitudes, and beliefs? Does it deal with feelings? Does it build interpersonal speaking and listening skills? Does it cultivate empathy? Is teamwork or collaboration being addressed here?

6. *Improving Performance: Learning Through Virtual Realities.* Is this a kind of learning that needs to be practiced in a safe environment? Does this learning involve activities that could cause damage, expense, or even loss of life? Will you feel more confident and be more competent if you have been able to work first in a simulated environment before going into the real world?

7. *Learning From Experience: Holistic Learning.* Is this a kind of learning that bubbles up from experience? Is this the holistic learning that occurs when you go out and get immersed in a new experience? Could you learn something more from this experience if you had a chance to reflect on it and construct meaning from it? Is there potential here for learning to see something in a new way?[26]

REFLECTION

Reflect on a program proposal or actual program at your institution. Can you identify within it a well-conceived understanding of learning? What type or combination of types of learning is being undertaken?

Leaders have a legitimate right and an obligation to ask of any program what concept of learning undergirds it. Sometimes the concept is clear and well-articulated; at other times it may be poorly expressed

or hidden as an unexpressed assumption. In this case, skillful leaders can help generate more precise expressions of what types of learning are involved and how they will be facilitated through the program.

The seven ways of learning described earlier are alternative means to some end. Nothing has been said yet about the end—the purpose of the learning—but this is also a legitimate question for leaders to raise about programs. What is the purpose and by inference the substance of the intended learning? Here leaders enter murky waters full of debates over educational philosophy, controversies about liberal versus professional education, skirmishes over the proper relationship of the discovery and transmission of knowledge, disagreements about the role of education in society, and exchanges of not always civil discourse about the definition of an educated person. Otherwise-peaceful creatures turn into snapping alligators in this swamp, but this is an insufficient reason to avoid raising the question of purpose. These are old debates, and they will continue in new forms in postsecondary education, but one has the sense that while the alligators are snapping, someone is draining the swamp. The societal conditions that framed the old debates have changed radically, so that many old issues are now moot, while new issues, as yet poorly understood, have arrived to replace them.

In a nutshell, educators, along with everyone else, live in a new era—not just a new century, but a radically different age—that has been vividly described in the literature on recent social change.[27]

At least three aspects of this new era have important implications for learning.

- *The new importance of knowledge.* In the information age, knowledge is now what raw materials were in the industrial age. As Peter Drucker points out in *Post-Capitalist Society,* "Formal knowledge is seen as both the key personal and the key economic resource. In fact, knowledge is the only meaningful resource today."[28] Drucker notes that the crucial difference now is that knowledge is not only being applied to the physical world, to production, and to management, but to knowledge itself, that is, to create *systematic innovation.*[29] At last, what academics have dreamed of for many years has come true: society recognizes the importance of knowledge. But along with this recognition has come a pervasive sense of the instrumentality of knowledge—it has utility—and this sets up a new orientation to knowledge shared by students and the society at large but not necessarily by professors. Most participants in postsecondary education are asking: What can I do with what I learn?

- *Rapid change.* The new era is characterized by rapid, high-order-of-magnitude change—one new thing after another—driven primarily by technology. The changes that came with advances in computers and telecommunications are now accompanied by other changes, including new developments in lasers, xerography, numerical control, speech recognition, computer vision, and liquid crystal and plasma displays.[30] The implication for education is that learning has "a short shelf life." Most knowledge becomes quickly outdated and most members of the society have no choice but to become perpetual learners. They are seeking new formats for learning that are efficient, effective and reasonably priced. Most participants in postsecondary education are asking: What can I do to catch up and keep from falling behind again?

- *Accessibility of information.* Information accumulates more rapidly in the new era, it is more accessible, and it is packaged in more usable forms.[31] Although the Internet with its World Wide Web sites and instantaneous links to other sites is in itself fascinating, consider that the Internet is but one resource in a truly awesome arsenal of resources for locating information in the modern university library. The focus of education no longer needs to be solely on receiving and remembering information, but on accessing, evaluating, and applying information to crucial problems. The implication for education is that the relationship of the learner to information is radically transformed, suggesting changed roles for professors and students alike. Learning to learn becomes a high priority. Most participants in postsecondary education are asking: How can I gain the skills needed to be effective in learning what I want and need to know?

The information age is surely upsetting the routines of the typical postsecondary institution, but the appropriate responses to the changes wrought by the new era are as yet unclear. Leaders know that knowledge is being given new importance in society for its instrumental value, that rapid change is making knowledge obsolete, and that the accessibility to information is calling into question the typical role of faculty as transmitters and students as receivers of information. Responses to this changed situation are clearly a "work in progress," but leaders have the obligation to ask program planners how their new proposals address learning in the information age. How is the proposed new program crafting a creative approach to learning appropriate for the new era?

REFLECTION

What is your response to this description of the new era? Can you add other examples to this description of influences that challenge traditional arrangements for teaching and learning? How would you further elaborate the educational implications of the information age?

The litmus test of the worth of any program is the learning it generates. Administrators turn into leaders when they ask program planners searching questions about learning in the information age.

Leaders may get involved directly in the task of planning programs or work indirectly with others who do so. In either case, they need to know what models to use or suggest and what processes to employ. They not only know how to plan programs but also how to assess and evaluate them. Leaders have a broad definition of learning, and they reflect seriously about how arrangements for teaching and learning need to change as society changes.

MARY'S MENTOR

Mary's mentor wants her to remember these things about program planning:

- As new ideas for programs emerge, leaders ask whether proposals align with institutional mission.

- Strategic choice criteria, such as quality, centrality, demand, cost-effectiveness, and comparative advantage, are useful when making decisions about adding or discontinuing programs.

- Rational planning models and flexible checklists are valuable when it is time to work out the details for a program.

- Some good ideas need to be expanded; others need to be contained.

- An important part of program planning is negotiating the power and interests of those who are involved.

- A plan for assessing program outcomes should be established in the beginning stages of planning.

- Models such as Angelo and Cross's Classroom Assessment Techniques, Astin's Input-Environment-Output approach, the NCA checklist, or Kirkpatrick's Four Levels of Evaluation are valuable for designing and carrying out assessment.

- Ongoing programs should be reviewed periodically to improve quality and maintain accountability.

- Leaders examine programs carefully to see if a clear concept of learning can be identified.

- Planners need to consider how a program addresses the altered environment of learning in the information age.

- The litmus test of any program is the learning it generates.

NOTES

1. Marvin Peterson, "Using Contextual Planning to Transform Institutions," in Marvin Peterson, David Dill, Lisa Mets, and Associates, *Planning Management for a Changing Environment: A Handbook on Redesigning Postsecondary Institutions* (San Francisco: Jossey-Bass, 1997).

2. David Dill, "Focusing Institutional Mission," in Marvin Peterson et al., *Planning Management for a Changing Environment*, p. 171.

3. Ibid., p. 172

4. Ibid.

5. Ralph Tyler, *Basic Principles of Curriculum Planning* (Chicago: University of Chicago Press, 1949).

6. James Van Patten, *What Is Instructional Design: New Alternatives for Effective Education and Training* (New York: Collier Macmillan, 1989), p. 18.

7. Ibid., pp. 26–28.

8. Rosemary Caffarella, *Planning Programs for Adult Learners* (San Francisco: Jossey-Bass, 1994).

9. Ibid., p. 17.

10. Ibid., pp. 19–22.

11. Peter Senge, *The Fifth Discipline: The Art and Practice of the Learning Organization* (New York: Currency Doubleday, 1990), p. 12.

12. James R. Davis, *Better Teaching, More Learning: Strategies for Success in Postsecondary Settings* (Phoenix: American Council on Education and The Oryx Press, 1993). See also James R. Davis and Adelaide B. Davis, *Effective Training Strategies: A Comprehensive Guide to Learning in Organizations* (San Francisco: Berrett-Koehler, 1998), p. 89.

13. Ronald Cervero and Arthur Wilson, *Planning Responsibly for Adult Education: A Guide to Negotiating Power and Interests* (San Francisco: Jossey-Bass, 1994).

14. Ibid., p. 13.

15. Ibid., p. 28.

16. Ibid., p. 30.

17. E. Grady Bogue and Robert Saunders, *The Evidence for Quality* (San Francisco: Jossey-Bass, 1992), p. 40.

18. Daniel Seymour, *On Q: Causing Quality in Higher Education* (Phoenix: American Council on Education and The Oryx Press, 1993).

19. Bogue and Saunders, *The Evidence for Quality*, p. 39.

20. Thomas Angelo and K. Patricia Cross, *Classroom Assessment Techniques: A Handbook for College Teaching*, 2nd ed. (San Francisco: Jossey-Bass, 1993).

21. Alexander Astin, *Assessment for Excellence: The Philosophy and Practice of Assessment and Evaluation in Higher Education* (New York: Macmillan, 1991).

22. Austin Doherty and Gerald Patton, "Criterion Three and the Assessment of Student Achievement," *NCA Quarterly* 66:2 (1991), pp. 409–412.

23. Peter Ewell and Dennis Jones, *Assessing and Reporting Student Progress: A Response to the "New Accountability"* (Denver, CO: State Higher Education Executive Officers, 1991).

24. Donald Kirkpatrick, *Evaluating Training Programs: The Four Levels* (San Francisco: Berrett-Koehler, 1996), Chapter 3.

25. Davis and Davis, *Effective Training Strategies*, p. 53.

26. Ibid., pp. 49–50.

27. See especially Peter Drucker, *Post-Capitalist Society* (New York: Harper Business, 1993); Paul Kennedy, *Preparing for the Twenty-First Century* (New York: Vintage, 1993); John Naisbitt and Patricia Aburdeen, *Megatrends 2000: Ten New Directions for the 1990s* (New York: William Morrow, 1990); Robert Reich, *The Work of Nations* (New York: Vintage, 1992); Lester Thurow, *The Future of Capitalism: How Today's Economic Forces Shape Tomorrow's World* (New York: William Morrow, 1996); and Peter Vaill, *Learning as a Way of Being* (San Francisco: Jossey-Bass, 1996).

28. Drucker, *Post-Capitalist Society*, p. 42.

29. Ibid., pp. 32–47.

30. William Davidow and Michael Malone, *The Virtual Corporation* (New York: Harper Business Books, 1992), p. 73ff.

31. James R. Davis and Adelaide B. Davis, *Managing Your Own Learning* (San Francisco: Berrett-Koehler, 2000), pp. 36–38.

CHAPTER 4

Meetings, Groups, and Teams: Learning to Collaborate

Today the dean's calendar is filled with meetings: the provost's council of deans at nine, the task force on new student orientation at eleven, a lunch meeting with the college alumni council, a two o'clock meeting with the teaching team for the high-enrollment general education course "Science and Social Issues," and an off-campus meeting on volunteer service with the community action board at four. Meetings, meetings, meetings—all day long! Dean Williams shakes her head as she pulls the file for each group from the clutter on her desk. No time for paperwork with so many meetings.

The meetings in themselves are not so bad. She enjoys the people, and the issues they address are important, but outcomes appear to be minimal when compared to the time and energy invested. Is it really necessary to have so many meetings? Is that the issue? Too many? Or is it the quality of what takes place? Surely, there must be some tricks of the trade for making meetings more productive.

The council of deans has come to be especially onerous. The same people in the same seats, meeting after meeting! She already knows the script—who will say what, the old axes they will need to grind, the petty power struggles, the pecking order of power. The provost consumes two-thirds of the meeting with announcements and reports. Seldom is a serious issue discussed in depth, and then only if it affects the deans themselves. Sometimes she wants to stand up on her chair and scream, "Hey, what about the education of our students!" But she's not the dean to make a scene, not just yet.

The orientation task force has a weak chair, so she falls into becoming the unofficial leader of that group. That's not so good. Someone on the student life staff needs to become the project manager, so to speak. The dean shouldn't have to meet with them every time they gather.

The alumni council appears to be full of talent—many of the members are managers in some very impressive organizations—but nobody appears to be in charge. They could accomplish things if they would just stay on task. Every meeting is like a reunion. Maybe they could designate a facilitator and rotate that role for each meeting.

The interdisciplinary teaching team badly needs help. It is difficult for them to get beyond their own disciplinary perspectives. There is a lot of conflict in that group, but they don't appear to want to face it. Have they grown to dislike each other? A little environmental warming might actually do them some good.

The meeting off-campus with the community action board is strange. Talk, talk, talk! And they always seem so discouraged. All these organizations appear to have their own special interests. The common denominator, right before their nose, is volunteer community service, but who is she to say; she's just one of several very impressive leaders. Well, the others are impressive at least. She's not sure if she is actually a leader in that odd coalition.

M ost colleges and universities are organized through boards, councils, senates, departments, committees, and task forces, and these bodies assemble frequently—some would say too frequently—for meetings. Henry Mintzberg, in his classic study of executive behavior, *The Nature of Managerial Work*, found that 59% of a manager's time was spent in scheduled meetings and another 10% in unscheduled meetings.[1] Other studies of managers in other settings confirm these rates and even suggest that when managers have been observed in order to verify their self-report rate, they often *underestimate* the amount of time spent in meetings.[2]

Meetings take time—the precious time of leaders—and they also have a cost. Eli Mina suggests in *The Complete Handbook of Business Meetings*, that these costs ought to be addressed and that a return on investment (ROI) ought to be calculated.[3] Direct costs include the wages of participants during the meeting, their efforts and those of their staff in preparing for the meeting, and sometimes travel expenses, facilities, food and beverages, and audiovisual support.[4] If administrators were to think carefully about costs, maybe there wouldn't be so many meetings.

Meetings appear to be, nonetheless, a universal phenomena, not only across types of organizations but also across cultures.[5] Many people detest meetings, claiming that they are ritualistic exercises where nothing gets done; whereas other people enjoy the exchange of views and information, the social contact, and the opportunity to solve problems in the context of a group.

REFLECTION

What meetings do you attend? Are they valuable? Do you like meetings? Why are meetings held? What do they accomplish? Can leaders make meetings more effective?

MEETINGS

Helen Schwartzman provides an interesting anthropological study of meetings in *The Meeting: Gatherings in Organizations and Communities.*[6] She begins with a useful definition of meetings as follows: "A meeting is defined as a communicative event involving three or more people who agree to assemble for a purpose ostensibly related to the functioning of an organization or group, for example, to exchange ideas or opinions, to solve a problem, to make a decision or negotiate an agreement, to develop policy and procedures, to formulate recommendations, and so forth."[7] Schwartzman points out that there are two distinct and contrasting ways to look at meetings. On the one hand, meetings are what most people believe them to be: tools for getting things done. Their purpose is to facilitate discussion and make collective decisions.[8] On the other hand, meetings can be viewed as focused gatherings, where status and hierarchy are worked out, organizational culture is communicated, and meaning is made of what the participants are doing and saying. Meetings in this sense are social and cultural validations, occasions that serve ritual functions for the tribal culture, and gatherings where people unscramble the things that are happening to them.[9]

If one were to take the first generally accepted view, then the goal is to improve meetings, that is, to make them function better as rational instruments of the organization. This has inspired an interesting genre of management literature that might be called the "how-to-make-meetings-better" books.[10] One of these books, by Michael Doyle and David Straus, *How to Make Meetings Work*, provides practical suggestions for improving meetings, such as using a facilitator to encourage full participation and keep the discussions on track, appointing a recorder to take down and post the "group memory," planning the meeting well in advance, developing an agenda, and arranging for the right space.[11]

John Tropman, Harold Johnson, and Elmer Tropman have generated useful principles for meeting management in their book, *Committee*

Management in Human Services: Running Effective Meetings, Committees and Boards, paraphrased as follows:

- *The Role Principle.* Meeting participants play roles, are often stuck in an expected role (devil's advocate, peacekeeper, cynic), but can change roles.

- *The Orchestra Principle.* For a concert there is a score, a hall, tickets sold ahead of time, and extensive rehearsal; similarly, meetings are ready to begin only after a period of extensive development and preparation.

- *The Three-Characters Principle.* Meetings usually have three types of topics—announcements, material for exploratory discussion, and matters for decision—and it is important to sort these topics into bundles and treat them differently.

- *The "No New Business" Principle.* New business is the enemy of an orderly meeting and invites meandering; it should be brought to the planners well in advance of the meeting.

- *The "No More Reports" Principle.* Reports are "oral newsletters" and might best be distributed prior to the meeting.

- *The Pro-Activity Principle.* Most of the meeting activity should be focused on the present and future not on a rehash of the past. [12]

The authors also suggest that when reports must be made, they should either follow the format of a one-page Executive Summary Technique or Options Memo Technique that summarizes the problem, states the options, and makes a recommendation.[13]

Recently, new technologies have been employed to make meetings more effective. James Creighton and James Adams describe these technologies in their book *CyberMeeting: How to Link People and Technology in Your Meeting.* Computers facilitate multimedia presentations, modeling, and simulations. They also provide immediate access to databases and can be used with whiteboard technology to make "working walls" for recording group memory. Groupware is now available to facilitate computer-supported collaboration. Amplified telephone, meeting room video conferencing, and desktop video conferencing, all bring participation in from a distance. Obviously, e-mail can also be used for calling meetings, arranging schedules, and sending out documents before and after meetings.[14]

Meetings can be improved by following simple guidelines and employing available technologies. Assuming that meetings are useful tools for getting the work of the organization done, the task is simply to work harder at making meetings better. On the other hand, if one were to take Schwartzman's second view, that meetings function in ways that go beyond their presumed purposes of information sharing and rational discussion, then one needs to use a different set of lenses to understand the behaviors of participants in meetings. Leaders learn to read this behavior and make sense of it.

Schwartzman's study of meetings, reported and elaborated in the work cited earlier, fits into the larger field of the " anthropology of occasions," and capitalizes on the anthropologist's ability to cause "us to question familiar and taken for granted assumptions in our society."[15] As rational tools for getting things done, Schwartzman argues, meetings don't have a very good track record. "It is assumed that most meetings in most organizations, are ineffective, unproductive, inept, chaotic, incompetent, wasteful, ridiculous, boring, tedious, silly, and so forth."[16] Perhaps meetings are viewed in this light because participants expect the wrong things from them. "It is possible to suggest that decisions, policies, problem solving, and so forth are *not* what meetings are about." What meetings *are* about, Schwartzman argues, is social validation, reconfirming status, and making meaning of things that have already occurred or are occurring.[17] They are essentially " communicative events" that are used to confirm a given social structure.[18]

If this is the case, what should one look for in meetings? A series of questions has been generated below based on Schartzman's discussion of the events and components of meetings:

- *Negotiating the Meeting.* Who called the meeting? Who has the right to call the meeting? Who are the participants and how many of them will be invited? When will the meeting be held? What if some people can't attend? Who must be there?

- *The Meeting Setting.* Whose territory will be the site for the meeting? Will it be a face-to-face meeting? What will be the seating plan?

- *Arrivals and Departures.* Who arrives first? Who arrives with whom? Who sits with whom? Who starts the meeting and permits breaks? What side issues are discussed before and after the meeting?

- *The Meeting Frame.* How is the meeting called to order (gavel, prayer, ritual) and who does this? How are agreements and disagreements framed for discussion? How does the meeting end?

- *Meeting Talk.* Who talks and how is the talk regulated? Which topics are discussed? What are the speaking and oratorical styles? What procedures are used for regulating debate and making decisions? Are decisions binding?

- *Participation and Interest.* Is participation required? What is done to instill duty and commitment as well as interest and enthusiasm? What conventions are used for maintaining interest?

- *Postmortems.* Who meets after the meeting? Where does the postmortem of the meeting take place and who participates? What is the format—chatting, gossiping, storytelling? How is the meeting being read?
- *Meeting Cycles.* What is the relationship of this meeting to previous and future meetings? What other related meetings do participants attend? What are the meeting patterns?[19]

Within the various components of the meeting, participants learn about power, status, their niche in the organization, how friendships are affirmed and antagonisms are played out, the way power struggles take place, where loyalties reside, and what the participants believe about the organization—"all in the guise of discharging business or work."[20] Schwartzman's view is that meetings "are not what they seem to be."[21]

REFLECTION

Which of the two views of meetings is most illuminating for you? Is it necessary to choose one view or the other? Are meetings what they seem to be or not?

Most meetings operate on two levels—as settings for rational discussion and as arenas for social validation. Perhaps this is what makes meetings so confusing and unsatisfying: one process keeps interfering with the other. Leaders learn to manage meetings and participate in them effectively, but they also know how to step back and ask: What is taking place here in this component of this meeting?

GROUPS AND TEAMS

Although meetings play an important role in colleges and universities, people also collaborate in other ways as members of groups and teams. Participants in meetings may come from across the institution to coordinate disparate activities, but may not in themselves constitute a functional group. Groups and teams are more often composed of people who work together on an ongoing basis, such as a faculty research team, an interdisciplinary teaching team, a residence hall staff, a special event task force, a committee that plans and carries out new student orientation, an emergency response team, or the president's senior management team. Groups and teams also meet, of course, but what they engage in is usually not so much a "meeting" with reports, agendas, and minutes, but rather an examination of the purposes and activities of their work with the intent to improve effectiveness. Sometimes groups and teams meet not only to talk about their work but also to do it.

Although *group or team* may not be the preferred nomenclature in colleges or universities—*department, committee, or task force* may be more common—much of the work done in postsecondary institutions takes place in what would be called *groups* and *teams* in other types of organizations.

Consider, for example, the college or university president's senior staff as a team. Estela Bensimon and Anna Neumann studied fifteen of these teams and reported their findings in *Redesigning Collegiate Leadership: Teams and Teamwork in Higher Education*.[22] They noticed that these teams have three functions:

- *The Utilitarian Function*—providing information, coordination and planning, and decision making.
- *The Expressive Function*—providing mutual support, giving counsel to the president.
- *The Cognitive Function*—viewing problems with multiple perspectives, questioning, challenging, arguing, monitoring, and feedback.[23]

Bensimon and Neumann observed that some presidents use these teams in complex ways in all three areas; and these can be designated *real teams*, as opposed to *illusory teams*, which focus mostly on the utilitarian function of doing.[24] The authors conclude that the strength of "real" presidential teams "lies in their ability to think together in ways that individuals typically cannot do."[25]

REFLECTION

What aspects of group behavior puzzle you? Does your group function effectively as a team? Are you a member of a group that works together as a team? What conditions are necessary for teams to perform well?

Group behavior was studied extensively during the second half of the twentieth century. The findings about so-called *group dynamics* are of interest to leaders because leaders so often find themselves in groups or leading groups. The research on groups helps leaders know what to expect from groups. Groups are used when individual effort is insufficient. When the total output is greater than the sum of individual efforts, there is an outcome called an *assembly* effect. What the group produces exceeds what individuals produce alone.[26] Groups also generate far more ideas than individuals do when they work alone.[27] Group discussion provides an opportunity to examine feelings and emotions, as well as ideas, and to alter what social scientists refer to as opinions, attitudes, and beliefs.[28]

It is known that groups go through various phases or stages over time. A classic formulation of these stages uses four catchy rhyming words:

- *Forming.* Testing member independence with emphasis on defining the task.
- *Storming.* Intragroup conflict and emotional expression.
- *Norming.* Development of group cohesion and establishing the rules.
- *Performing.* Functional role relatedness and emergence of solutions.[29]

Persons that enter a group after it has passed through certain stages may have considerable catching up to do and the other group members will need to make adjustments to the new member. Likewise, a group changes when a member leaves.

Scholars who study groups have noted also that communication takes place at two levels. At one level, members are communicating about the task to be completed; at another level, they are dealing with the *process* (sometimes referred to as social or maintenance needs) of the group members.[30] It is not surprising, then, that groups are not always "on task." They need the process interaction to build cohesion. *Cohesion* refers to the ability of the group members to get along, including their loyalty, pride, and commitment to the group. More simply put, cohesiveness is the degree of liking that members of the group have for each other.[31]

Participants also take on *roles* within the group, such as information seeker, elaborator, recorder, and energizer.[32] Groups also have *structure*; the composition of the group helps determine its structure and the group's communication reveals it. Some people play a more central role in the group; others end up on the periphery.[33] Groups also establish *norms* although the rules will vary from group to group. What may appear to be bold and abrasive confrontation in one group may be viewed simply as open and direct self-disclosure in another. The rules only need to work for that group, but once established, group members should try to abide by them.[34]

Groups also generate certain typical problems. *Conflict* is generated when group members disagree. When tension reaches high levels it can be destructive. *Apathy* occurs when the group loses interest in the task or when members perceive the goal to be unattainable. *Group think* occurs when they have failed to consider risks or alternatives. *Social loafing* occurs when one or more participants fail to carry out their responsibilities in the group.[35] All of these problems are natural and can be solved by being aware of them and dealing with them through open discussion.

All teams are groups, but not all groups are teams. When people get together on a Friday night and enjoy square dancing, they are referred to as a group, not a team. A team is a group with a mission. A group that has the responsibility for achieving or producing something, such as a heart transplant, is called a team.[36] Carl Larson and Frank LaFasto, authors of the classic work, *Teamwork: What Must Go Right, What Can Go Wrong*, offer this definition: "A team has two or more people; it has a specific performance objective or recognizable goal to be obtained; and coordination of activity among the members of the team is required for the attainment of the team goal or objective."[37] As noted earlier, teams share many properties with groups. Most of what happens in groups also happens in teams, but teams usually have a more focused mission. Larson and LaFasto examined teams in a variety of work settings and were able to generate a list of characteristics of high-performance teams. These include:

- Clear and elevating goal
- Results-driven structure
- Competent team members
- Unified commitment
- Collaborative climate
- Standards of excellence
- External support and recognition
- Principled leadership.[38]

In a college or university setting this translates into a clearly identified and challenging task, the right people on the team, evolving commitment, high expectations, a qualified and accepted leader, and sufficient administrative support.

Larson and LaFasto also noticed that not all teams have the same purposes nor do they function in the same way. They identified three types of teams based on function:

- *Problem-solving teams*—for identifying, defining, and solving problems
- *Creative teams*—for generating new ideas, services, or products
- *Tactical teams*—for carrying out a routine though sometimes-complex activity efficiently[39]

A slightly different support structure and means of operation is required for each type of team, but each can become a high-performance team in its own way.

Leaders learn to observe and understand group dynamics and team behavior, and they know how to distinguish between normal and unproductive activity of participants. A leader is often called upon to help groups function more effectively from within as a skilled participant or from outside as a facilitator.

GROUP FACILITATION

Leaders often facilitate the work of groups and teams. This may come about as part of the leader's established role or because an individual with a certain talent or expertise has stepped forth or been called upon to help a group or team do its work more effectively. Although no fixed rules are available to guide the facilitator because every group is different and needs its own type of help, many group facilitation techniques are available to those who want to learn what they are and develop the ability to use them. As with other aspects of learning to lead, the skills needed for effective facilitation can be learned and practiced.

Trevor Bentley provides a valuable compendium of these techniques in his book *Facilitation: Providing Opportunities for Learning*.[40] The word *facilitation* derives from the Latin verb *facilis*, which means *to make easy*.[41] A facilitator should help make it easier for the group or team to succeed in reaching its objectives. To do this, Bentley notes, the facilitator must first of all be able to identify certain communication patterns in the group such as monologue, conversation, dialogue, discussion, debate, or argument. The facilitator spots these different forms of exchange and ponders why they are being used and whether they are useful.[42] The effective facilitator also becomes a sensitive listener, not only to the type of communication, but also to its content and accompanying feelings and nonverbal behavior. Facilitators put forth great effort to be attentive and often summarize and restate what has been said. Without putting words into a particular speaker's mouth, the facilitator often captures in a more succinct and clear way what the speaker may be struggling to say. When the facilitator interprets what the speaker says, an opportunity usually is provided for the speaker to disagree or clarify.[43] Facilitators also listen to the level of listening within the group, and may encourage members of the group to listen more carefully to each other and to build on the previous speaker's comments.

A facilitator is faced at any given moment with a decision about whether and how to intervene. Should one let the seemingly pointless discussion continue or the heated argument rage? Bentley proposes a useful spectrum of intervention techniques ranging from gentle to forceful, paraphrased here:

- *Doing nothing* means "sitting quietly and not reacting." It allows the group members to "work things out for themselves."
- *Silence* is "saying nothing," but perhaps "using movement, gesture, or posture to influence what is happening."
- *Support* is acting in a way that encourages what an individual is doing or where the group is going.
- *Questions to clarify* are designed to gain understanding about something that has been said by an individual or about the group's intent.
- *Questions to move the group* ask if the group is ready to continue or change direction.
- *Questions on where next* clarify exactly where the group wants to go next.
- *Suggesting choices* provides options for the group to consider
- *Suggesting paths* gives the group an idea (when they are lost) about new directions they might take.
- *Suggesting ideas* takes place when the facilitator shares his or her own personal view of what the group is doing or what it might do.
- *Suggesting action* involves providing options when the group is divided or "at a loss for what to do next."
- *Guiding the group* occurs through telling the group what the facilitator would do if he or she was "in their situation."
- *Choosing for the group* is done when the group "is heading for a cliff edge" and needs to stop and think.
- *Directing the group* means telling the group what to do next, and is usually used as a last resort.[44]

As Bentley points out, "the facilitation spectrum is a continuum" involving at the upper-end a more forceful and more directive intervention.[45] The facilitator's challenge is to understand what might work best at a particular moment and to select the most appropriate intervention.

Participants in groups or on teams often comment on the *energy level* of the group, and this is another aspect of group behavior for facilitators to monitor. Bentley notes that "individual members bring their own physical, intellectual, emotional, and spiritual energy to the group. The resulting combination of energies becomes the group energy.[46] *Physical energy* is characterized by gestures, body movements, laughing and joking, or by people slouching down in their seats or dozing off. *Intellectual energy* is manifest by thoughtful probing and questioning. *Emotional energy* is shown through open and sometimes intense expression of feelings such as anger, joy, or sadness. *Spiritual energy* has to do with being willing to be exposed, take risks, and change, and may be displayed in openness to vulnerability or defensiveness.[47] Facilitators should understand that the various forms of energy are interrelated (high intellectual energy may be correlated with low emotional energy), and that the group's energy will ebb and flow. It is difficult for a group to sustain high energy for long periods of time, and it is not the facilitator's job to pump up the energy level of the group, but to let the group know how its energy level is being perceived.[48]

Facilitators need to be on guard against their personal need to manipulate the group or team. Manipulation is likely to occur when the facilitator has predetermined outcomes for the group, or even worse, a hidden agenda.[49] The group will spot manipulation and will tend to become uncooperative. This is especially important in settings where the person serving as facilitator is also serving in an administrative role, such as the provost facilitating the discussion of a group of deans. In such cases, the administrator may wish to call on a neutral party to facilitate the discussion or rotate the role of facilitator. Bentley quotes this wise advice from the *Tao of Leadership:* "Facilitate what is happening rather than what you think ought to be happening."[50]

REFLECTION

> Have you been in a position to observe good or poor facilitation? Do you have in mind the effective facilitator's toolbox of techniques? With a little practice could you become an effective facilitator? When should you call in a seasoned specialist?

Groups and teams need facilitation. A skilled facilitator can help a group achieve its purposes more efficiently and effectively. Leaders learn this skill and recognize when a group needs help.

PROJECT MANAGEMENT

Often a committee, task force, or team is appointed to work on a particular project with a fixed time duration. A special project team may be assembled to make plans for and carry out a new advising system, an annual giving campaign, a technology transition, a celebrity visit, or a full weekend of graduation events. In such cases a very specialized team is called together to plan and execute the project within a specific time frame. Although the term *project management* may not be used widely in colleges and universities, short-term projects that require diverse forms of expertise are numerous. Much can be learned about how to engage in such activities from the literature on project management.

Jack Meredith and Samuel Mantel, Jr., have produced a classic text on the subject entitled *Project Management: A Managerial Approach*.[51] There is a tendency to bring to mind very large projects when considering project management, such as building a nuclear power plant or sending an astronaut to the moon; but most projects, the authors point out, are comparatively small. A project is not necessarily characterized by size, therefore, but by complexity, by the need for a team of diverse individuals to produce an outcome called a *deliverable*.[52] The deliverable must meet three primary criteria: *performance, time, and costs*.[53] The project must include certain outcomes of a designated quality, and these must be delivered within an established time frame at a specified cost. It is not surprising, therefore, that projects need good management

REFLECTION

Have you ever watched a building being built? What do they do first? What next? How do the materials arrive at just the right moment? Who organizes all of that activity? What system is used?

The concept of *project management* grew out of the vast military efforts of World War II, and although one can bring to mind certain ancient projects, such as the Egyptian pyramids, that probably needed management, writers in the field trace the modern origin of the concept to the Manhattan Project, which produced the atomic bonb.[54] A project is "a specific finite task to be accomplished within a given time frame and cost. It has a purpose, a life cycle (beginning and end), certain interdependencies that make collaboration necessary, and a uniqueness that requires special organizational arrangements for its accomplishment."[55]

Leaders often participate in selecting projects, and as with program planning, they need to ask if the project is a good fit with the institutional mission. Sometimes one doesn't have much choice about projects such as "sacred cow" projects (the president wants it done), operating necessity projects (the old boiler system needs to be replaced), or competitive necessity projects (if we don't do it, they will). But sometimes there is a choice, not only about whether to do a particular project, but also about which project to choose to do among many that could be done.[56] In some cases, rather careful numerical and financial modeling needs to be undertaken, including the calculation of risks, before a decision is made even to become engaged in a particular project.[57]

Deciding where to lodge a project in the organizational structure presents a challenge. Some projects find their home in an existing functional unit, as in a college, reporting to a dean, even though the project may draw on personnel from other units. Other projects, sometimes referred to as *pure projects*, have their own home in a center or institute, reporting perhaps to a provost or president, or even floating a bit within the organization, such as a research project with a faculty member as principal investigator. Larger projects—perhaps several of them—may cut across several units simultaneously, creating a matrix model.[58] Whether a project has a functional, pure, or matrix organization can have important implications for obtaining resources and cooperation; and advantages and disadvantages exist for each arrangement.

Successful projects need a project manager. A project manager differs in important ways from a functional (line) manager. A project manager is usually a generalist with overall knowledge, as opposed to specialized knowledge; takes a systems approach, as opposed to an analytical approach to planning and problem solving; and facilitates cooperation, rather than applying specialized knowledge directly.[59] Project managers need to be good at fighting for resources, selecting and obtaining the right people for the project, and motivating them to work together.[60] As project management processes have grown more sophisticated through the years, several accepted techniques have emerged, and these may be adapted to projects in postsecondary settings. A useful source for ideas about such techniques is James Lewis's *Fundamentals of Project Management*.[61]

The first step, after the project has been conceptualized in a general way is to describe the mission of the project in writing. Lewis suggests three key questions to ask while the mission is being established:

1. What do we do?
2. For whom do we do it?
3. How do we go about it?[62]

Once established, the mission is elaborated into specific *objectives* and *subobjectives*. Objectives should be **SMART**:

Specific

Measurable

Attainable

Realistic

Time-limited.[63]

Objectives are the first step in breaking the project into manageable parts. When the mission and objectives are clear, these provide the basis for the *Work Breakdown Structure* (WBS).[64] The WBS consists of tasks, and subtasks broken down into the smallest chunks beyond which no further breakdown makes sense. The WBS provides a detailed description of the work that actually needs to be done to achieve the objectives. The description of these tasks includes the time to do them and the cost. The tasks are then arranged in a chronological order, with some tasks done in parallel (at the some time) and others following and depending on completion of antecedent tasks. The WBS is a logical interrelated web of activities.

A well-designed WBS can then be converted into a *schedule*. The schedule puts the time required for tasks and subtasks into an actual calendar of activities. Various events (discrete activities with defined beginning and ending times) are networked into a system that is sometimes illustrated with bar graphs or diagrams with boxes and arrows. The network of events defines the *critical path*—the overall timeframe that will be required to complete the project.[65] Naturally, the project manager must initiate control systems to see that all of the parts of the project are of high quality, are done on time, and stay within the budget. Progress is monitored all along the way and sometimes an *earned value analysis* is completed to show how much dollar value has been added at certain stages of the project.

Although sophisticated project management today uses engineering principles, mathematical theory, and computer modeling, and even though it may appear to be highly rationalized, cold, and abstract as a process, it takes human resources to apply it. As Paul Dinsmore points out in *Human Factors in Project Management,* successful projects depend on human factors, such as effective communication, successful negotiation, and good problem solving and decision making.[66] When a project fails to meet the deadline or overruns the budget, the system may be at fault, but more likely it is the people who are executing the system. Project management requires skilled people management.

Project management, therefore, involves juggling quality, costs, time and people. It can be and often is, stress-producing. In *Customer-Driven Project Management* Bruce Barkley and James Taylor note that a key fact about a project is that it is almost always customer-driven. Usually "it focuses on total customer satisfaction through the highest quality deliverables, whether products or services, at the lowest life cycle costs to compete in the global environment." That means that the organization must focus on "improving quality, increasing productivity, and reducing costs to satisfy customers."[67] That is usually stressful!

REFLECTION

Have you ever been involved in an activity that more or less fits the definition of a project? Were any project management techniques used? Was the project successful? Was it stressful? Was the project manager effective?

Colleges and universities usually have a number of projects underway simultaneously and although administrators may not call them projects or think of leaders of these activities as project managers, managing projects is often an aspect of what leaders do. No real leader will try to muddle through, but instead will try to help the project team become clear about the mission and objectives, will define the network of events that form the work breakdown structure, and set up a schedule of completion tied to actual calendar dates. Some leaders do this naturally, almost by instinct, but the more complex the project, the more sophisticated the engineering it will need. Sometimes members of project teams need to speak up when the project management is weak. That is another way to lead. Leaders refuse to watch a project fail.

COMMUNITY COLLABORATION

Not all teamwork takes place on campus within the boundaries of a particular institution. Today, colleges and universities increasingly find themselves as participants in larger community efforts, involving diverse groups of participants. This can happen as the campus tries to relate to its immediate neighborhood—the so-called "town and gown" relationship—or to various forms of civic engagement, most often through school or community improvement projects. Some collaborations even have international dimensions, depending on how *community* is defined. College and university administrators often find themselves engaged in complex forms of collaboration with community members in planning the work of centers or institutes, adult education programs, research and training grants, or other special projects. In such activities the emphasis shifts from team cooperation to community collaboration. The institution is one player among many.

David Chrislip and Carl Larson report on their study of an array of such community projects in, *Collaborative Leadership: How Citizens and Civic Leaders Can Make a Difference*.[68] They note a number of reasons why traditional forms of political leadership often fail—corrupt "old boy" networks, special interest groups, complex issues, diffusion of responsibility, and a culture of individualism—and suggest that in many communities new forms of organization are emerging based on collaboration. The word *collaboration*, rooted in the Latin words *com* and *labore*, literally suggests *working together*. Chrislip and Larson's definition of *collaboration* is as follows: "It is a mutually beneficial relationship between two or more parties who work toward common goals by sharing responsibility, authority, and accountability for achieving results." Collaboration is more than simply sharing knowledge and information (communication) and more than a relationship that helps each party achieve its own goals (cooperation and coordination). The purpose of collaboration is to create a shared vision and joint strategies to address concerns that go beyond the purview of any particular party.[69]

REFLECTION

Have you been involved with projects that take you beyond the campus and require collaboration among several groups? What makes such projects succeed or fail? What type of leadership do they need?

After studying forty-six cases of community collaboration, plus six additional exemplary cases in depth, Chrislip and Larson were able to draw conclusions about what makes collaboration succeed. These are paraphrased as follows:

- *Good timing and clear need*—stakeholders with a sense of urgency
- *Strong stakeholder groups*—well-organized groups that can represent many interests credibly
- *Broad-based involvement*—many participants from many sectors
- *Credibility and openness of process*—a process seen as fair and credible by participants and with ground rules for open participation
- *Commitment and/or involvement of high-level, visible leaders*—officials committed by actual presence or representation
- *Overcoming mistrust and skepticism*—increasing trust and belief that something significant can happen
- *Strong leadership of the process*—leadership of the process as opposed to leadership through advocacy of a particular point of view
- *Interim success*—acknowledgment and celebration of small gains
- A *shift to broader concerns*—less focus on narrow interests and more on broader community interests.[70]

One can see that collaborative leadership may require an orientation and set of skills that is quite different from the old vision of top-down hierarchical leadership. To begin with there is no top, but a diverse conglomeration of people with many interests trying to find and elaborate a common interest. What kind of leadership is called for when the goal is not a goal but a process? Chrislip and Larson were able to define four things that collaborative leaders do, as paraphrased in the following list:

- *Inspire commitment and action.* They "catalyze, convene, energize, and facilitate others to create visions and solve problems." They overcome cynicism and convince people that "something can be done."
- *Lead as peer problem solvers.* They relinquish command and control ideas about leadership, reduce power and status differences, share ownership, and help peers solve problems.
- *Build broad-based involvement.* They include the relevant community of interests, consciously encouraging inclusiveness by adding more people rather than fewer.
- *Sustain hope and participation.* They seek "incremental and attainable goals" and "keep people at the table." When frustrations and difficulties occur, they sustain confidence by promoting and protecting the process."[71]

As Chrislip and Larson note, collaborative leaders often "initiate a process that brings people together when nothing else is working."[72] The authors also acknowledge that "effective leadership in a world of peers may be the most difficult of all leadership roles."[73]

Colleges and universities, depending on their mission and the way they perceive their role in the community and the world, may find themselves in unusual forms of collaboration that require new approaches to leadership. Leaders in established roles may need to learn new leadership behaviors while others in the organization who participate in collaborative ventures may discover new leadership opportunities behind the scenes that they find comfortable and satisfying.

As Jon Katzenbach and Douglas Smith point out in their book, *The Wisdom of Teams: Creating the High Performance Organization,* "most models of the 'organization of the future' that we have heard about—networked clustered, nonhierarchical, horizontal, and so forth—are premised on teams surpassing individuals as the primary performance unit in the company."[74] Is that something that companies have learned from colleges and universities, or vice versa? In any case, committees, groups, and teams will probably continue to have an important place in the work of administrators. Leaders have no choice but to learn the skills of an effective facilitator and contributing participant.

MARY'S MENTOR

Mary's mentor wants her to remember these things about meetings, groups, and teams.

- Meetings have costs that can be weighed against the benefits.
- Meetings can be viewed as rational tools for getting work done, but also as occasions for social validation.

- Meetings can be made more effective through careful advance planning; sorting topics for announcement, discussion, and decision; restricting unscheduled new business and eliminating lengthy reports.
- Meeting behavior has its deeper meanings, so participants watch for such things as how and where the meeting is set, arrivals and departures of key players, how the meeting begins and ends, the talk of the participants, and the postmortems.
- The output of the group is greater than the sum of individual efforts.
- Groups go through stages, their members engage in process as well as task behavior, and they take on roles that give the group structure and cohesion.
- Groups generate typical problems such as conflict, apathy, groupthink, and social loafing.
- A team is a group with a mission.
- High-performance teams have definable characteristics, such as a clear and elevating goal, a unified commitment, and principled leadership.
- Purposes and structure vary for problem solving, creative, or tactical teams.
- Groups and teams sometimes need the skill of a facilitator to help participants understand better what they are saying and what the group should do next.
- Projects have deliverables that meet the criteria of performance, time, and costs.
- Project managers take a systems approach and are good at finding resources, selecting the right people, and getting them to cooperate.
- Community collaboration involves peer problem solving and requires a different style of leadership that focuses on process.
- Leaders learn to collaborate in many different ways, both as effective facilitators and savvy participants.

NOTES

1. Henry Mintzberg, *The Nature of Managerial Work* (Englewood Cliffs, NJ: Prentice-Hall, 1980), p. 41.

2. Helen Schwartzman, *The Meeting: Gatherings in Organizations and Communities* (New York: Plenum Press, 1989), p. 56.

3. Eli Mina, *The Complete Handbook of Business Meetings* (New York: American Management Association, AMACOM, 2000), pp. 7–12.

4. Ibid., p. 8.

5. Ibid., pp. 273–307.

6. Ibid.

7. Ibid., p. 7.

8. Ibid., pp. 47–59.

9. Ibid. pp. 41, 44, and 58.

10. Ibid., p. 53.

11. Michael Doyle and David Strauss, *How to Make Meetings Work* (New York: Jove Books, 1982).

12. John E. Tropman, Harold R. Johnson, and Elmer J. Tropman, *Committee Management in Human Services: Running Effective Meetings, Committees and Boards* (Chicago: Nelson-Hall, 1992), pp. 221–226.

13. Ibid., pp. 244–246.

14. James L. Creighton and James W.R. Adams, *CyberMeeting: How to Link People and Technology in Your Meeting* (New York: American Management Association, AMACOM, 1998), pp. 49–50.

15. Schwartzman, *The Meeting*, pp. 4, 39.

16. Ibid., p. 53.

17. Ibid., p. 40.

18. Ibid., p. 65.

19. Ibid., pp. 70–85.

20. Ibid., p.78.

21. Ibid., p. 86.

22. Estela Bensimon and Anna Neumann, *Redesigning Collegiate Leadership: Teams and Teamwork in Higher Education* (Baltimore: The Johns Hopkins University Press, 1993).

23. Ibid., pp. 34–43.

24. Ibid., pp. 44–45.

25. Ibid., p. 135.

26. Barry E. Collins and Harold Guetzkow, *A Social Psychology of Group Process for Decision Making* (New York: Wiley, 1964), p. 58.

27. Irving Lorge, "A Survey of Studies Contrasting the Quality of Group Performance and Individual Performance, 1920–1957," *Psychological Bulletin* 55 (1958), pp. 337–372.

28. Bernard Berlson and Gary Steiner, *Human Behavior: An Inventory of Findings* (New York: Harcourt, Brace, and World, 1964), p. 557ff.

29. Bruce W. Tuckman, "Developmental Sequence in Small Groups," *Psychological Bulletin* 63 (1965), pp. 384–399.

30. Alvin Goldberg and Carl Larson, *Group Communication* (Englewood Cliffs, NJ: Prentice-Hall, 1975), p. 46. The distinction is made earlier as well by George C. Homans in *The Human Group* (New York: Harcourt, Brace, and World, 1950).

31. Aubrey Fisher, *Small Group Decision Making: Communication and the Group Process* (New York: McGraw-Hill, 1980), pp. 39–43.

32. Kenneth D. Benne and Paul Sheets, "Functional Roles of Group Members," *Journal of Social Issues* (Spring 1948), pp. 4, 41–49.

33. Larry L. Barker, Kathy J. Wahlers, Kittie W. Watson, and Robert J. Kibler, *Groups in Process: An Introduction to Small Group Communication*, 3rd ed. (Englewood Cliffs, NJ: Prentice-Hall, 1987), p. 53ff.

34. James R. Davis and Adelaide B. Davis, *Effective Teaching Strategies: A Comprehensive Guide to Maximizing Learning in Organizations* (San Francisco: Berrett-Koehler, 1998), pp. 293–294.

35. Leland Bradford, Dorothy Stock, and Murray Horowitz, "How to Diagnose Group Problems," in Robert T. Golembiewski and Arthur Blumberg, eds. *Sensitivity Training and the Laboratory Approach* (Itasca, IL: Peacock Publishers, 1970), pp. 142–147.

36. Davis and Davis, *Effective Training Strategies*, p. 289.

37. Carl Larson and Frank LaFasto, *Teamwork: What Must Go Right, What Can Go Wrong* (Newbury Park, CA: Sage, 1989), p. 19.

38. Larson and LaFasto, *Teamwork*, p. 26.

39. Ibid., p. 42ff.

40. Trevor Bentley, *Facilitation: Providing Opportunities to Learn* (New York: McGraw-Hill, 1994).

41. Ibid., p. 27.

42. Ibid., p. 39.

43. Ibid., pp. 41–42.

44. Ibid., pp. 64–66.

45. Ibid., p. 67.

46. Ibid., p. 77.

47. Ibid., pp. 77–80.

48. Ibid., pp. 80–82.

49. Ibid., pp. 33–34.

50. Ibid., p. 20, The quotation is cited by Bentley as John Heider, *The Tao of Leadership* (Aldershot: Wildwood House, 1986).

51. Jack R. Meredith and Samuel J. Mantel, Jr., *Project Management: A Managerial Approach*, 3rd ed. (New York: John Wiley & Sons, 1995).

52. Ibid., p. 3.

53. Ibid., p. 4.

54. Ibid., p. 7.

55. Ibid., p. 8.

56. Ibid., p. 48.

57. Ibid., p. 49.

58. Ibid., pp. 153–162.

59. Ibid., pp. 110–111.

60. Ibid., pp. 119–122.

61. James R. Lewis, *Fundamentals of Project Management.* (New York: AMACOM, 1995).

62. Ibid., p. 30.

63. Ibid., p. 32.

64. Ibid., pp. 37–42.

65. Ibid., pp. 49–54.

66. Paul Dinsmore, *Human Factors in Project Management* (New York: AMACOM, 1984), pp. 1–8.

67. Bruce T. Barkley and James H. Taylor, *Customer-Driven Project Management* (New York: McGraw-Hill, 1994), p. 12.

68. David D. Chrislip and Carl E. Larson, *Collaborative Leadership: How Citizens and Civic Leaders Can Make a Difference* (San Francisco: Jossey-Bass, 1994).

69. Ibid., p. 5.

70. Ibid., pp. 52–54.

71. Ibid., pp. 138–141.

72. Ibid., p. 139.

73. Ibid., p. 140.

74. Jon R. Katzenbach and Douglas K. Smith, *The Wisdom of Teams: Creating the High Performance Organization* (New York: Harper Business, 1993), p. 19.

CHAPTER 5

Communication and Conflict Resolution: Finding Agreement

At the end of the first term, Mary realizes that she has been able to develop several important and satisfying relationships. The other deans have been especially cordial. She goes to lunch with faculty regularly. A warm relationship has developed with Dolores; and even Fred, though he has less to say, is becoming a close colleague. People appear to trust her more now that she has established solid relationships.

She spends a lot of time listening to faculty and to students, one-on-one, and that appears to have a high payoff. People like to be understood. She also takes great care with the college newsletter and makes sure that at least one article about faculty from her college appears in each issue of the University Sentinel. Even so, there are one or two faculty members who insist that they have a communication problem with her.

Sometimes she is called upon to resolve conflicts between students and faculty, usually about a grade, but sometimes about teaching methods or tests. In general, the little disagreements aren't so difficult to mend.

Then there are the ongoing conflicts that never seem to get resolved. This is the third time now that she has met with the economics professors from her college and the core curriculum professors from the college of business. The business faculty insist that their students need a practical, applied brand of economics while her faculty insist that they know what the field is about—numbers, graphs, and formulas—and if the students find that dismal, they should be thankful they only have to learn it and not teach it. Mary smiles to herself as she recalls that the business dean calls her economists the futile warlords.

Today's calendar shows a meeting in the provost's conference room on the proposed customized undergraduate degree completion program with

G & P Industries. That session could really blow up. Some of her faculty leaked the proposal to students who put a very unflattering article in the student newspaper about "selling out the undergraduate degree for half tuition." So the provost is bringing together representatives from the undergraduate council, student government, continuing education, the faculty senate, and G & P to resolve the conflict. The provost has asked a professor from the communications department to facilitate the discussion. That will be interesting. Mary would like to be able to support the new program, but not in its present form. What creative ideas can she bring to that meeting?

Then there is the ongoing battle with Duckworth about his salary. He has an excellent research record, but he wants to be bought out of all of his courses and paid overload, too. That's impossible! He's threatening to take his grants elsewhere or even to sue. He always wants to negotiate something and appears to enjoy it. She hates it, but if that's the game, she will learn to play.

LEADERS AND RELATIONSHIPS

When people are asked what is important and motivating in their lives, *personal relationships* lead the list.[1] Leaders depend on good relationships to achieve desired goals, and in some societies —particularly in Asian countries—good relationships must precede any agreements to do business. Relationships don't occur in a vacuum;[2] they develop over time in a context where people have the opportunity to meet and get acquainted. They occur within a network of other relationships, within the life cycle stages of young and old, and according to the rules of the culture.[3] "They all start in the same broad way—as a meeting of strangers."[4]

Leaders try to develop good relationships with the people with whom they work. What does it mean to "develop" a relationship and what is it exactly that develops when a relationship grows? Social psychologists study these questions and some of the answers can be found in the interesting text by Steve Duck, entitled *Relating to Others*.[5]

The way a relationship develops depends on several factors. "Relationships derive much of their essence from the things that partners do together"—the activities that individuals engage in jointly.[6] If one set of interactions is repeated frequently—attending the same meeting together—these are called *uniplex relationships*. On the other hand, people who share several different types of activities are said to have *multiplex relationships*. Relationships also depend on the frequency and the quality of interactions. Obviously, relationships will not develop as quickly when encounters are infrequent and superficial. Relationships grow when there is a degree of reciprocity, (each receives something similar), complementarity (a help giver and help seeker), or an unfolding intimacy based on self-disclosure. Relationships also grow when there is a perception of a relationship that can be identified and described, and when a sense of commitment develops.[7]

Relationships can break down, of course, for all the same reasons that they develop. People are no longer working in the same proximity or with the same interests, or the "glue" of reciprocity is no longer present. Sometimes relationships dissolve as a result of inept social skills or through boredom and the need for new social stimulation.[8] Regular patterns of dissolution can be traced when relationships break down, and these include phases of mental preparation, confrontation and discussion, seeking social support, and post-relationship evaluation.[9] In workplace settings, relationships often come apart as a result of miscommunication and unresolved conflict.

REFLECTION

What workplace relationships do you have? Are certain relationships developing while others are breaking down? What are the associated reasons? Are relationships important to leaders?

Much of the work of both leadership and administration takes place through relationships with colleagues. Effective leaders build those relationships and depend on them.

LEADERS AND COMMUNICATION

Effective leaders, so it is said, need to be good communicators. If this is so, what is good communication, and is that a skill that can be learned? Although one would hope that leaders would already have good communication skills, a periodic review and reminder about basic principles may help and can never hurt. These "rules" can be gleaned from any good basic text on communication, such as Kittie Watson and Larry Barker's *Interpersonal and Relational Communication*.[10]

Communication theorists remind us that a communication event involves both a sender and receiver of a message, and that this transaction can occur through several channels (sound, sight, touch) simultaneously. In addition, communication often includes some form of feedback about whether understanding is taking place. Verbal communication involves a triad of object, thought, and symbol; because symbol making employs abstraction, misunderstanding can occur easily. A message contains description, sometimes called *naming*, but it also involves the making of meaning, called *inference*, or at higher levels, *generalization*.[11] Good communicators realize that there is no one-to-one correspondence between what they say and what the listener perceives, and vice versa. People are always busy constructing their own meaning for the message.

Effective communicators also observe certain protocols for conversation. They try to send direct and congruent messages, as opposed to mixed or oblique messages with regard to content. They also try to maintain congruent verbal and nonverbal communication. They observe basic conventions about turn-taking and interrupting.[12] They look for communication clues in body language such as facial expression, gestures, and posture, as well as in tone of voice and rate of speech and they monitor this behavior in themselves as well.[13]

Although sending clear messages and obeying protocols is important, the key to effective communication is not so much in telling as in listening. People in high office especially, who have the authority to speak while others listen, may need to work hard at being good listeners. Serious listening involves being attentive. At a minimum this means not interrupting or rehearsing a reply while the other person is speaking.[14] Good listeners also encourage others to speak through *door openers* that invite conversation (tell me about it), *encouragers* that invite the speaker to continue (and then . . .), and *attentive silence*, which allows the speaker time to think.[15] Good listeners are also effective followers who listen for details throughout the entire account. Perhaps the most important aspect of listening, however, is in providing a response that demonstrates understanding. This can be done by reflecting—restating feelings, content, or both—and paraphrasing—distilling the essence of the speaker's message in one's own words.[16] Sometimes, the listener will seek confirmation of the reflection by asking: Did I understand you correctly?

REFLECTION

> On a scale of one to ten, how would you rate yourself as a communicator? As a listener? Can you identify leaders who are either good or poor communicators? How do others value communication skills in leaders?

Sometimes poor communicators don't even get the opportunity to be leaders. Otherwise well-qualified candidates for administrative positions are often turned down because of poor communication skills—speaking too fast or too slow, making assertions with an inflated sense of authority, or simply talking too much and failing to listen. Followers expect leaders to be good communicators.

ORGANIZATIONAL COMMUNICATION

Leaders are often called upon to communicate beyond the one-on-one exchange of personal conversation. They are asked to speak in public, write memos, make announcements, develop reports, and follow up on details. They often play a special role in keeping many constituents well-informed and sometimes find themselves at the center of a communications hub. This requires both good written and oral communication skills and an astute sense about who needs to know what. A leader today has many communication options, including mail (hardcopy), telephone (often resulting in voice mail), fax, e-mail, and live face-to-face conversation. Selecting the right medium for the right message and using it well is an art to be cultivated.

David Shenk suggests in *Data Smog: Surviving the Information Glut*, that we are all faced with information overload.[17] College and university administrators are no exception, receiving on a busy day forty or fifty e-mails, ten or twenty voice mails, and a stack of incoming letters, memos, and publications. Keeping up with all of this communication while one spends most of the day in conferences and meetings requires a heightened ability to discern the important amidst the trivial. Whether one perceives the amount of information available in an organizational setting today as an advantage or a threat, or both, almost everyone agrees that there is now a veritable deluge of information and that coping with the sheer volume of it requires an extensive commitment of time.

Even more challenging, the emerging new high-technology communications culture is spawning a different set of rules and expectations for communication. Immediate access and instant response are increasingly perceived as a right. Growing expectations for attention—including a justification for anger if one doesn't get it—bring a host of issues to the busy administrator's desk that might never have arrived there ten years ago. The ease in sending communications is sometimes accompanied by the expectation that the message must have been read simply because it was sent and the odd conclusion that if there is no reply, the request must have been approved. Although communication is faster, much of it is unclear, imprecise, full of error, and sometimes downright annoying.

The wise administrator is proactive about communication, setting rules about how and by what means communication will best be received, establishing boundaries regarding accessibility, and making clear exactly what may and may not be assumed. Careful choices are also made to fit the message to the right medium. E-mail may be a wonderful way to make travel plans with a colleague in a foreign country, but may not be the best way to negotiate a sensitive issue with someone across campus or down the hall. An exchange of four voice mails may or may not equate to one productive phone conversation. Above all, some messages requiring clear and detailed explanation need to appear in writing, perhaps in a memo, report, or formal publication. One universal challenge that leaders face today is in getting anyone's attention.

On most campuses, administrators can turn to a publications office for help with communication to internal as well as external constituencies. As Ann Granning Bennett points out, an effective publications office has "writers who can take institutional and academic information and translate it into copy that communicates effectively with all constituencies."[18] For administrators who need to communicate in writing, whether by e-mail, memo, or report, and choose to do so without assistance, following certain basic principles will enhance effective communication. Norman Darais provides these good suggestions:

- Be clear about the *objective*, the outcome that a particular piece of communication is attempting to accomplish.
- Know the *subject* intimately so that you are comfortable in writing about the people, facts, and details.
- Identify the *readers* and consider their interests and needs to know.
- Select an appropriate way to *package* the material in an appropriate medium.
- Develop a plan for *organization* of the message.
- Conduct *research* if necessary to gather up the important facts and details.
- Consider carefully the *elements of style* such as point of view (narrative voice), tone, verb tense, word choice, and sentence structure.
- Attend closely to *beginnings and endings* to capture attention and draw a clear conclusion.
- Engage in serious *revision and editing* to obtain a clean final copy.[19]

Leaders also manage their communication to prevent or reduce conflict by avoiding stereotypes, slang, excessive jargon, threats or implied threats, joking, sarcasm, or hostile questioning. As Deborah Borisoff and David Victor note in *Conflict Management: A Communication Skills Approach*, "Unlike speech, writing allows the luxury of one-sided communication—a monologue weighted in the writer's favor. While writing can prove to be among the strongest tools to reduce the likelihood of conflict, inappropriate writing styles may not only increase existing levels of conflict but also, often create conflict where none existed before."[20]

REFLECTION

> Locate an example of written communication in your organization
> and evaluate it for effectiveness. Can you find desirable elements?
> What is missing? Is language used that might provoke unnecessary
> conflict?

**Leaders never give up their search for open, inclusive, and effective
methods of communication.**

CONFLICT

Even when leaders put forth their very best efforts to communicate directly and clearly, communication sometimes breaks down; when that happens frequently, relationships can be affected. Sometimes people say, "There is a communication problem here," and occasionally there is; but very often actual, substantive disagreement exists. How do people respond in organizations when serious conflict arises?

One response is to deny that there is conflict and to try to gloss over differences. In colleges and universities, where there are often deeply held beliefs about rationality, harmony, and collegial governance—we are, after all, a community of scholars—there is a natural tendency to regard conflict as inappropriate, abnormal, and even dangerous. William Wilmot and Joyce Hocker in their text entitled *Interpersonal Conflict*, point out that in general people don't like conflict and that it brings to mind unpleasant metaphors: that conflict is warlike, violent, explosive, and adversarial (as in a trial); and that it involves struggle, brings out the animal side of human nature, and usually ends in a mess.[21]

Another response is to regard conflict as natural and normal, as something to be faced and resolved—and even managed. M. Afzalur Rahim, in his useful book, *Managing Conflict in Organizations*, provides this practical definition: Conflict is "an interactive process manifested in incompatibility, disagreement, or dissonance within or between social entities."[22] Those social entities produce *intrapersonal conflict*, seen as conflict within an individual, usually about some choice; *interpersonal conflict*, manifest between two or more individuals; *intragroup* conflict, appearing among individuals or subgroups within a group; and *intergroup* conflict, manifest between two or more divisions or departments within an organization.[23] Rahim also suggests that even though there may be differences in the way writers define conflict, scholars are in general agreement that conflict usually involves the following elements: opposing interests, recognition of disagreement, beliefs that the other side will thwart their interests, a process that grows out of actual experiences of conflict, and specific actions where both sides have thwarted the other's interests.[24] Rahim also distinguishes between affective conflict driven by feelings and emotions and substantive conflict about content, task, or action.[25] Conflict can brew beneath the surface, but it is not usually called *conflict* until it reaches a recognizable threshold level of intensity.[26]

Rahim is among those scholars who believe that conflict is not necessarily a bad thing. Too little conflict may encourage stagnation, mediocrity, and groupthink, "but too much conflict may lead to organizational disintegration. . . . A moderate amount of conflict, handled in a constructive manner, is essential for attaining and maintaining an optimum level of organizational effectiveness." This belief in the positive value of restrained conflict supports the concept of conflict management. Rahim concludes, "What we need for contemporary organizations is conflict management, not conflict resolution" to enhance "the constructive functions of conflict."[27]

REFLECTION

Can you identify "incompatibility, disagreement, and dissonance" between individuals and within and among groups in your organization? What is your "gut-level" reaction to conflict? How can leaders play a constructive role in conflict resolution and conflict management?

Leaders are able to identify the people in organizations who provoke conflict for the sake of conflict and will take steps to constrain destructive disagreement. On the other hand, leaders will acknowledge and help manage healthy differences. They will surely encourage honest confrontation of issues that bring about repeated conflict.

INFORMAL NEGOTIATION

Sometimes leaders are called upon to facilitate conflict resolution or participate constructively in a process being facilitated by someone else. At times, a case from an appeals process lands in the leader's office, or a dispute between a faculty member and a student, two faculty members, or two other administrators beckons for resolution. The leader is expected to play a role in resolving these conflicts. At other times, a leader is a party to a conflict—one of the antagonists—and needs to be skillful in working with others to bring about a favorable resolution.

Excellent advice on conflict resolution through negotiation can be found in a popular work by Roger Fisher and William Ury entitled *Getting to Yes: Negotiating Agreement Without Giving In.*[28] The authors offer several guidelines that make conflict resolution more likely:

- *Don't Bargain Over Positions.* Often the parties to a conflict come together with well-established positions—predetermined ideas about what they will or will not accept. It is important to get beyond these positions to address underlying concerns and interests.

- *Separate the People from the Problem.* Try not to attack the people involved in the disagreement or to personalize the issues. Think about the issues apart from the personalities of the participants in the conflict.

- *Focus on Interests, Not Positions.* Each party has underlying interests— the things that they most want to gain from the resolution. Sometimes the parties even have common interests. The task is to discover the underlying interests and if at all possible to serve these interests through the resolution.

- *Invent Options for Mutual Gain.* The creative part of conflict resolution is in finding options that enhance the interests of both parties. For these options to surface the disputants must give up their premature conclusions about solutions, stop searching for a single answer, abandon the idea of a "fixed pie," and stop thinking that "solving their problem" is the problem. The goal is mutual gain through new and creative arrangements.

- *Insist on Using Objective Criteria.* Principled negotiation involves using objective criteria for evaluating the agreement, including fair standards for judging the process and the outcomes. Objective criteria are often independent of the will of either party and may include such things as efficiency, precedent, costs, reciprocity, or the common good.

Although Fisher and Ury also provide suggestions about what to do when there is an imbalance of power, a refusal to cooperate, and deception,[29] their model generally assumes and works best when the participants are reasonable and want to cooperate. In some respects it is the ideal model for conflict resolution in college and university settings, where these conditions are usually present.

REFLECTION

Consider a conflict you know about and ask yourself if the principles in *Getting to Yes* would work. Have you seen them work? Do you have doubts?

Under conditions where people are honestly seeking rational resolutions of conflict, informal negotiation can be used to craft solutions that not only satisfy the participants but also enrich and enlarge the scope of endeavor over which there had been conflict.

ADVERSARIAL NEGOTIATION

Sometimes conflict occurs in a setting where the participants view the disagreement as adversarial, that is, as a zero-sum game "in which positive outcomes to one party are directly and equally matched by negative outcomes to the other."[30] In some cases this may be only a perception, and the disputants may discover that they can create outcomes that are in fact "win/win."[31] At other times a true zero-sum situation exists, with winners and losers, and in these adversarial cases the disputants may not be reasonable and will rely on whatever power they think they have.

Power, like conflict, is another concept that people in general prefer not to discuss, especially in a democratic society in which all persons are supposedly created equal. Power, however, is acknowledged in the everyday language of organizations when people use the terms *power struggle*, *power politics*, or *power play*.[32] Often the parties to a conflict have different types and amounts of power available to bring to the negotiation, and these are referred to as *power currencies*. Just as a particular currency (marks, dollars, pounds) works chiefly in the country where it is used, the power one has must be valued by others in the negotiations for it to function as power. "Power depends on having currencies that other people need."[33] What are the sources of power? Some power derives from the position itself, from controlling resources and information, from being in the right place at the right time, or from not being easily replaced.[34] Power currency theory suggests, however, that power is situational, and in negotiation that means having control or at least influence over what someone else wants.

Often adversarial negotiation takes place in a context where recognizable inequalities of power exist. When a power imbalance exists, people with high power can use it, or they can employ restraint, focus on interdependence, and share power by delegating and consciously empowering others. People with low power can exercise calm and rational persistence and are urged not to give up, that is to stay actively engaged over time.[35] Remember, however, that power can be significant or insignificant in negotiations depending on its currency value in a specific context.

REFLECTION

Have you been in conflicts where you feel powerless? Were some power currencies available to you that you might not have recognized? Have you been in conflicts where you felt powerful? How did you choose to exercise your power? Were your choices effective?

Assume for a moment the worst scenario: a situation in which the parties are in an intense zero-sum conflict, power is clearly a factor, there is no facilitator, and the rational guidelines for "getting to yes" have been subverted by the cynical Machiavellian principles of expedience, craftiness, and duplicity. However inappropriate this may appear in a postsecondary setting, the conflict has come to this point, and serious recognizable losses could occur for either party. What strategies are likely to be used and how does a person prepare for this kind of tough-minded adversarial negotiation?

A useful review of these strategies and tactics is presented in James C. Freund's book, *Smart Negotiating: How to Make Good Deals in the Real World.*[36] Freund's advice is to begin by assessing whether the playing field is level or not, and in either case trying to tilt it to one's advantage.[37] What is there to bargain with in this situation and how can these factors be leveraged?

In thinking about the adversary, Freund suggests, ask how necessity, desire, competition, and time could work to one's advantage or disadvantage. If it is absolutely necessary that Party A achieve the goal, that is an advantage to Party B. If achieving the goal is not a necessity but is deeply desired, that is also an advantage to Party B. Does Party B have competition—that is, can Party A get what is desired somewhere else? Then that's an advantage to Party A, unless Party B can eliminate or neutralize the competition. Is time a factor? If Party A is under a deadline, Party B may have an advantage.[38] The important first step is to become aware of all of the strengths and weaknesses on both sides. Freund's advice is: "If you are strong, make sure your counterpart knows it. If you're weak, work hard to keep him from realizing it."[39] Catalogue advantages and leverage them—that is, make the most of them. Remember, however, that "leverage factors aren't necessarily permanent. They can change swiftly in the course of negotiations."[40]

Success in negotiation also depends on information. Who knows what? Who is bluffing? Information can be gathered in many ways. Some information is public, some is available from knowledgeable third parties, but some must be obtained from one's counterpart. When the latter is necessary, a low-key, indirect approach with general, open-ended questions may encourage revelation of what one needs to know. At other times one must ask directly. Lying is discouraged, but protecting sensitive information is something both parties will try to do.[41] Both also need to balance secrecy with honesty as they try to maintain credibility and not be caught bluffing. If Party B is bluffing and Party A knows it, Party A will go elsewhere to make a deal, and Party B will have lost out when they might have been willing to negotiate.[42]

Once the negotiation actually begins to take place, specific offers and counteroffers appear on the table, and both parties are faced with serious questions: Is this what I want? What tradeoffs am I willing to make? Am I sacrificing too much? Can I make a better deal if I wait or is this my last chance? Is this really a compromise? Freund suggests that effective negotiation involves good judgment—"the ability to strike the right balance between vying and compromise."[43] He suggests that the goal is "to achieve a functional balance between what you do to gain an advantage at your counterpart's expense and what you do to move the two of you closer to an eventual compromise."[44] The goal is the outcome, not the process of winning. Although good negotiators use perseverance in pursuing the details of what they want, they temper it with perspective, a healthy realization of what is possible. Freund advises: "You're not going to prevail on all the issues that arise in negotiation, so save yourself for the significant ones. Let your counterpart take home a few trophies."[45] This is especially good advice when the parties have an ongoing work relationship that brings them back to continuing negotiation over time. No one wants to face an adversary who is still bitter from the last round of negotiations.

REFLECTION

> Have you ever been involved in adversarial negotiations? Do you expect to be? Are you comfortable with Machiavellian negotiation? If not, what bothers you?

Naturally, certain ethical issues arise when one is engaged in Machiavellian-style negotiation, certainly concerning honesty and deceit, but also about whether any desirable end warrants such shameless means. These are difficult choices in any organization, but in colleges and universities, hard-nosed negotiation violates certain sensibilities about honesty and integrity that are fundamental to the academic enterprise. The goal, of course, is to resolve conflict (or manage it) in less confrontational ways.

If negotiation becomes a necessity, then one must weigh carefully the desirability of the end and the means that must be used to achieve it. There are, after all, many worthwhile causes to fight for on a college campus. Maintaining one's freedom to act effectively is important: It is one thing for leaders to relinquish cherished dreams because they refuse to play the power game to achieve them, but it is quite another matter for leaders to be vanquished because they didn't know *how* to play the game. Leaders who consistently lose through negotiation sometimes have trouble maintaining their reputation as leaders.

SELECTING AN ALTERNATIVE DISPUTE RESOLUTION METHOD

In some instances, administrators become involved as third parties to help resolve other people's conflicts; at other times they need to seek outside help themselves for unresolved conflicts in which they are participants. In recent years, in an effort to resolve conflict before it turns into litigation, several mechanisms for settling conflict have developed under the general designation of *alternative dispute resolution* (ADR). The movement has been initiated, interestingly enough, at law schools; and The Harvard Program on Negotiation has produced a useful book edited by Lavinia Hall entitled *Negotiation: Strategies for Mutual Gain*.[46]

ADR is the umbrella term used for a wide array of methods now used for addressing conflict, including the more familiar methods described above as informal and adversarial negotiation. In addition, several types of third-party interventions can be used to help reach agreements when there is conflict. The most common roles are as follows:

- A *facilitator* helps with logistics in the proceedings of meetings.
- A *mediator* guides or helps people come to a voluntary agreement.
- An *arbitrator* tries to understand the issues on all sides and then imposes an agreement, as a judge.[47]

A mediator is often helpful in focusing and speeding up a negotiation process where the parties to the conflict want to reach an agreement but may need some help in doing so. An arbitrator is used when agreement can't be reached by the disputants and they agree to an imposed solution.[48] Binding arbitration is used when the parties agree in advance to accept the recommendation, but nonbinding arbitration is also a choice. Several hybrid varieties of these basic roles have generated useful techniques. *Fact finding* involves determining and presenting the facts but not imposing a solution, although an opinion may be offered. *Final offer arbitration* asks both parties to submit their best offer, knowing that the arbitrator will pick the one that appears to be most reasonable. In some states, for certain kinds of legal cases, ADR is required before the case comes to court and this may be applied as a general rule to certain categories of cases or on an individual referral basis by the judge. These efforts have also generated some useful techniques. A *special master* is sometimes assigned to conduct fact finding, supervise a decree, or make recommendations to a judge. A *neutral expert* is sometimes assigned when technical issues are involved. A *minitrial* involves going through the pretrial procedures, including sharing information; and a *summary jury trial* is like a minitrial but takes the case before a mock jury to gain a sense of how the case might come out.[49]

REFLECTION

Have you used or observed the use of ADR principles and techniques? What have been the results? Can you think of a conflict where some adaptation of an ADR technique would be useful? What criteria might you use for selecting the best technique?

ADR methods vary across a continuum that includes informal negotiation, adversarial negotiation, mediation, and arbitration. Some of these options may be voluntary, some mandatory; some may include third parties. Effective leaders have a repertoire of ADR techniques, and they develop a keen sense of when to use which techniques.

Leaders hope to avoid conflict through effective communication skills, but they also realize that conflict will occur in spite of these efforts. Some conflict is useful to the organization and some is destructive. Productive conflict needs to be managed and destructive conflict needs to be contained. Most conflict can be and should be resolved through open discussion of interests and by generating creative win/win solutions. Sometimes conflict requires difficult hard-nosed negotiation. When conflict occurs, it is always useful to ask why; when it has been resolved, it is important to ask how it might have been avoided. Most administrators would agree that conflict takes too much of their time—hours they would prefer to reserve for other forms of leadership. Leaders also recognize, however, that "positive conflict . . . celebrates diversity and encourages opposing views, and that conflict can be managed more easily when there is "a common mission and unified direction."[50]

MARY'S MENTOR

Mary's mentor wants her to remember these things about communication and conflict resolution:

- Building relationships is important.
- Leaders are effective communicators both verbally and in writing.
- Good communicators observe standard protocols for conversation and are active listeners.
- Leaders play a special role in keeping people well informed, particularly those affected by decisions.

- Substantive differences are often wrongly cast as a breakdown in communication.
- Conflict is normal and need not be denied.
- Conflict can take the form of intrapersonal, interpersonal, intragroup, or intergroup conflict.
- Conflict can be resolved, managed, or even encouraged.
- Conflict can be resolved when the focus is not on positions or people, but rather on interests, and when participants in the conflict work together to invent options for mutual gain that measure up to objective criteria.
- Some conflict involves adversarial negotiation, which requires skill in assessing and leveraging advantage, gaining information, and exercising good judgment about vying and compromise.
- Leaders ask whether the end justifies the means and learn how to play the adversarial negotiation game, even if they sometimes choose not to do so.
- As third parties, leaders often take on the role of facilitator, mediator, or arbitrator.
- Leaders sometimes use or adapt other ADR techniques, such as fact finding, final offer arbitration, special master, and neutral expert.
- Leaders develop a repertoire of ADR techniques and know how to choose among them.
- Court *is* the last resort.

NOTES

1. Steve Duck, *Relating to Others*, 2nd ed. (Buckingham, England: Open University Press, 1999), p. 1.
2. Ibid., p. 18
3. Ibid., pp. 16–19.
4. Ibid., p. 26.
5. Ibid.
6. Ibid., p. 41.
7. Ibid., pp. 41–43.
8. Ibid., pp. 88–89.
9. Ibid., pp. 93–98.
10. Kittie W. Watson and Larry L. Barker, *Interpersonal and Relational Communication* (Scottsdale, AZ: Gorsuch Scarisbrick, 1990).
11. Ibid., pp. 106–107.
12. Ibid., p. 12.
13. Ibid., pp. 136–142.

14. Ibid., p. 188.

15. Ibid., p. 189.

16. Ibid., p. 190.

17. David Shenk, *Data Smog: Surviving the Information Glut* (San Francisco: HarperEdge, 1997).

18. Ann Granning Bennett, "The Publications Office: Perspectives on Quality and Professionalism," in A. Westley Rowland, ed., *Handbook of Institutional Advancement*, 2nd ed. (San Francisco: Jossey-Bass, 1986), p. 533.

19. Norman A. Darais, "Writing Effectively for Advancement Publications," in Rowland, *Handbook of Institutional Advancement*, pp. 546–554.

20. Deborah Borisoff and David Victor, *Conflict Management: A Communication Skills Approach* (Englewood Cliffs, NJ: Prentice Hall, 1989). The quotation is from p. 165 and the list of things to avoid from pp. 33–36.

21. William W. Wilmot and Joyce L. Hocker, *Interpersonal Conflict*, 6th ed. (New York: McGraw-Hill Higher Education, 2001), pp. 17–22.

22. M. Afzalur Rahim, *Managing Conflict in Organizations*, 3rd ed. (Westport, CT: Quorum Books, 2001), p. 18.

23. Ibid., p. 23. See also chapters 6–9 for a full description of each type of conflict.

24. Ibid., p. 18.

25. Ibid., p. 21.

26. Ibid., p. 19.

27. Ibid., p. 76.

28. Roger Fisher and William Ury, *Getting to Yes: Negotiating Agreement Without Giving In* (New York: Penguin Books, 1981). The summaries that follow are drawn from Chapters 1–5.

29. Ibid., Chapters 6–8.

30. Rahim, *Managing Conflict in Organizations*, p. 20.

31. Wilmot and Hocker, *Interpersonal Conflict*, p. 100.

32. Ibid., p. 97.

33. Ibid., p. 107.

34. Ibid., p. 111.

35. Ibid., pp. 121–126.

36. James C. Freund, *Smart Negotiating: How to Make Good Deals in the Real World* (New York: Simon & Schuster, 1992).

37. Ibid., p. 42.

38. Ibid., pp. 43–45.

39. Ibid., p. 46.

40. Ibid., p. 47.

41. Ibid., pp. 55–66.

42. Ibid., pp. 67–68.

43. Ibid., p. 79.

44. Ibid.

45. Ibid., p. 82.

46. Lavinia Hall, ed., *Negotiation: Strategies for Mutual Gain* (Newbury Park, CA: Sage Publications, 1993).

47. Howard Raiffa, "The Neutral Analyst: Helping Parties to Reach Better Solutions," in Hall, *Negotiation*, p. 14.

48. Frank E.A. Sander, "The Courthouse and Alternative Dispute Resolution," in Hall, *Negotiation*, p. 46.

49. Ibid., pp. 45–58.

50. Dean Tjosvold, *The Conflict Positive Organization: Stimulate Diversity and Create Unity* (Reading, MA: Addison-Wesley, 1991), p. 143.

CHAPTER 6

Problem Solving and Decision Making: Employing Rational, Legal, and Ethical Criteria

Friday afternoon! Dean Williams comes to the end of this week completely exhausted. The week began with two students—both women—coming to her office to inquire about their grades for a workshop that they took in the summer session. They had completed the required assignments, but still after all these months, no grades appeared on their transcripts. They told her that their tuition had been paid through a grant, but that other students who had initially been registered for no credit had already received grades. Upon further investigation conducted by her Associate, Fred Newton, Dean Williams learned that the grant had no provisions for training, that noncredit fees had been charged to some students, and that Professor Watkins had deposited the fees in a special holding account for the grant. On top of that, Professor Watkins had told the noncredit students, they could receive credit if they made "special arrangements" with his teaching assistant, Chip Merritt. What was this all about? Was something illegal taking place? Something unethical? Every day, almost every hour, Fred and Dolores had come up with some shocking new tidbit of evidence. Today it is that Professor Watkins earned a perfect 5.0 on all of his course evaluations for that workshop. Were these being doctored by his TA?

So much valuable time being devoted to this one mind-boggling problem when there are so many important decisions pending! The search committees for three new faculty positions are meeting and that process needs to be monitored. A recommendation for tenure—it was negative—deserves her careful attention. A student's honor code case has landed on her desk: a questionable recommendation for expulsion without much respect for due process for the student. And now—this is new—a threatened lawsuit by

one of the faculty over intellectual property rights to materials developed
for a distance learning course.

She listens to the chimes from the bell tower at Harkness Hall. Five
o'clock. Finally, this part of the campus has grown quiet. She leans back
against her desk, folds her arms, and slips into a lonely meditation on de-
cision making. There must be some way to be more systematic, more ra-
tional, more data driven, so that her decisions produce better outcomes
and are less fraught with risk. Naturally, she must stay out of court. But
beyond that, what bothers her most is whether her decisions are "right"—
not only for the individuals involved, but also for the institution. Many
decisions she faces appear to have ethical ramifications. On top of every-
thing else is she expected to be some kind of moral leader, too? She's not
so sure she's comfortable with that role. Who's to say what's right and
wrong? Besides, she's no saint. On the other hand, she can't let that mess
with Professor Watkins go unresolved, can she?

Most leaders in colleges and universities find themselves spending significant amounts of time—usually more time than they
wish—on problem solving and decision making. As with other
skills that leaders need, these can be learned. Leaders who are near the
top of the organizational chart surely need these skills, but leaders at all
levels of the institution, whether as individuals or as members of committees and task forces, find themselves making decisions—or at least
shaping recommendations for decisions—that need to be reasonable, legal,
and ethical. What do leaders do when they address problems and make
decisions? What do they take into account?

USING RATIONAL MODELS

A problem is a question proposed for solution or discussion, usually a
matter involving doubt, uncertainty or difficulty. Diane Halpern cites a
classic example of a problem in her book *Thought and Knowledge: An In-*
troduction to Critical Thinking.

> Suppose you are driving alone at night on a long, dark stretch of free-
> way that is infrequently traveled when you suddenly hear the famil-
> iar thump-thump of a flat tire. You pull onto the shoulder of the road
> to begin the unpleasant task of changing a tire, illuminated only with
> the light of the moon and a small flashlight. Carefully, you remove
> the lug nuts and place them in a hubcap by the roadside. A speed-
> ing motorist whizzes past you hitting the hubcap and scattering the
> lug nuts across the dark freeway and out of sight. Here you sit, spare
> tire in hand, a flat tire propped against the car and no lug nuts, on a

dark and lonely stretch of freeway. To make matters worse, a cold rain
is beginning to fall. What would you do?[1]

The problem is "classic" in many respects. There is a *desired outcome* at
the center of it: get the spare tire on the wheel. There is *information given*
in the problem, some of it relevant, some not. The loss of the lug nuts
makes the situation *problematic*, and the problem may have to be *recast*
or worked on *systematically* to arrive at a *solution*.

Halpern reports that one of her students claimed to have had this problem occur in another setting, during daytime, with the following resolution:

> The flat tire occurred alongside a large mental institution near our
> college. While the hapless motorist sat pondering his problem, he
> attracted the attention of several "residents" of the institution, who
> gathered near the motorist along the chain link fence that separated
> them. One resident offered this solution to the motorist's problem:
> Remove one lug nut from each of the other tires and use them to
> attach the spare. Each tire should hold securely with three lug nuts
> until the motorist reaches a gas station. The grateful motorist
> thanked the institution resident and then asked, "How'd you think
> of such a good solution to this problem?" The resident replied, "I'm
> not dumb, I'm just crazy."[2]

Problem solving is different from decision making. People make decisions by selecting among choices about what course of action is best. Problem solving comes first and is focused on generating solutions that will
make a change for the better. Problem solvers make recommendations;
they say how they think a particular problem can be addressed with a
particular solution. Then it is up to decision makers to decide what to do.
Once the solution to the lug nut problem has been offered, someone still
has to decide whether that is the preferred solution and what probability
it has of succeeding.

Most problem solving and decision making gets complicated. The more
influences (variables) relevant to the situation, the more difficult it is to
keep them all straight. Picture the juggler keeping several tenpins in the
air or the circus performer spinning a dozen plates simultaneously. It
"boggles the mind" we say, and *boggle*, the dictionary tells us, is to alarm,
astound, shock or stagger; and so our mind must find some alternative to
getting boggled. Psychologists call this boggling "cognitive overload." Our
mind needs some system for dealing with complexity. That is why we turn
to mental models.

We operate with mental models all the time, of course, in our daily life.
Usually these are fairly simple pictures of how things work. As Thomas
Ward, Ronald Finke, and Steven Smith have put it well:

> We actively construct mental models to comprehend complex phe-
> nomena, and we use our general knowledge about the workings of
> the world to do so. We might want to understand the nature of the
> digestive process in humans, how a clutch or brake system operates,
> or why the sun, moon, and stars appear and disappear in a consis-
> tent sequence. The mental pictures we form of the component parts
> of these systems and how those parts interact are called mental
> models.[3]

Mental models are sometimes referred to by other names. They may be
called mental tactics, rational systems, languages, programs, or strategies.
The important point is not what they are called but how they function
as tools for problem solving and decision making.

Administrators are often required to deal with complex problems for
which a mental model would be useful, such as planning the budget for a
new program, delivering a course in a new way, developing a more effective staff utilization plan, reassigning space, reducing attrition, or managing a raise pool more equitably. Recognizing the need for a mental
model is usually not difficult: one's mind begins to go in circles as cognitive overload sets in and confusion and anxiety increase. The tendency
is to want to rush in with a premature solution or to escape screaming
"let me out of here!" The first step is to place the problem in a tried and
true framework for problem solving.

The classic study of problem solving is Newell and Simon's *Human
Problem Solving*.[4] They provide the theory and a general problem solving
model represented in most texts on the subject, outlined briefly here.

- *Goal State*. Most problems call for solution. In the flat tire problem,
  having the spare tire on the wheel is the goal state, or even more generally, driving the car again. It is possible to observe people in organizations engaged in a flurry of problem-solving activity without first
  having arrived at clear concept of the goal state, some idea of what
  things will be like when the problem is solved.

- *The Initial State*. The conditions that are given along with the statement
  of the problem describe the initial state. They are what the problem
  solver has to work with initially. The initial state includes all the givens
  that people bring to the problem: conditions, boundaries, and information currently available.

- *Problem Space*. The decision gap between the initial state and the goal
  state is the problem space—the area within which the problem can be
  worked out.

- *Solution Paths*. Within the problem space a number of options can be
  generated. Options are the potential solutions or the steps in the pro-

cess that might add up to a solution. Solution paths are the creative ideas that people in organizations generate as possible solutions or steps toward a solution of the problem.

- *Operations.* Also within the problem space, certain operations must be performed to move from the initial state to the goal state. Mental models become very useful in performing operations because usually the operations are quite challenging.

- *Barriers.* The problem space is filled with barriers. It is not so easy to move from initial state to goal state; if it were easy, there would not be a problem. If there were no barriers, these operations might best be referred to as tasks, algorithmic activities for which the solution methods are already known. If there are no barriers there is no problem.[5]

Newell and Simon's general framework for thinking about problem solving provides a useful overall model into which more specific mental models fit. What happens within the problem space is crucial, of course, and this is where mental models come into play directly. These are some of the mental models that can be used to attack problems.

- *Random Search.* Random search is sometimes called trial and error. Random search works when the actual number of options is small.[6]

- *Systematic Random Search.* This mental model consists of classifying the random search efforts, writing them down, and noticing the degrees of effectiveness that certain options may have.[7] These efforts take the randomness out of random search to make it more systematic.

- *Hill-climbing.* When the exact goal is unknown, as in trying to reach a mountain peak hidden in the clouds, one can at least take steps in what is presumably the right direction.[8] Physicians sometimes use hill-climbing to arrive at the right dose of medication for a chronic patient. The drug can be increased or decreased in small doses until the unspecified goal has been reached. Unlike trial and error, there is at least some feedback in this situation as the goal is approximated a step at a time.

- *Means-End Analysis.* If the goal is the end, and the means for getting there are not clear, it is sometimes useful to find subgoals and then devise the means for reaching these. One might say more simply that this is a way of dividing a problem into subproblems in order to work on the easier parts first.[9]

- *Working Backward.* The natural question to ask is, What comes first? With certain kinds of problems, it may be best to ask, What comes last? next to last? And so on, back to the beginning. The paper-and-pencil mazes that children enjoy working are usually more easily solved by starting at the goal and working backward.[10]

- *Simplification.* Some problems are complicated, and simplifying them, by temporarily suspending the rules or cutting down on the details, may help. In organizations, complicated problems often need to be stripped down to manageable terms, by going to the essence of the problem.[11]

- *Using Actual Data.* Many problems are hard to deal with in the abstract, but they sometimes become more manageable if actual numbers or objects are used.[12] Problem solving in organizational settings often involves plugging in the numbers to see whether a proposed solution will work or not work. A good approach to many problems is to try out a solution using real data to see how it works.

- *Contradiction.* For some problems it is easy to get overwhelmed with the number of solution paths, and it may be necessary to eliminate some of them. One way to do this is to see if the potential solutions are contradictory to the givens in the initial state or incompatible with what might be reasonably expected in the goal state.[13] In some cases an eyeball comparison will generate the awareness: It couldn't be that! The method of contradiction, therefore, is very much like estimating and it is used to sort out impossible or absurd solutions from promising ones.

- *Graphs and Diagrams.* No rule says that all problem solving has to take place exclusively in one's head. The use of mental models can be enhanced by writing things down or using a diagram or chart.[14] There are many ways to chart information. A simple bar graph, pie diagram, or matrix may be useful. Putting data on paper takes the mental model out of the head and helps portray the problem visually.

- *Analogies.* Perhaps the problem at hand is analogous to another. This does not mean that the two problems are similar necessarily; in fact, they can be quite remote from each other, but something can be learned from one problem that might be applied to another.[15] The trick, of course, is to generate good analogies and to have the ability to learn from them to help solve the problem.

At a certain stage it may be important to back away from the problem itself to engage in some careful reexamination of the mental model being used, to reassess the effectiveness of a particular mental model, and to consciously select another. Effective problem solvers monitor their selection and use of mental models—the term for such monitoring is *metacognition*—and they know how to switch effectively from one model to another.

Certain common pitfalls are associated with problem solving, things to watch out for and avoid:

- *Misunderstanding the problem.* Rushing to find solution paths can lead to confusion about the goal state or an inadequate reading of the initial state. When one rushes the search for solution paths, good information gets ignored or irrelevant information is regarded as valuable.[16]

- *Unrecognized presuppositions.* Presuppositions are the constraints imported to the problem from general knowledge or lack thereof usually without an individual's being aware of them. Presuppositions tend to narrow down the number of options within the problem space.[17] Recognizing and discarding presuppositions allows more potential solutions to flow into the problem space.

- *Functional fixedness.* The tendency to employ the learned labels for the use of certain objects or concepts in such a rigid way that one cannot think of using them for anything else is called *functional fixedness.* A screwdriver is for twisting in screws, so it is hard to think of using a screwdriver for anything else. But if we stop thinking of it as a *screwdriver* and call it a *gadget* or *doohickey,* that rethinking opens up many more possible functions for it. "When the name of the thing is left open, the possibilities for using the device seem also to remain open."[18] Finding creative solutions often requires getting beyond standard definitions.

REFLECTION

Think about an administrative problem you are facing in the context of your institution. What is the goal state? What are the givens? Can you use certain mental models to find more creative solutions or new approaches to the problem? How can you avoid the common pitfalls that confront problem solvers?

Effective problem solvers use mental models to become more rational and systematic in the way they address problems. They try to define the problem carefully and not become overwhelmed by the dimensions of the problem. They focus on finding creative yet reasonable solutions.

Whereas problem solving requires moving through various solution paths to get to the desired goal state, decision making involves weighing various pros and cons and selecting the best (or lesser of the evils) among alternatives. Decision making differs from traditional problem solving and it is important to know which process one is engaged in at any given time. What problem solving and decision making have in common, however, is that they both use up cognitive capacity. Most decisions involve many different variables and require multidimensional comparison.[19] Consider, for example, a personnel decision such as hiring a new dean or department chairperson

A useful ten-step model for basic decision making is provided by Diane Halpern.[20] The steps are paraphrased as follows:

1. *Determine values.* In decision theory, values have to do with what the organization believes is desirable, and these values drive the decision process. To avoid the word *values,* some decision models use the term

utility. What utility will the decision produce? What does the organization value, for example, that a new leader might add?

2. *Determine outcomes.* What outcomes will fulfill established values? The important part of this step is to designate outcomes that fulfill values. Specifically, what outcomes does one hope for in the new leader: more effective organization, financial management, or program planning?

3. *Weight the outcomes.* If several outcomes are identified, they may not all be equally desirable. Some outcomes may be assigned greater weight than others. Outcomes can be ranked, or they can be assigned numerical weights to reflect importance (most important gets assigned the number 1, with lesser outcomes assigned decimals such as .80, .75, and so forth). With or without numbers attached, the weighting process establishes the relative importance of different outcomes. For example in the choice of a new leader is financial management more important than creative program planning?

4. *Generate options.* Decisions involve choices among the best options available. Sometimes options grow out of effective problem solving. Not all decisions have good options, and some choices are among the least damaging options. Naturally, decision making is enhanced by having a large number of suitable options. In a personnel decision, one hopes to have a sufficient number of excellent candidates.

5. *Identify attributes of options.* Options always have attributes. For example, in personnel selections the candidates all have different strengths and weaknesses.

6. *Match attributes to outcomes.* Next, the decision maker wants to examine what attributes of the options appear to fit the outcomes. In a rational decision, the attributes of the options are matched to the weighted outcomes. What qualities of the candidates, for example, best fit the desired outcomes?

7. *Make a choice.* Consider carefully the attributes of various options and how they will produce desired outcomes. Make a choice and frame the choice as a recommendation for action. Which candidate, for example, is to be recommended?

8. *Cast the choice as a probability and consider the consequences.* No one knows for sure how decisions will work out. That is why prediction is part of decision making, and recommendations are cast as probabilities. Because outcomes are uncertain, one must ask how uncertain they are and then consider the consequences. Decision theorists call this *expected utility theory.* How much usefulness (or potential disaster) is there in the consequence? What are the chances, for example, that a particular candidate will work out well?

9. *Predict the likelihood of outcomes.* In most decision making, people think the work is done when they come up with options. The hardest work may lie in trying to predict outcomes. Probability has been described as a "willingness to bet." If the decision maker is willing to bet, is the bet a sure thing or is there some risk? If there is a risk, how much? Predictions can be made through careful measurement and use of statistics or through more subjective impressions, but the point is that somehow someone has to predict the outcomes of a decision and base those predictions on something.

10. *Align the steps.* Check the alignment of values, weighted outcomes, options, attributes of options, and actual choices. For example, in what ways does the candidate being recommended actually show promise for producing the right outcomes and adding desired value?

The tendency in using the decision-making model is to focus too much on one aspect of the process, such as weighting outcomes or generating creative options. For the model to work, all of the steps need to be brought into play and kept well aligned. As with problem solving, decision making also has its pitfalls. Consider the following:

- *Wishful thinking.* Sometimes known as the *Pollyanna Principle*, wishful thinking is the tendency to overestimate the chances of being successful, to see the wonderful things that could happen from a particular decision, and to minimize or deny the risks.[21] Expert decision makers evaluate risks realistically, and they ask what the consequences will be if a decision proves to be wrong.[22] It is possible to be wrong, of course, in choosing a certain option, but it is also possible to be wrong in not choosing it. Risks show up both as opportunities missed as well as blunders made. In terms of the general decision-making model, wishful thinkers tend to overvalue the attributes of particular options, exaggerate the way the options will attain outcomes and fulfill values, or overproject the utility and probable success of a particular option.

- *Entrapment.* Most decisions exist within the context of other decisions, and one decision, especially a bad decision, can affect another.[23] Sometimes previous decisions that have turned out badly have already cost a great deal in time, money, and effort. If people in the organization have already made a big investment in a decision, they can become trapped in that previous decision so that a free, fresh, rational choice becomes difficult in the situation at hand. The best way to avoid this pitfall, of course, is to separate decisions and view each on its own terms.

- *Tradeoffs.* Tradeoffs occur when people are willing to give up one outcome for another, or forgive a weak or missing attribute because it is compensated by another.[24] The questions to be asked include: What is being given up and how important is it? Is the tradeoff truly compensating?

There is also a tendency, once one tradeoff has been made, to make others. Sometimes known as the *slippery slope tendency*, engaging in a series of compromising tradeoffs can eventually lead to a collection of bad decisions. To counteract this tendency in a personnel decision, for example, a bottom line can be set that defines characteristics of applicants that will not be traded off, even if it means starting the search all over again.

- *Aversion to loss.* Aversion to loss refers not to the prospect of losing, but to the loss suffered from having to give up something as part of the decision. People often hate to give up some position, space, or privilege and will resist a decision that involves a loss, even when that loss is adequately compensated.[25]

- *Missing information and uncertainty.* A decision will sometimes be avoided because important information is missing.[26] It makes sense to want to postpone a decision to get more information, but what happens when information is truly missing and unavailable? The tendency is still not to select that option, even though it may otherwise be a good option. Lack of information and uncertainty tend to move decision makers toward conservative decisions or postponement.

- *Gambler's fallacy.* In so-called wheel-of-fortune games, there is a tendency to say, "If number seven has come up twice already, it is unlikely to come up again," or "If number seven hasn't come up lately, it is about time for it." In a truly random situation, however, every number on the wheel has a chance of coming up on every spin because the wheel has no memory. This irrational tendency to impute memory in situations involving chance has been called *Gambler's fallacy*.[27] Symptoms of irrational decision making will show up in phrases such as, "We're due," "It's our turn," or "We've had our share of bad luck."

- *Misinterpreting trends.* Another pitfall associated with predicting outcomes relates to understanding trends.[28] Trends are tricky because the trend can always change as new factors come into play. Trends are reliable only if all the factors producing them stay the same. Projecting probable outcomes of a decision includes careful use of trend data.

REFLECTION

Bring to mind a decision that proved not to be a good one. In retrospect, can you identify what happened? Was there a tendency to short-change the process and move prematurely to consideration of options? What pitfalls came into play? What would you do differently?

Effective decision makers follow logical steps as they work toward a decision. They ask what values and outcomes are important before they consider options. They recognize that all decisions carry the risk

of failure; therefore, they consider expected utility and weigh carefully the probable success of each decision.

LEGAL IMPLICATIONS

Administrators work within a legal context, and the decisions they make should not only be rational but should also stand up if challenged in a court of law. Unfortunately, Americans love to litigate, and in spite of promising new efforts to resolve disputes outside of court, people often seek legal recourse. Higher education institutions are not immune from the court system; and legal rights, responsibilities, and duties are manifest continually in daily operations. Although private universities have greater latitude to regulate the rights of students and faculty, it is easier to end up in court than one might initially think possible. For this reason, administrators must learn to consider the potential legal implications of their decisions. Although there is no way to avoid completely the risk of lawsuits, taking the preventative approach can reduce the risk of litigation and improve the chances of a favorable outcome in the event that a case goes to court.

The types of law that administrators need to be concerned about when they make decisions come from three sources: statutory law, administrative law, and case law. *Statutory law* refers to laws that are passed by legislative bodies at the federal, state, and local levels. *Administrative law* usually comes in the form of regulations or directives and originates from the administrative branch of government, for example, executive orders or regulations issued by departments and agencies of the government. *Case law* refers to a body of cases accumulated over time that set precedent for how a given law or set of laws will most likely be interpreted by the courts. Such interpretation becomes the standard for that particular jurisdiction on matters of law, fact, or procedure. The appellate process gives litigants an opportunity to challenge the interpretations of the lower courts.[29]

The grounds for suits that colleges and universities are most likely to encounter are those related to contracts and torts. People who are employed in colleges or universities seldom commit crimes—a crime being a public wrong, such as robbing a bank or committing a murder—at least not on duty or in behalf of the institution. Postsecondary administrators are more likely to commit private wrongs associated with contracts and torts. Contracts are formal or informal agreements made as promises between parties that are enforceable in a court of law, such as a contract between an institution and a faculty member.[30] *Torts* refer to civil wrongs or actions, either intentional or accidental, that cause harm or injury to another person for which the court may provide a remedy in the form of an action for damages.[31]

Courts generally hold that the relationship between a postsecondary institution and its employees, including faculty, flows from such sources as contracts or employment manuals.[32] Accordingly, most institutions maintain and update the faculty handbook and staff policy manual to cover many of the legal issues surrounding contracts, including terms of employment and procedures and standards for promotion. Administrators must not only follow the practices included in such handbooks and manuals, but must make sure that faculty and staff are aware of the policies contained therein. In the absence of written policy, issues such as employment, promotion, and tenure will generally be reviewed on the basis of institutional custom or be subjected to common law (custom and tradition codified by state legislation), leaving the outcomes to the discretion of the court. In order to avoid or at least minimize employment lawsuits, administrators also need to keep in mind several other legal concerns, such as avoiding inappropriate questions during the interview process, respecting individual privacy rights, and following immigration laws.[33] As a contract is being entered into, the parties should know what the terms of the contract are, what type of appointment is being made (tenure track, term, part-time, probationary, at will), and conditions of dismissal.[34]

In a very different sense, the institution also has a contract with students implied in what the institution offers and hopes to deliver for them. More recently, the student has been looked at as a client or even as a consumer. This issue is explored by Robert Hendrickson in his useful work, *The Colleges, Their Constituencies, and the Courts*.[35] As Hendrickson points out, the institution is now seen as having a fiduciary relationship with students, one in which there is special confidence, like that between doctor and the patient or lawyer and client.[36] Although this may be difficult for some faculty and administrators to accept—education is neither a commodity nor a service—there is such a thing as educational malpractice in the eyes of the courts, which can come in the form of a breach of contract suit for failing to provide students with promised skills.[37]

Many lawsuits in higher education stem from an institution's failure to follow its own prescribed rules and procedures.[38] Preventive law would therefore encourage administrators to make decisions that abide by institutional policies and to check periodically to see that these policies are in accordance with federal and state statutory and regulatory requirements.

REFLECTION

What are the important handbooks and policy manuals that affect contract relationships in the areas where you serve the institution? Have these been reviewed and updated recently? What are key policies that you need to follow in contractual matters? What is the nature of your contract with students?

Contracts are relatively straightforward compared to tort liability, that murky area of civil duties and responsibilities imposed by legislation and case law traditions that are not so obvious or well-known. For example, a college or university needs to exercise responsibility to see that the chemistry lab does not blow up or that students are not injured on a university-sponsored field trip. Hendrickson maintains that the key issue in tort liability in higher education revolves around the standard of care used under the circumstances.[39] Was the institution careful in providing and maintaining exhaust hoods in the chemistry laboratory? Were the worn tires on the van changed before becoming the "proximate cause" of an accident on a field trip? Case law is clear, for example, that insufficient campus security responses, to everything from disruptive students to dormitory rapes, may create liability under tort law.[40] Clearly a reasonable standard of care must be used across all university activities both inside and outside the classroom, and practices that fall outside of what the court may regard as "reasonable" can potentially subject the institution to tort liability and could result in required payments for damages.

Another aspect of the law that affects colleges and universities in important ways is what the courts refer to as *due process*. Students, faculty, and staff have certain rights and prominent among these is the right to be treated appropriately when accused of something serious or in some matter under dispute. The concept of *due process*, which can differ significantly for public and private universities, includes specific requirements, such as notice of the charges, a hearing, the opportunity to hear witnesses testify, and the opportunity to provide one's own testimony or witnesses.[41] This holds true for disciplinary action taken against students for cheating, plagiarism, or violation of any of the institution's policies as set forth in the student handbook. It can include such things as drinking on campus property, engaging in hazing activities, offenses against the person such as battery (touching people inappropriately or striking them), or destruction of property. There are areas where the institution's administration has the right and responsibility to step in, but when they do so, they must keep in mind that the student (or any other party to the alleged incident) has a right to due process. The student's right to due process is accompanied also by a right to privacy, which means that investigations must be undertaken with care.[42]

In general, the legal system is designed to safeguard fairness, and although there is room for improvement in the procedures, establishing and maintaining fairness is in itself inherently problematic because the disputants in any case bring to it different ideas about what is fair. That is mostly what a legal dispute is about in the first place. Consider three examples that affect colleges and universities.

In the area of admissions, financial aid, and what has been called affirmative action, colleges and universities have struggled to give extra needed support to disadvantaged or historically oppressed populations, while at the same time being fair to all students. When dealing with issues of race, gender, age, sexual orientation, or handicap, administrators strive for diversity "while ensuring that suspect criteria do not result in violations of federal statutes."[43] The admissions office is often called upon to assemble a class that is academically capable as well as diverse. Today, colleges and universities need to defend their policies on the basis of educational and institutional purposes being served, and although institutions still need to be proactive in seeking diversity across the campus, they need to ensure that such policies do not run the risk of spurring reverse-discrimination charges.[44] The courts are increasingly entering into such cases, to such an extent that institutions must be very careful about the decisions they make in these areas. What appears to be fair to one may not be fair to another—and that is how such cases land in court.

The second example of the complications associated with fairness grows out of recent legal issues about computer technology and use of the World Wide Web. Here the law can barely keep up with new issues that arise almost daily. Most students have access to computers in the residence hall or library, allowing them access to a vast amount of information, potentially good and harmful, as well as a highway for communicating their own thoughts and feelings. Should there be limits on what students have access to or how they use the institution's computers? A thoughtful review of these issues can be found in a pamphlet published by the National Association of College and University Attorneys by Michael Sermersheim, entitled "Computer Access: Selected Legal Issues Affecting Higher Education."[45] Many institutions are beginning to draft rules about computer use to diminish confusion, establish policy, and reduce the likelihood of misuse. The challenge for the institution, notes Sermersheim, is to draft a policy that is "fair, reasonable and consistent."[46] To aid in this effort, the American Association for Higher Education (AAHE) has produced a Bill of Rights entitled "Ethics and Technology Initiative," chiefly the work of Frank W. Conley.[47] The document gives suggestions about and examples of prohibited uses such as harassment of computing facilities, violation of another's privacy, use of accounts without authority or appropriate access codes, inappropriate mass-mailings, running programs that may cause damage, and transferring pornography or posting hate mail. Most of these issues have or will have legal dimensions, and balancing the great potential of open access against potential abuse is once again an issue of fairness that will result in many court cases.

The third and somewhat related issue is intellectual property rights. Four primary types are subject to legal protection: patents, copyrights, trademarks, and trade secrets.[48] Colleges and universities usually have policies for dealing with these rights, although they also support wide dissemination of materials used for educational purposes. One key question today is about the ownership and control of the scholarly materials created by faculty, particularly for Web-based courses. Do faculty own these materials; or does the institution, particularly when providing major support for development, also share in this ownership?[49] What is fair and how will the courts enter into determining what is fair? A useful starting point is for the institution to develop its own policies.

REFLECTION

> What legal issues underlie the decisions you make in your work? Are they issues related to contracts, torts, due process, or fairness? What should you do when you don't know what to do?

Administrators make decisions every day that have potentiality huge legal implications. No administrator can be a legal expert in all areas, and that is why colleges and universities employ or retain legal counsel. As Douglas Toma and Richard Palm point out in *The Academic Administrator and the Law: What Every Dean and Department Chair Needs to Know*, most administrators should not try to make difficult decisions on their own. The areas of potential error are vast and the sources of law governing these issues are numerous.[50] Seek counsel.

Responsible decision makers anticipate the legal consequences of their decisions. They learn enough about higher education and the law to see the legal issues appearing in their work. Although they will seldom become experts in a particular area, they will learn enough to know when to get advice or defer to legal counsel. Sometimes they will learn the hard way, in court, and then they will discover how much time they could have saved by taking time to learn or ask.

ETHICAL RAMIFICATIONS

Conscientious administrators put forth sincere efforts to make decisions in a rational rather than arbitrary manner and they check these decisions for legal implications, but decisions can also be reviewed for their ethical ramifications. What are the dimensions of a decision that can be called ethical and what help can be found in the field of ethics for testing a decision for its morality?

Morality refers to a standard of right or wrong in evaluating behavior or potential action. James Rachels, the author of *The Elements of Moral Philosophy*, offers this definition: "Morality is, at the very least, the effort to guide one's conduct by reason—that is, to do what there are the best reasons for doing—while giving equal weight to the interests of each individual who will be affected by one's conduct."[51] Although some philosophers also stress the importance of sentiment (feeling) and volition (will) in ethical decision making, reason clearly plays an important part, not only in assembling and evaluating pertinent information about the issue at hand, but also in sifting through the reasons that might be used to support a particular decision.

Ethics is, of course, a branch of study within the field of philosophy, along with such areas as logic, metaphysics, and aesthetics. Moral philosophy, which is what Rachels calls ethics, is the "attempt to achieve a systematic understanding of the nature of morality."[52] Ethics is the normative study of what people ought to do and why they should do it. Cynthia Brincat and Victoria Wike in their book, *Morality and the Professional Life: Values at Work*, note that ethics goes beyond law and runs deeper than etiquette, the study of manners.[53] They provide a useful distinction between morality and ethics: morality is what people do and ethics is the *study* of what people ought to do; thus "morality is like eating" and "ethics is like nutrition."[54] When people study the moral decisions made in the context of the workplace or a particular profession such as law, medicine, or clinical psychology, the term *professional ethics* is generally used, whereas the term *general ethics* is usually reserved for more universal issues such as "abortion, euthanasia, war, and censorship."[55]

How does an administrator know whether a decision has ethical ramifications or not? Tom Beauchamp in his text *Philosophical Ethics* offers four "Marks of the Moral" for identifying ethical issues, paraphrased and simplified as:

1. *Importance*—an overriding value consideration in the decision
2. *Prescriptive form*—action-guiding imperatives about what ought to be done

3. *Universalizability*—guidelines that apply to other similar circumstances

4. *Moral content*—reference to the welfare of others.[56]

Conscientious administrators examine their decisions to see if they have the marks of the moral. In a chapter in William May's *Ethics and Higher Education*, Charles Reynolds and David Smith use the term *discerning ethical judgment* to describe the process of discovering the ethical ramifications of decisions.[57] Although such discerning is not easily cultivated, it is the important first step in ethical decision making.

REFLECTION

> Using the definitions provided above as well as the four "marks of the moral," identify what you believe are ethical ramifications of a decision you have faced or are facing. Describe the ethical aspects of the decision.

What are some of the ethical issues that an administrator might find in the context of a college or university? Several textbooks on ethics and higher education provide useful catalogs of areas in which ethical issues typically arise. The list below is compiled from the following books, many of which contain the same issues treated in different ways: Steven Cahn, *Morality, Responsibility, and the University: Studies in Academic Ethics*; William May, *Ethics and Higher Education*; Kenneth Strike and Pamela Moss, *Ethics and College Student Life*; and George Vaughn, *Dilemmas of Leadership: Decision Making and Ethics in the Community College.*[58]

- *Admissions*—standards, fairness of process, financial aid, equity and access, integrity in marketing
- *Faculty*—appointment, promotion, tenure, academic freedom, truth telling and role modeling, student faculty relationships, letters of recommendation
- *Instruction*—academic honesty, expertise and credentials, professionalism, granting of academic credit, extent of preparation, student testing and grading
- *Student behavior*—freedom of expression and campus publications, tolerance of diversity and hate speech, privacy and dignity, excessive drinking and related behavior, drug abuse, respect for property, consensual sex, secret keeping and promise making, academic honor codes, discipline procedures
- *Athletics*—fair play vs. winning, scholarship aid, compensation of staff, academic achievement, character modeling, commercial uses of sporting events

- *Research*—sources of funding, integrity in analysis of data, use of assistants, overload payment and released time, rights of human subjects
- *Community linkages*—business alliances and partnerships, integrity of mission, political commitment or neutrality, objectivity and compensation
- *Trustees and governing boards*—selection and composition, conflicts of interest, mission and program integrity, presidential selection process, character and reputation, accountability
- *Institutional policies*—sexual harassment, hiring/firing processes, diversity and equity, travel and reporting of expenditures, use of institutional equipment, profit making in auxiliary enterprises
- *Institutional advancement*—donor interest and intent, mission integrity, investment of endowment, counting of achievements

Obviously, ethical issues abound in the institutional practice of higher education, but why not just to avoid these sticky issues? One frequently hears what sound like convincing arguments about the futility of ethical decision making. Scholars in the field of ethics have heard these familiar arguments, catalogued them, and countered them.

Simon Blackburn elaborates seven threats to the enterprise of ethics in his intriguing book, *Being Good: A Short Introduction to Ethics*.[59]

1. *The death of God.* The assumption is made that ethics is tied to religion and that without a religious orientation there is no place for ethics. Blackburn argues, however, that there is a long, sound tradition of secular philosophical ethics dating from Plato and Aristotle. Blackburn concludes that "religion . . . is not the source of standards of behavior, but a projection of them . . . and is not a prerequisite to ethical thought."[60]

2. *Relativism.* Because "rules may be made in different ways by different people at different times," the assumption is that "there is no one truth" but "only different truths of different communities." Blackburn points out, however, that relativism has its limits, and that the core of ethics is found in the search for the universal "norms or standards that are transcultural." Relativism itself is a vulnerable absolute. It is often said, Blackburn notes, "When in Rome do as the Romans do—but what if the Romans go in for some rather nasty doings?" Are there not some things that are "not OK, anywhere or anytime?" Blackburn concludes "there must be a course between the soggy sands of relativism and the cold rocks of dogmatism."[61]

3. *Egoism.* Because we are often egotistical, the assumption is that we are all *only* egotistical, that "concern for others, or concern for principal, is a sham." With an eye for hypocrisy, "we get the view that pacifism

conceals aggression, or a desire to help masks a desire for power." But such interpretations Blackburn notes, "kidnap the word *self-interest*" and apply it in a "Grand Unifying Pessimism." He concludes that people often genuinely "neglect their own interest or sacrifice their own interest to other passions and concerns."[62]

4. *Evolutionary theory.* Our animal origins belie our capacity for true altruism. We only do what is adaptive and functional. Blackburn argues that we *are* capable of altruism, even when it is not adaptive or goes unnoticed, just as "the human propensity for art and music are puzzling because we cannot find a survival function" for them.[63]

5. *Determinism and futility.* Because we are influenced by culture and upbringing, the assumption is that everything is determined and "we just do as we are programmed to do it." Blackburn observes that we may be programmed genetically to grow long hair, but we are not programmed to wear it that way. Whatever our "makeup programs us to do, it leaves some . . . room for us to vary our behavior in response to what we hear or feel or touch or see . . . in accordance with what we learn."[64]

6. *Unreasonable demands.* Because ethics sometimes expects a great deal of human beings, the assumption is that it demands too much, thus creating a "natural reaction to shrug off its demands." On the other hand, Blackburn notes, ethics is not so much about *extreme* demands as *reasonable* demands. He concludes that "the absoluteness of the fanatic or the hair shirt of the saint lie on the outer shores. Not wanting to follow them there, or even not able to do so, we still have plenty of standards left to uphold."[65]

7. *False consciousness.* Because some ethical theories are the product of particular interests, the assumption is that ethics is an enterprise "whose real function is other than it seems," a "diffuse exercise of power and control" that deserves to be deconstructed. Blackburn agrees that sometimes ethical principles are touted by those that don't live them, but also observes that simple emotions, such as "gratitude to those who have done us good, sympathy for those in pain or in trouble, and dislike of those who delight in causing pain or trouble, are natural to most of us, and are good things. Almost any ethic will encourage them. Here there is nothing to unmask: these are just features of how most of us are, and how all of us are at our best."[66]

When facing difficult decisions with complex ethical ramifications, leaders sometimes want to run for cover, hiding behind handy rationalizations. The excuses mount: I'm not religious. There is no ultimate right or wrong. Everyone acts out of self-interest. Altruism is an illusion. There is no real choice or free will. Besides, I'm no saint. Ethics is bunk.

Leaders are able to discern ethical decisions and do not avoid them.

REFLECTION

> What do you think about Blackburn's list of threats to the enterprise
> of ethics? Have you found yourself using these excuses? Do leaders
> have some special responsibility for ethical behavior? Why?

Leadership may indeed carry with it special responsibility for ethical
decision making. As George Vaughn notes, "At any level, in any sector
in society, a public leader automatically takes on the responsibility of
moral or ethical leadership."[67] One might say: it goes with the turf! It is
not so much that leaders seek out this responsibility, but that it is expected
of them. Daniel Perlman, writing on the ethical challenges of college or
university presidents captures this expectation well:

> It does not take many scandals for the public and the press to call
> for the president's resignation and insist upon new leadership, and
> for the trustees to respond. Apart from the desire a president may
> have to build a more just, open, fair, and moral community, self-
> protection and self-interest alone will motivate the president to
> monitor and to elevate the institution's awareness of ethical issues
> and its attention to ethical behavior.[68]

Not just presidents, but leaders at all levels of the institution are inevita-
bly in the glare of the ethical spotlight when decisions are made, even if
the issue is only a matter of simple fairness. More important than this
expectation, however, is the genuine desire that most leaders have to exert
positive influence through their decisions. Effective leaders try to be conscientious moral agents, and as James Rachels describes well:

> The conscientious moral agent is someone who is concerned impar-
> tially with the interests of everyone affected by what he or she does;
> who carefully sits back and examines their implications; who accepts
> principles of conduct only after scrutinizing them to make sure they
> are sound; who is willing to "listen to reason" even when it means
> that his or her earlier convictions may have to be revised; and who
> finally, is willing to act on the results of this deliberation.[69]

Although leaders are often called upon to act as moral agents or find
themselves in situations where they have opportunities to do so, they are
not necessarily the wisest or the most virtuous persons in the organization, and they sometimes struggle with their ethical responsibilities.
Knowing what to do is not easy, and having guidelines against which to
measure a particular decision can be valuable. Fortunately, the great thinkers in the field of ethics—a long chain of philosophers from Plato and
Aristotle to the present day—have pondered the many reasons that can

be provided for "doing the right thing" and have provided a series of intriguing justifications for moral decisions.

Justifications are reasons. As Brincat and Wike observe, "A reason is something that contributes to the making or defending of a decision" and "an explanation is just a collection of reasons offered in defense of a decision."[70] To justify ethical decisions, leaders often turn to moral rules or principles growing out of carefully developed moral theories. The study of these theories and rules is called *general normative ethics*, and the basic purpose of this aspect of moral philosophy is "to provide a theory or justification of those rules."[71] Decision makers recognize that "not all moral reasons and explanations are equally good."[72] In fact, philosophers through the ages have been merciless in their criticisms of each other's theories. Decision makers have two tasks: to be aware of the rules and theories, and to discern which of the theories are most applicable to and useful for a particular decision.

Several texts provide interesting discussions of these theories, and although some authors focus on particular theories and exclude others from their discussion, a general list of typical moral justifications can be established. The composite list of ten moral theories and the discussion of each provided below is drawn from the work of Beauchamp, Blackburn, Brincat and Wike, and Rachels.[73]

1. *The Nonmaleficence and Beneficence Principle.* The first rule of the physician's Hippocratic Oath is " Above all, do no harm."[74] The goal is, at a minimum, not to do damage (or further damage) through a particular decision. As Blackburn points out, it may also be easier to get agreement initially about what *not* to do.[75] Beneficence, on the other hand, involves letting at least some good—perhaps some happiness—come out of the decision. As Brincat and Wike note: "Beneficence and nonmaleficence express the same thing. They are both expressions of a commitment to bringing about good outcomes." They are "like opposite ends of a continuum. . . . Doing good is not fundamentally different from preventing harm"[76] **At the most basic level, leaders are trying to prevent harm and do good.**

2. *The Utilitarian Principle.* What are the useful consequences of the decision? Rachels notes that the "Principle of Utility . . . requires that whenever we have a choice between alternative actions or social policies, we must choose the one that has the best overall consequences for everyone concerned."[77] This is sometimes referred to as the principle of the greatest happiness of the greatest number.[78] The utilitarian theory has its roots in the work of the philosophers David Hume, Jeremy Betham, and John Stuart Mill.[79] As Betham puts it, one asks to what extent the decision will "augment or diminish the happiness

of the party whose interest is in question."[80] Sometimes referred to as *consequentialism*, utilitarianism "asserts that actions are right or wrong according to their consequences, rather than because of any intrinsic features they may have."[81] The concern, therefore, is with actual outcomes, and as Blackburn points out, "the cast of mind is that of the engineer, not the judge."[82] **Leaders ask about the consequences of a decision and how it affects the common good.**

3. *The Principle of Duty and Responsibility*. Certain decisions involve obligations. This theory, and others that stress duties as opposed to consequences, are called *deontological theories*, from the Greek word *deon*, meaning *duty* or *obligation*. As Beauchamp points out, "deontologists . . . argue that moral standards exist independently of utilitarian ends, and that the moral life is wrongly conceived in terms of means and ends."[83] An act is right or wrong in itself according to principle. This theory has roots in the work of the German philosopher Immanuel Kant who believed that morality "provides a rational framework of principles and rules that guides and places obligations on everyone."[84] Kant is known for the concept of the *categorical imperative*, a prescription that enjoins someone to do something or not do something apart from consequences simply because it is a responsibility. **Leaders recognize that they are often responsible to or for someone or something, and that they have obligations.**

4. *The Social Contract Principle*. Some decisions have implications for the entire community and are required to maintain a peaceful and cooperative social order. Imagine what life would be like if no one cared about anything but his or her own interests. Thomas Hobbes, the British philosopher noted for setting forth the social contract theory, suggested that without some general agreement about social order, life in a state of nature would simply be nasty, brutish, and short. "Moral rules," as Rachels notes in describing social contract theory, "are simply the rules that are necessary if we are to gain the benefits of social living. . . .To escape the state of nature, then, people must agree to the establishment of rules to govern their relations with one another."[85] The social contract is the foundation of civilization, but it is also what enables organizations to function in an organized rather than chaotic way. **Leaders know that some decisions are for the good of the institution and maintaining the larger society it serves.**

5. *The Communitarian Principle*. Sometimes decision makers take into account the mores and values of a particular community. The roots of the communitarian philosophy are found in the work of David Hume. Beauchamp points out that Hume's theory springs from the simple idea that "conventions or traditions . . . are observed and enforced" because the community—the family, institutions, the government—has found them valuable. Rules, therefore, do not come from

an external source or obligation, but from "communal values or practices."[86] Academic communities, for example, place special emphasis on academic freedom and integrity and on the personal development of the individual. **Leaders are often expected to support and defend the values of the community.**

6. *The Principle of Justice.* Justice implies fairness. *Distributive justice* refers to equality of opportunity or treatment, while *retributive justice* involves corrective actions, remedies, or punishments.[87] Because benefits are often scarce within an institution or in the society, the competition for or distribution of those benefits needs to be fair, and this is often referred to as *comparative justice*. The fair treatment of individuals through unhindered operations is called *procedural justice*.[88] One of the foremost expositors of the theory of justice is the contemporary philosopher, John Rawls. As Rawls points out: "The natural distribution is neither just nor unjust; nor is it unjust that men are born into society at some particular position. These are simply natural facts. What is just and unjust is the way that institutions deal with these facts."[89] To deal with these inequalities, Rawls suggests a hypothetical "veil of ignorance" that assumes one might land within a particular social situation—rich or poor, male or female—without knowing it beforehand. The goal is to adopt principles of justice that would serve a person well in any status in which they found themselves. In describing Rawls' theory, Blackburn notes: "It is rather like cutting a cake and not knowing which bit you might end up with: developing a procedure that enforces a fair distribution."[90] As Brincat and Wike point out, "Equality means sameness, but justice, which is about equity, means fairness . . ." which sometimes requires "fair, but unequal treatment of persons."[91] **Leaders ponder what is just and try to distribute resources equitably; but sometimes they support inequality in the name of fairness.**

7. *The Principle of Rights.* Sometimes basic rights are at stake in a decision. The language of rights is rooted in the political philosophy of the Enlightenment, but has taken on a new meaning recently in the global concern for human rights through "moral protections for persons who are vulnerable to abuse."[92] Human rights include the constitutionally protected rights of democracies, such as life, liberty, and property, but many people "now believe that these rights transcend national boundaries and particular forms of government."[93] More controversial is the expansion of the concept of rights to include such things as rights to housing, clothing, medical care, food, and even the right to die.[94] As Blackburn points out, the language of rights is "apt to be controversial. It pits *me* against *them*, encouraging a sense of *my* rights against others, *my* sense of just grievance when things don't go my way."[95] Although the concept of *rights* stresses what is good for the

individual as opposed to the community, some would say that this is the very strength of the principle of rights. "Rights, they argue, protect us against the encroachment of society."[96] **Leaders ask whether basic rights are involved in a decision and are concerned about protecting and not violating rights.**

8. *The Principle of Respect for Persons.* Sometimes a decision involves fundamental concern about a person based on their nature as a human being. The focus is not so much on their rights, but on their need to be treated with dignity and respect. Because human beings have the freedom to act and capacity for moral action (unique in the animal kingdom), it is argued that they should be treated in ways that respect this unconditional value. At issue in particular is the need to respect the autonomy of individuals to make their own decisions and create their own destinies, free from paternalistic care.[97] Respect for individual autonomy generally means "to leave the choice up to the individual" or "generally not interfering" with people "as they carry out the goals of their life."[98] **Leaders respect the dignity and autonomy of individuals.**

9. *The Principle of Caring and Compassion.* Sometimes a decision expresses caring and compassion. Caring involves authentic concern for those around us. *Compassion* comes from Latin words meaning *suffer together.* Compassion "begins with a shared feeling of suffering and ends with acting in the best interests of the person suffering."[99] The roots of this principle are in the recent feminist writings of Nell Noddings and Carol Gilligan, who react against the deontological theories and principles of justice, which often appear abstract and distant.[100] **Leaders identify suffering and ask: How can I help?**

10. *The Virtue and Integrity Principle.* Virtues are character traits that are socially valued. "A *moral* virtue is a character trait that is morally valued—for example, truthfulness, honesty, gentleness, politeness, and the like. . . . Calmness and competitiveness are virtues but not moral virtues."[101] The idea of virtue goes back to Aristotle who suggested that virtue is sustained by repetitive action. A person who tells the truth or keeps promises only some of the time is not considered virtuous. Thus, virtuous behavior is rooted in unchangeable character.[102] **Leaders cultivate consistency in their decisions and over time develop qualities that are respected by others as virtues.**

REFLECTION

Consider an issue within your scope of activity that has ethical ramifications. Which of the theories described above are most applicable as justifications for a decision you might make (or have made) about the issue? Does more than one theory apply? Are the theories har-

monious or are they sometimes in conflict? What is the proper relationship among moral theories?

Knowing about moral theories is the first step; applying them is another
matter. Decision makers do everything they can to analyze choices carefully, making sure they understand the facts of the situation as fully as
possible while generating appropriate options. They then scan the list of
moral theories to see which may be especially useful as justifications for
a particular choice. At this point, however, decision making becomes
complicated. One quickly discovers that the moral explanations, like the
options themselves, are not of equal weight. Some are better for a particular situation than others. (Philosophers also argue that some moral
theories are essentially more supportable than others, but they tend not
to agree on which ones.) Furthermore, more than one explanation may
be appropriate. As Beauchamp points out: "To satisfy the requirement of
comprehensiveness, a strong moral explanation will probably have to have
several strong moral reasons, not just one."[103]

The more challenging problem in applying moral justifications, however, is that the choices themselves often involve inherent conflicts. Such
choices present *moral dilemmas*. As Brincat and Wike describe them, these
are situations "where the decision maker is faced with choosing between
two alternatives, both of which may be backed up by moral reasons. It is
a kind of moral no-win situation."[104] Although leaders sometimes find
themselves making clear-cut choices between good and evil, the more
likely predicament is one in which leaders must choose between two goods
or between two bads. Moral dilemmas involve two or more "moral explanations leading to appropriate courses of action, between which a decision must be made."[105] What one hopes to do in such situations is to find
the "greatest obligation" and the "greatest balance" of right over wrong,
so that some aspects of the decision become "overriding."[106]

REFLECTION

When you make decisions, do you find yourself contemplating com-
promises and tradeoffs? Do you feel that your choices are often between the lesser of two evils? How do you establish the overriding
good? Is it easy or difficult to harmonize rational, legal, and ethical
outcomes?

**Leaders recognize the complexity and ambiguity involved in decision
making, and they know that many decisions involve hard choices.**

As problem solvers and decision makers, leaders strive for congruence
among rational, legal and ethical perspectives. A rational decision may

not always be legal, and a decision that is legal may still not be ethical. Perhaps the main outcome of systematic reflection on problem solving and decision making is increased awareness of implications. The novice will say: I never dreamed that was going to happen. The experienced leader will say: I knew that was going to happen, but I made the right decision anyway.

MARY'S MENTOR

Mary's mentor wants her to remember these things about problem solving and decision making:

- Mental models keep the mind from getting boggled.
- Effective problem solvers identify the goal state and initial state before seeking solutions.
- Random search, systematic random search, hill-climbing, means-ends analysis, working backward, simplification, using actual data, testing for contradiction, making diagrams, and using analogies are mental models that are useful in generating solutions.
- Problem solving pitfalls include misunderstanding the problem, failure to recognize assumptions, and functional fixedness.
- Leaders distinguish between problem solving and decision making and know which process they are engaged in at the moment.
- Effective decision makers identify values and outcomes, weigh the outcomes, generate options, identify their attributes, match the options to outcomes, and cast choices as probabilities.
- Decision making pitfalls include wishful thinking, entrapment, making tradeoffs, aversion to loss, missing information, gambler's fallacy, and misinterpreting trends.
- Decisions often have legal implications, especially in situations that involve contracts, potential tort liability, and due process requirements.
- In the eyes of the law, decisions need to be fair, reasonable, and consistent.
- Decision makers know when to seek expert legal advice.
- Leaders become skilled in identifying ethical issues by looking for marks of the moral and by discerning situations that call for ethical judgment.
- Leaders know that ethical issues are scattered throughout administration in many diverse settings.
- Leaders are aware of the typical excuses made for avoiding ethical leadership, but also know that, like it or not, leaders are expected to be ethical.

- As students of moral philosophy, leaders learn useful justifications for ethical decision making, such as nonmaleficence, utility, duty, justice, rights, caring, and so forth.

- Leaders know that ethical decision making usually involves hard choices characterized by complexity and ambiguity.

- Congruence among rational, legal, and ethical dimensions of decision making is the impossible dream of dedicated leaders.

NOTES

1. Diane Halpern, *Thought and Knowledge: An Introduction to Critical Thinking* (Hillsdale, NJ: Lawrence Erlbaum, 1984), p. 160.

2. Ibid.

3. Thomas Ward, Ronald Finke, and Steven Smith, *Creativity and the Mind: Discovering the Genius Within* (New York: Plenum Press, 1995), p. 53.

4. Allen Newell and H.A Simon, *Human Problem Solving* (Englewood Cliffs, NJ: Prentice Hall, 1972), pp. 53–63, 787–791.

5. Norbert Jausovec, *Flexible Thinking: An Explanation for Individual Differences in Ability* (Cresskill, NJ: Hampton Press, 1994), p. 10.

6. Halpern, *Thought and Knowledge*, p. 189.

7. Wayne Wickelgren, *How to Solve Problems: Elements of a Theory of Problems and Problem Solving* (San Francisco: B.H. Freeman, 1974), pp. 46–47.

8. Jonathan Baron, *Thinking and Deciding* (New York: Cambridge University Press, 1994), p. 68.

9. Halpern, *Thought and Knowledge*, pp. 182–184.

10. Ibid., pp. 184–185.

11. Wickelgren, *How to Solve Problems*, pp. 124–126.

12. Ibid., p. 26.

13. Ibid., pp. 109–110.

14. Halpern, *Thought and Knowledge*, pp. 167–174.

15. Keith J. Holyoak and Richard Nisbett, "Induction, " in Robert Sternberg and Edward Smith, eds., *The Psychology of Human Thought* (New York: Cambridge University Press, 1988), pp. 82–83.

16. Halpern, *Thought and Knowledge*, pp. 199–201.

17. Anthony J. Sanford, *Cognition and Cognitive Psychology* (New York: Basic Books, 1958), p. 357.

18. Sam Glucksberg, "Language and Thought," in Robert Sternberg and Edward Smith, eds., *The Psychology of Human Thought* (New York: Cambridge University Press, 1988), p. 225.

19. Halpern, *Thought and Knowledge*, pp. 225–226.

20. Ibid., pp. 1–5, 55–66.

21. Ibid., pp. 221–222.

22. Raymond Nickerson, David Perkins, and Edward Smith, *The Teaching of Thinking* (Hillsdale, NJ: Lawrence Erlbaum, 1985), p. 32.

23. Halpern, *Thought and Knowledge*, pp. 167–174.

24. Baron, *Thinking and Deciding*, pp. 346–349.

25. Ibid., pp. 382–384.

26. Ibid., pp. 375–376.

27. Halpern, *Thought and Knowledge*, p. 123. (See also Baron, *Thinking and Deciding*, pp. 229–230.)

28. Ibid.

29. Jane P. Mallor et al., *Business Law and the Regulatory Environment: Concepts and Cases*, 10th ed. (Boston: Irwin McGraw-Hill, 1995), pp. 3–4.

30. William L. Prosser, John W. Wade, and Victor E. Schwart, *Cases and Materials on Torts*, 8th ed. (Westbury, NY: The Foundation Press, 1988), p. 1.

31. E. Allen Farnsworth and William F. Young, *Cases and Materials on Contracts*, 3rd ed. (Mineola, NY: The Foundation Press, 1980), p. 1.

32. Kent M. Weeks and Derek Davis, eds., *Legal Deskbook for Administrators of Independent Colleges and Universities*, 2nd ed. (Notre Dame, IN: University of Notre Dame Press, 1999), p. II-2.

33. Douglas J. Toma and Richard L. Palm, *The Academic Administrator and the Law: What Every Dean and Department Chair Needs to Know* (Washington, DC: ERIC Clearinghouse on Higher Education, ED427627, 1998), p. 2.

34. Weeks and Davis, *Legal Deskbook*, pp. IV-9, IV-10.

35. Robert Hendrickson, *The Colleges, Their Constituencies, and the Courts* (Topeka, KS: National Organization on Legal Problems, 1991).

36. Ibid., p. 127.

37. Ibid., p. 133.

38. Weeks and Davis, *Legal Deskbook*, p. II-1.

39. Hendrickson, *The Colleges, Their Constituencies, and the Courts*, pp. 137–138.

40. William Kaplan, *The Law and Higher Education* (San Francisco: Jossey-Bass, 1980), p. 123.

41. Hendrickson, *The Colleges, Their Constituencies, and the Courts*, p. 125.

42. Ibid.

43. Ibid., p. 83.

44. Ibid., p. 83.

45. Michael D. Sermersheim, "Computer Access: Selected Legal Issues Affecting Higher Education" (Washington, D.C.: National Association of College and University Attorneys, 1998).

46. Sermersheim, "Computer Access," p. 2.

47. URL: *http://www.luc.edu/sae/bill-of-rights.html*. The principal architect for the Bill of Rights is Dr. Frank W. Connelly, an associate professor at American University in Washington, D.C.

48. Weeks and Davis, *Legal Deskbook*, p. XII-2.

49. Ibid., p. XII-1.

50. Toma and Palm, *The Academic Administrator and the Law*, p. 1.

51. James Rachels, *The Elements of Moral Philosophy*, 3rd ed. (New York: McGraw-Hill College, 1999), p. 19.

52. Ibid., p. 1.

53. Cynthia A. Brincat and Victoria S. Wike, *Morality and the Professional Life: Values at Work* (Upper Saddle River, NJ: Prentice Hall, 2000), pp. 34–38.

54. Ibid., p. 34.

55. Ibid., pp. 55–59. The quotation is from p.59.

56. Tom L. Beauchamp, *Philosophical Ehthics: An Introduction to Moral Philosophy*, 2nd ed. (New York: McGraw-Hill, 1991), pp. 16–20.

57. Charles H. Reynolds and David C. Smith, "Academic Principles of Responsibility," in William May, ed., *Ethics and Higher Education* (New York: The American Council on Education and Macmillan, 1990), pp. 45–46.

58. Steven M. Cahn, ed., *Morality, Responsibility, and the University: Studies in Academic Ethics* (Philadelphia: Temple University Press, 1990); William May, ed., *Ethics and Higher Education* (New York: American Council on Education and Macmillan, 1990); Kenneth A. Strike and Pamela A. Moss, *Ethics and College Student Life* (Needham Heights, MA: Allyn and Bacon, 1996); George B. Vaughn, *Dilemmas of Leadership: Decision Making and Ethics in the Community College* (San Francisco: Jossey-Bass, 1992).

59. Simon Blackburn, *Being Good: A Short Introduction to Ethics* (New York: Oxford University Press, 2001).

60. Ibid., pp. 10–19.

61. Ibid., pp. 19–29.

62. Ibid., pp. 29–37.

63. Ibid., pp. 37–43.

64. Ibid., pp. 43–46.

65. Ibid., pp. 47–50.

66. Ibid., pp. 50–55.

67. Vaughn, *Dilemmas of Leadership*, p. 53.

68. Daniel H. Perlman, "Ethical Challenges of the College and University Presidency," in May, *Ethics and Higher Education*, p. 365.

69. Rachels, *The Elements of Moral Philosophy*, p. 19.

70. Brincat and Wike, *Morality and the Professional Life*, pp. 85, 91.

71. Beauchamp, *Philosophical Ethics*, pp. 35–37.

72. Brincat and Wike, *Morality and the Professional Life*, p. 99.

73. Beauchamp, *Philosophical Ethics*; Blackburn, *Being Good*; Brincat and Wike, *Morality and the Professional Life*; and Rachels, *The Elements of Moral Philosophy*.

74. Brincat and Wike, *Morality and the Professional Life*, p. 325.

75. Blackburn, *Being Good*, pp. 93–94.

76. Brincat and Wike, *Morality and the Professional Life*, p. 323.

77. Rachels, *The Elements of Moral Philosophy*, p. 97.

78. Blackburn, *Being Good*, p. 86.

79. Rachels, *The Elements of Moral Philosophy*, p. 96.

80. Ibid., p. 97.

81. Beauchamp, *Philosophical Ehthics*, p. 129.

82. Blackburn, *Being Good*, p. 88.

83. Beauchamp, *Philosophical Ehthics*, p. 171.

84. Ibid., p. 178.

85. Rachels, *The Elements of Moral Philosophy*, pp. 143, 146.

86. Beauchamp, *Philosophical Ehthics*, pp. 267–270.

87. Ibid., pp. 342–343.

88. Ibid., pp. 343, 357.

89. Beauchamp, *Philosophical Ethics*, pp. 368–369. The selection quoted from Rawls in Beauchamp is the reading "An Egalitarian Theory of Justice" from John Rawls, *A Theory of Justice* (Cambridge, MA: The Belknap Press of Harvard University Press, 1971).

90. Blackburn, *Being Good*, p. 127.

91. Brincat and Wike, *Morality and the Professional Life*, p. 254.

92. Beauchamp, *Philosophical Ethics*, p. 305.

93. Ibid.

94. Ibid.

95. Rachels, *The Elements of Moral Philosophy*, p. 106.

96. Ibid., p. 107

97. Ibid., p. 101.

98. Beauchamp, *Philosophical Ehthics*, p. 196.

99. Brincat and Wike, *Morality and the Professional Life*, pp. 280–281.

100. Strike and Moss, *Ethics and College Student Life*, p. 10.

101. Beauchamp, *Philosophical Ethics*, p. 213.

102. Rachels, *The Elements of Moral Philosophy*, pp. 177–178.

103. Beauchamp, *Philosophical Ethics*, p. 102.

104. Brincat and Wike, *Morality and the Professional Life*, p. 94.

105. Ibid., p. 95.

106. Beauchamp, *Philosophical Ethics*, p. 189.

CHAPTER 7

Financial Management:
Seeing Dollars Everywhere

Dean Williams comes out of the provost's budget and planning office, her heart heavy with discouragement. So much detail. Inscrutable technical language. It's easy for the "bean counters"—that's what some of her faculty call them—to overpower with obfuscation. In any case, the projections for the rest of the year are not promising. It seems like the accountants love to forecast doom and gloom so they can bring you good news later on and take credit for having saved you. At least that's her perception. As she stops in the restroom, she looks in the mirror and notices that her face has a stricken, ashen look, as if she were grieving for a close friend or relative. Losses. Losses! Are there no profits in this business? Only prophets with their jeremiad predictions?

Actually, she has been pleased with what she believes is her growing awareness of financial matters. She is learning to identify the financial implications of the proposals brought to her for decisions, and she now sees dollar signs everywhere—in the plans for a new major, in the move of a unit to more appropriate space, even in the simple addition of new phone lines and services. She reads and understands the monthly reports. She is becoming more proficient as a financial manager and she is eager to help the faculty and others who work with her to gain a better appreciation of the budgeting process.

Balancing the budget is only one part of the problem. The budget will balance, even if she has to cut things that she knows are essential. The real problem is in finding the resources for new programs and budgeting far enough ahead. People have so many good ideas; she hates to turn them down. As she walks back to her office she is reminded of the story she heard somewhere about the old lion and the young lion. How does that go? Each

*day the zookeeper brings the old lion a generous portion of meat to his cage,
while dropping off for the young lion next door a pitchfork of hay. After
several days of this, the young lion voices his complaint. "What's going
on here? I'm young, full of energy, and eager to grow, yet all I get is this
small portion of hay!" The wise old lion paces over to him and replies,
"Well-spoken, my friend, but the problem is that you are in the budget as
a zebra!" Ah, yes, Dean Williams reflects, I have many young lions to
feed and some old lions who need a change of diet.*

*Still thinking of the story as she enters her office, Dean Williams greets
Dolores with a smile on her face. "You must have good news," Dolores
remarks.*

*"Actually, Dolores," Dean Williams replies, "it's a little indigestion."
The dean flops into her leather desk chair as Dolores asks her if she can
bring her anything.*

*"Money, Dolores. Just money. I am beginning to wonder if the bud-
get is the solution or the problem. If it's the solution, I'm going to need to
learn how to get much more proactive during the budget planning process.
On the other hand, maybe the challenge is to increase the size of the resource pool. Surely, there must be some way for me to get beyond this
role I have inherited as Divider of the Shrinking Pie.*

Although most colleges and universities do not exist to make money,
neither can they lose money, at least not for long, or they will cease
to exist. As we have noted, many participants in organizations
use the organization for their own purposes. Often their knowledge or concern about the overall financial health of the institution is quite limited,
not extending much beyond payday or perhaps the resources available to
the programs with which they are most directly associated. Although some
of this studied disregard for financial matters is to be expected in an institution in which the main business is not business but academics, leaders
will usually find that managing the constraints of financial resources is
part of their job. If not, they must at least understand how to access financial support for the projects they hope to carry out.

Fortunately, the professional association for postsecondary administrators who manage and exert leadership over financial affairs has produced
readable introductions to the field. The organization is the National Association of College and University Business Officers (NACUBO), and
the key works are *College and University Budgeting: An Introduction for
Faculty and Administrators*, by Richard Meisinger, Jr.,[1] and a three-volume
work—the key reference for the field—edited by Deirdre McDonald
Greene entitled *College and University Business Administration*.[2] As with
other aspects of leadership, this is an area that can be learned. No leader
can afford not to know how the budget is developed and controlled. Fur-

thermore, even financially strong units within an organization will not actually prosper unless the overall institution is in good financial health. How does a college or university achieve and maintain financial vigor? To a great measure through careful development and management of its budget.

THE FORM AND FUNCTION OF THE BUDGET

The word *budget* derives from an old Middle English root designating a bag or pouch wherein the king or his officials kept the receipts of taxation or spoils of war, and from which funds were withdrawn periodically for expenditure.[3] The metaphor of a secret pouch, difficult to locate and access, has carried forth in some institutions to the present day, but for those with a more enlightened mentality, the budget is recognized as the instrument that helps to set and reflect priorities as well as provide a plan of action for a given time period. As Meisinger points out, the budget establishes a control mechanism and informal contract about what will and will not be done. It is a gauge of risk—a considered bet on income sources and expenses—and a means of communicating intended activities. It is also a political device and a focal point for negotiation, wherein decisions about who gets what are turned into numbers that reflect a consensus, however derived, about a unit's "fair share."[4]

Colleges and universities generate a lot of financial information, but two documents are especially important: the statement of financial position and the operating budget. At a particular point in time after the end of the fiscal year (which often does not correspond directly to the calendar year), the institution takes stock of everything it owns and owes. This financial snapshot is communicated in a report called a *statement of financial position* (balance sheet) and summarizes all of the institution's assets and liabilities and displays the difference between them, known as *net worth*.[5] This would be comparable to an individual's net worth, derived by subtracting everything owed from the current value of everything owned. The statement of financial position lets the institution know where it stands with its property values, the amount of its endowment, and the balances in its fund accounts at a given point in time. From year to year, one can compare these balance sheets to assess changes in the net worth of the institution.

During the year, the institution operates with a plan of expenditure commonly referred to as the *operating budget*. Accounts of similar types (all faculty salaries, all travel, and so forth) have been grouped into funds and these funds have been further categorized into fund groups.[6] "Higher education institutions have typically combined their funds into the following fund groups: current funds, loan funds, endowment and similar funds, annuity and life income funds, and plant funds."[7] This has changed for private institutions and is in the process of changing for public institutions, allowing institutions more autonomy in developing fund groups. General categories are now being used to differentiate current unrestricted funds, board-designated funds, current restricted funds, restricted endowment funds, fixed asset funds, and other funds. Legally, restricted funds may be used only for purposes designated by the donor.[8] Current funds are subdivided by the institution into specific income and expenditure accounts.[9] These accounts have names designated by words such as *tuition and fees* or *travel*, but they also have an alpha-numeric name, a string of numbers for encoding purposes referred to as budget numbers.[10] At the end of the fiscal year all of the balances are tallied up by carefully keeping track of all income and expenditures from the fund group, and these figures provide the basis for the statement of financial position—the snapshot at a point in time.

REFLECTION

> With which specific accounts are you most familiar? Does it depend on your niche in the organization? Have you ever seen your institution's statement of financial position or summary of the operating budget? Do you have certain budget numbers memorized?

The categories of funds, as well as the rules for managing them, are not made up at the whim of an accountant within each institution. The "rules" are established by national bodies, most notably the Financial Accounting Standards Board (FASB), generally for private institutions, and the Governmental Accounting Standards Board (GASB) for public, both of which are designated as authoritative by certain federal and state agencies.[11] This helps to explain the differences in procedures for fund accounting and the changes underway mentioned above. Furthermore, the general system of financial control is audited, as are individual accounts, for accuracy and appropriate documentation by internal (employees of the institution), independent, and governmental auditors. Many outside organizations want to know about the institution's true financial status, including those who make loans to the institution, those who make appropriations or gifts, and various government agencies, including the Internal Revenue Service. Once again, the standards for auditing are established by an association, in this case the American Institute of Certified Public Accountants (AICPA).[12] When employees of the institution are asked to verify expenses (keep all travel receipts), it is not because they are regarded as untrustworthy, but because the institution must document its financial activities.

Effective leaders learn the terminology and systems for financial management. They acknowledge that budget control involves precision and they recognize that many of the rules that the institution follows have their origins elsewhere. Not all aspects of the process are friendly or agreeable, and many are quite time-consuming, but in a general way they are necessary and therefore not only tolerated but embraced.

BUSINESS AS USUAL AND UNUSUAL

Many aspects of the financial life of postsecondary institutions look like a business, although the organization's status, as we have seen, may be business, government, or not-for-profit. Many units of the institution have an operating budget that has standard categories of income and expense, and much of the financial life of the unit is expressed through accounts that are clustered in funds. Each unit projects revenue and expenses, tries to stay within the expenditure budget, and ends the year with a surplus or deficit—business as usual. Several other aspects of a college or university, however, do not fit this usual pattern; and it is important for administrators to have at least some knowledge that other types of financial activity also exist.

Consider, for example, research and other sponsored programs, "the activities of a college or university that are financed by external funds and that support various instructional, research, or public service functions of the institution."[13] When an institution receives such funds, it must administer them with stewardship and accountability, recognizing that this is not really the institution's money but the sponsor's. Sometimes this is done in the business office, or in a larger institution, through an office of sponsored programs responsible for administrative as well as financial oversight of the funds. The types of sponsors could be any cabinet-level departments of the federal government, independent federal agencies, and nonfederal sources of support.[14] Support may come in the form known as a *grant* to support an activity at the institution, such as research or training, or in a form known as a *procurement*, a contract to perform certain services on behalf of the government.[15] In each case, administrators need to know what the terms of these agreements are, who is involved and in what ways, what the institution is required to provide, and what benefit (usually in overhead or "soft money" personnel) the unit is likely to derive. It is not surprising therefore that sponsored programs have separate accounting procedures.

Certain operations known as *auxiliary enterprises* provide another example of a different kind of financial activity. These include such operations as residence halls, the food service, college stores, college unions, parking services, university presses, athletics, wellness centers, vending machines, daycare centers, and even golf courses. "An *auxiliary enterprise* is an activity that charges individuals for its services as distinct from a *service department* that charges other campus departments for its services or is funded from central resources."[16] In general, auxiliary enterprises are intended to be self-sufficient operations that usually generate net revenues budgeted to support other aspects of the enterprise. That is why athletics and student health services may or may not be considered auxiliary enterprises. Some of these enterprises may be contracted out or operated as a cooperative, but most are run directly by the institution. They require their own accounts and accounting procedures.

Student financial aid is yet a different type of financial activity in that the institution manages aid funds on behalf of students, but the money does not appear as income until the student registers for courses and is billed for tuition. In a sense then, the institution runs a "lending subsidiary" and has separate loan accounts to manage student financial aid.[17]

Colleges also have separate fund accounts for endowment and similar funds. These are essentially accounts to keep track of investments and they have strict rules for accounting. When certain portions of the income on endowment are spent, they are transferred to the operating budget and appear as revenue. Some endowment income is restricted to specific purposes, other funds are put there for investment purposes and are "functioning as endowment, but can be removed at a later time."[18]

Colleges and universities also have separate accounts for plant funds, not just for their gardens but for all aspects of the physical plant, which includes buildings, roads, and campus landscaping. Certain operating funds are transferred to plant funds, and vice versa, and these funds provide an important mechanism for managing building projects, depreciation, and maintenance.[19]

In summary, postsecondary institutions are complex organizations engaged in many diverse activities that require unique financial arrangements. A leader needs to understand these basic arrangements to answer questions raised by people who have very little understanding of or interest in such matters. Sometimes people will ask such questions as: How can the university build all these buildings and still give such a small annual raise? Why don't we get the profits on textbooks from the bookstore?

Leaders need to have a working knowledge of the institution's basic financial systems and should be able to ask intelligent questions about the system as well as function effectively within it.

THE BUDGET CYCLE

If an item is not in this year's budget, what needs to be done to get it into next year's budget? When does planning for next year's budget begin? The answers to these questions vary from institution to institution, but in some respects the budget might be thought of as an ongoing process. Revisions are made during the budget year and new budgets are being developed well in advance of the fiscal year they serve.[20] Although budgets are viewed as fixed, they often need to be adjusted during the year in light of shrinking income, rising costs, or both.[21]

The budget planning cycle is driven by the fiscal year, which may begin July 1, September 1, or in rare cases, January 1.[22] Decision points are then tied to the calendar year, and will vary by institution. The most important determinant for the new budget is usually the previous year's budget, so planning begins with a careful analysis of how the institution performed under that budget. A concurrent step is to determine overall *planning parameters*, sometimes called the *budget protocols* or *budget instructions*, that grow out of important decisions about enrollment levels, tuition increases, charges for room and board (if a residential campus), targeted gift endowment income, anticipated state appropriation levels, faculty salary increases, fringe benefits, and energy costs—the big-ticket items.[23] Sometimes these parameters are established within guidelines set for multi-year budget plans or by using long-range forecasting models that anticipate conditions and project consequences over several years.[24] This is especially true for capital budgets involving buildings, multi-year consequences of program changes, or other long-range projects. Another useful exercise for this phase of the process is *benchmarking*, searching for useful comparative data and best practices in comparable "peer" institutions, although as Rhonda Epper has pointed out, "True benchmarking . . . encourages us to look beyond our peers for processes that are similar, and perhaps implemented better, in quite different types of organizations."[25] Useful in this regard is the cooperatively developed Higher Education Price Index (HEPI) for comparing cost trends at other institutions.[26]

Once the planning parameters have been set and useful forms of modeling and benchmarking have been completed, the actual budget development process begins. Usually this involves some type of hearing or information gathering at the unit level to gain an understanding of actual needs. Institutions vary in the way they handle this, and internal units within a particular institution may differ in the degree of participation encouraged. Kent Chabotar categorizes this involvement into three approaches:

- An *informational approach*. Updates faculty and staff through memoranda and meetings but does not invite feedback
- A *consultative approach*. Actively seeks opinion and encourages debate of important issues, sometimes resulting in altered decisions
- A *participative approach*. Involves faculty and staff in producing budget drafts through committees and hearings.[27]

After appropriate input, draft budget requests go forward from the various units to the budget planning office and a period of significant negotiation begins to take place. Here the "cutters" and "spenders" will take on their natural roles,[28] and the decisions that are made should not be taken personally, even though fierce disputes may rage. Naturally, a unit will not always get what is requested, but this is the time for serious discussion of such points as number of faculty "lines" (positions), adjunct faculty, full-time and part-time staff, amount of travel funds, and above all, new initiatives—the programs a unit hopes to unveil in the new fiscal year. Usually these negotiations are carried on with deans or vice presidents in smaller institutions or by deans or unit heads with provosts in larger ones. During the negotiation process, the invisible hand of the president or chancellor—more visible at some institutions than others—is at work in the process, because the chief executive officer and chief financial officer want to present to the board a balanced budget with a modest surplus. In public institutions they may be required by law to do so. Producing a balanced budget, when needs and wants always exceed revenues, is not always a pleasant job.

Although a budget and planning committee of the board may be kept involved or at least well-informed throughout this process, eventually a draft of the budget goes through that committee to the full board. What does the board of trustees (or other designation for the governing board) look for in the budget? Chabotar suggests these three questions that the board should ask:

1. How does the recommended budget articulate with the mission and long-term financial plan?
2. What long-term capital and other commitments does the budget entail, and do sufficient revenues exist to cover them?

3. What contingencies exist in the budget, and how does the institution propose to handle unexpected shifts in revenues and expenses during the year?[29]

Naturally the board is also asking whether the assumptions about revenues and expenditures underlying the budget—the reasoned bets—are justified. Eventually the budget is approved through a process called *ratification*.

The next step in the process is called *implementation* and the key activity is control. Most institutions have a controller or office of budget control that monitors revenues and expenditures, updates income projections, flags problem areas, and controls transfers across funds.[30] Monthly reports provide information about the percent of revenues and expenditures projected against the total budgeted amounts.

An administrator is usually involved in three budget cycles simultaneously: closing out the previous fiscal year, managing the budget for the current fiscal year, and planning for the new fiscal year.[31] Budget planning and implementation is endless. That's why it is called a *cycle*.

REFLECTION

Can you identify various aspects of the budget cycle at your institution? To what extent have you been involved? How do you rate the relative importance of budget planning and budget control?

Leaders are called upon in various ways to participate in or perhaps oversee various aspects of budget planning. The budget process that governs financial management at most institutions requires a "plan-ahead mentality." Budgets are not fixed in stone, but neither are they easy to change once approved. Leaders learn how to impact the budget cycle favorably.

FLEXIBILITY

Because a very high percentage of budgeted expenditures in postsecondary institutions involve fixed costs—usually ongoing commitments to faculty and staff salaries—most administrators are looking for the few degrees of freedom where some flexibility can be found—the so-called "wiggle room." This is true not only in planning the budget but also in implementation. Where can the extra money—the uncommitted funds—be found for new opportunities?

As Meisinger points out, one significant goal in budget planning is flexibility. "A mark of a well-regarded institution is its ability to take advantage of opportunities and to respond to unanticipated problems."[32] One way to do this is by actually building in resources called *contingency funds*, pools of money to be used for emergencies or general purposes.[33] How much should be reserved in this way? Having no contingency results in a budget that is too rigid, but too much contingency is another name for lack of planning and control. Most institutions have rules about the extent and use of contingency funds, but most administrators at the top have these pools of uncommitted money.

Faculty or staff positions provide another area where unspent funds may reside, at least for a given duration. An unfilled vacancy usually has funding in the budget. An unpaid leave of absence will have uncommitted funds. Sometimes a sabbatical leave has salary savings, and very often a grant or contract has salary savings in amounts greater than needed to replace the researcher's course or courses with a part-time faculty member. In the longer term, when a senior faculty member leaves or retires, savings are effected by replacing an older, experienced, and higher-salaried person with a younger, less-experienced person at a lower salary, with a net savings to be applied to another position or to other purposes. In some cases early retirement incentives are given to effect net salary savings.[34] A common yet controversial practice is to fill a vacancy with part-time faculty and save the difference in salary. In some institutions, however, vacant positions revert to a dean or provost for redistribution; and if that is the case reversion diminishes the incentive for early retirement or other salary saving options through faculty positions.[35] All these sources, sometimes called *breakage*, provide a bit of flexibly in the current year's budget.

Sometimes money can be transferred from one fund to another or one program to another. Fund transfers during the budget year, depending on the budget system and policies of the institution, may be allowed across closely related accounts, but major reallocations usually need approval and are often discouraged.[36] After all, surpluses in one account are often used to cover deficits in another, and spending off surpluses as a general policy won't help the institution balance the overall budget. Reallocating funds during the budget *planning* cycle, however, is strongly encouraged, especially if it means reducing funding for certain continuing programs to undertake new ones. *Reallocation* usually means moving resources from one program to another without closing programs down, whereas *retrenchment* means elimination of programs or whole units, and often has serious legal, public relations, and morale implications. The American Association of University Professors (AAUP) provides important guidelines for closing programs under financial exigency when tenured professors are involved.

In general, institutions that close programs are encouraged to do so "essentially upon educational considerations, not just enrollment."[37]

Institutions using performance-based budget systems (see below) often return a fixed percentage of income to the central administration, sometimes called *revenue-sharing*.[38] Usually this percentage is negotiated and even a small downward change in the percentage can result in significant increases in unbudgeted dollar amounts available to the unit. Often institutions using this budget system also make arrangements for the unit to keep (at the end of the fiscal year) a portion of actual net income earned over and beyond the budgeted projection, a practice usually referred to as *gain-sharing*. Gain-share funds can usually be used, with approval, for quite general purposes as the unit chooses.

Naturally, one productive way to find additional resources is to cut costs. Important clues come from more careful analysis of non-financial data, such as student/faculty ratios, class size, number of adjuncts, average teaching loads, credit hours generated, rotation of courses, course duplication, and distribution of faculty expertise by lower division, upper division, and graduate teaching.[39] Sometimes the combined analysis of data—for example, comparing teaching loads, number of adjuncts—often produces interesting relationships. Savings in nonpersonnel areas can be effected on purchasing, service agreements, and technology purchases through institution-wide cooperative arrangements. It is always wise to monitor closely phone, travel, and copying costs, which may expand exponentially if unwatched.

Leaders know where to find money and how to save money. They don't intentionally hide money, but they can pull a rabbit out of a hat at important moments. They also know when they have run out of rabbits.

TYPES OF BUDGETS

The processes and practices described above will all vary according to the type of budget the institution uses. Meisinger provides useful descriptions of budget types as well as a summary of their strengths and weaknesses in the appendix to *College and University Budgeting*.[40] They are paraphrased here as follows:

- *Incremental Budgeting.* Using the previous year's budget to make small additions and deletions. Assumes that most things change in modest ways from one fiscal year to the next and that costs are fixed. Makes increments and decrements in relation to a fixed base budget. Simple, natural, and easy to apply. Is what many institutions in fact use. Does not encourage examination of the full spectrum of choices.

- *Planning, Programming, and Budgeting Systems (PPBS)*. Begins with program goals and plans. Considers costs and benefits of alternative ways of reaching goals. Uses rigorous analysis of policy alternatives. Groups activities by function and fosters multi-year planning. Relates costs to benefits. More appealing on paper than in practice. Costly process.

- *Zero-Based Budgeting*. Assumes no budget from prior year. Each new budget starts with zero. Begins planning with the consequences of not performing a particular activity again. Uses decision packages to be ranked and reviewed at higher levels for costs, benefits, and alternatives. Stresses performance. Requires continual justification for program continuation. Budgeting history not taken into account. Lacks sense of commitment.

- *Performance Budgeting*. Focus is on program performance and efficiency. Examines ratios of expenditures to outputs and improvements. Old idea with new interest. Sometimes used as a percentage of the budget dedicated to improvement.

- *Formula Budgeting*. Uses mathematically derived formulas and ratios, such as costs of instruction formulas, student credit hour productivity, students served by the library, or costs of physical plant per square foot. Based on actual historical data and experience or available comparison norms. Reduces differences to averages. Discourages innovation and rewards units with increasing enrollments.

- *Responsibility Center Budgeting*. Focuses on individual units as revenue or cost centers. Units return a share of income through a subvention pool (tax) to support central administrative functions. Provides incentives to local units for entrepreneurial activity and effort. Less central control. Maximizes local effort, but can reduce or complicate cross-unit collaboration or campus-wide cooperation.

Responsibility Center Budgeting deserves further description because it is one of the relatively new budget types, is widely discussed, and serves as an interesting case study of how differing types of budgets influence incentives. The key reference on the topic is Edward Whalen's *Responsibility Center Budgeting: An Approach to Decentralized Management for Institutions of Higher Education*.[41] The subtitle is interesting because it suggests that various budget types carry with them implications for organizational arrangement and management systems. Whalen points out that Responsibility Center Budgeting first appeared in postsecondary settings at Harvard University and the University of Southern California at approximately the same time, the late 1970s and early 1980s.[42] The central idea is often expressed in the phrase *every tub on its own bottom*, meaning that "each academic unit (the tub)" generates "its own income" and is "responsible for covering . . . its own expenses (the bottom line)."[43]

Although the "tub" metaphor conveys the essential message, in fact the arrangements for each tub will vary across the institution because the return rate (tax) is negotiated according to the special circumstances of each unit. One of the key issues with Responsibility Center Budgeting, therefore, is how to determine the appropriate responsibility for each unit, given varying capabilities, ranging from an actual need for support to a strong ability to produce net income. Responsibility Center Budgeting is probably not a useful system at a small college where there is already only one tub and the bottom line is easily discerned; but in large institutions with many departments, schools, colleges, and institutes, a decentralized budget may be more appropriate.[44] Each academic unit manages its own finances and has more autonomy than in most other systems to allocate and reallocate resources to achieve its goals. What about other units, particularly those that generate little or no income? They are supported in one of two ways: by charging other units directly a portion of the costs for the facilities and services provided, or by receiving a percentage of their income from the general administration. The central administration supports the units that function primarily as service units, including itself. That's what the tax is for.

Whalen notes that Responsibility Center Budgeting rests on certain axioms and basic concepts summarized here as follows:

- *Proximity.* "The closer the point of an operating decision is to the point of implementation, the better the decision is likely to be."

- *Proportionality.* Decentralization relates to size, and "not everything should be centralized" or "decentralized."

- *Knowledge.* "Correct decisions are more likely to occur in an information-rich environment."

- *Functionality.* "Authority and command over resources should be commensurate with responsibility for the task assigned, and vice versa."

- *Performance recognition.* Clear "rewards and sanctions" are required.

- *Stability.* Consistent rules and clear consequences need "to be known before a course of action is undertaken."

- *Community.* "The relationship of the parts to the whole and to one another has to be explicitly reflected in the assignment of responsibility and authority, and in the allocation of resources."

- *Leverage.* "The legitimacy of both institutional and local responsibility has to be recognized" and "certain services" must be provided for the collective benefit of the academic community."

- *Direction.* An "academic and administrative plan" with a "clear set of objectives for the short and long run" is "assumed."[45]

Responsibility Center Budgeting, therefore, turns out to be more than a new arrangement for a system of accounts. It is based upon a set of assumptions about organizations, motivation, and even human nature. Its most basic assumption is that people in organizations will work together with an entrepreneurial spirit if given the autonomy and proper incentives to do so.

REFLECTION

> What budget system, or pieces of budget systems, do you recognize in the institutional setting with which you are familiar? Do budget arrangements provide incentives and affect effort in negative or positive ways? At what levels does your budget system inspire or impede cooperation?

Every type of budget system, not just Performance Budgeting, provides incentives and disincentives for particular kinds of behavior. The design of the budget pushes action in a particular direction and encourages the institution to focus on what is regarded as important, such as the relationship of costs and benefits, program justification, program improvement, current performance, the development of revenue streams, future plans, the self-interest of the unit, or the common good.

Budget systems reward or discourage particular forms of behavior. People within the institution soon figure out what the incentives are and where the rewards for their effort are located. The mice will make their way toward the cheese. Leaders know where the cheese is, but they also have a broad perspective on the system and how it tends to create rewards and disincentives. They know when the system needs to be modified and how to work toward changing it.

EXPANDING THE RESOURCE BASE

Although leaders need to understand the budget system and be wise and fair in allocating existing resources, they are also called upon increasingly to find ways to expand the total resource pool. To do this they may employ a local variation of essentially three strategies: increase enrollment, develop entrepreneurial (money-making) programs, or seek outside funding.

Regularly established degree programs sometimes receive additional funding for more faculty, staff, or equipment when enrollments increase. The operative word here is *sometimes* because income from expanding programs is often used to offset the losses of struggling programs or support centrally determined initiatives, depending on the budget model.

Furthermore, in some public institutions that operate under funding formulas or enrollment caps, there is little immediate incentive for increased enrollments within a particular program. In general, however, an astute leader will explore whether more students will likely result in more funding. If so, this is one way to increase the resource pool.

Some leaders become skilled in developing entrepreneurial programs that bring in not only the resources to support a worthwhile activity but also generate a surplus of net income over expense (never say *profit*) to be used for other purposes. As we have seen, most institutions manage auxiliary enterprises that generate net income. Entrepreneurial programs are like these, but they are usually mission-related programmatic activities that have a strong enough demand and low enough expense to generate net income. Typical examples are programs for children and youth, adult fitness and youth sports activities, continuing professional education (legal, executive, medical), customized training, and special events or activities designed for identifiable constituencies, such as alumni or senior citizens. Usually the central administration will want (and deserve) a share of the net income for overhead, but even so, certain programs are still worth doing if the net income they generate is significant and truly available to be used for other purposes. This is a second way to increase the resource pool.

The third way is through outside funding, the most common and perhaps most productive way of generating additional resources, and therefore worthy of more extended discussion. Faculty in large universities with extensive funded research programs are usually quite experienced in this process, and although the "flowback" for overhead, funding for soft money enterprises, and support for student assistants can contribute significantly to a unit's budget, the income from research grants is restricted exclusively to the purposes of the research. Usually when a leader is seeking to enlarge the resource pool, it is for support of programs, not research, and although the source is sometimes federal (for example, the Fund for Improvement of Postsecondary Education—FIPSE) the more typical sources are individual donors, corporations, or foundations.

Most colleges and universities have administrative units or at least an office responsible for fundraising. The preferred term today is *institutional advancement* and includes such functions as "alumni relations, internal and external communications, public relations, fund raising, government relations, and enrollment management"—anything the institution does to "develop understanding and support" in order to secure resources.[46] The term *development* is used interchangeably with fundraising but implies a sophisticated process of identifying and cultivating donors.[47]

REFLECTION

How is the function of institutional advancement organized at your institution? What services are provided to help identify and approach funding sources?

"Philanthropy and charity are as old as humankind itself," going back to the biblical concept of aiding the poor, and the Roman corn law to provide food for the masses.[48] American higher education, unlike the national systems of other countries where universities are "owned, operated, and funded by the federal government,"[49] has long depended on a system of external support. Although private colleges and universities historically have relied more heavily on outside sources, today both public and private institutions have sophisticated mechanisms for raising money, and many public colleges and universities refer to themselves as *state-assisted* or *state-affiliated* to make clear that only part of their support comes from public funds.[50] The most frequent targets for support are individual donors, corporations, and foundations.

Although one usually associates individual donations with buildings, donors also have other interests, and in fact "more than 70 percent of the money given to American higher education comes from individuals."[51] The challenge is in getting to know prospective donors well enough to understand their interests and perspectives. Cultivation of individual donors often takes a long time and involves a series of steps involving the development of a vision, negotiation of project support, and the actual asking for dollars—all of which usually require professional support from the office of institutional advancement.[52]

Corporations, like individuals, receive tax deductions for giving, but unlike foundations, their business is business, not giving, and they are often "interested in a *quid pro quo*—that is, what is in it for them."[53] They may give annual gifts, capital gifts, or may offer expertise through consultation, instruction or gifts-in-kind, such as equipment.[54] In return, the company receives such benefits as well-prepared applicants for employment, faculty expertise through consultation, visibility (as in the case of corporate sponsorship), or recognition for social responsibility. Giving usually relates to well-established corporate objectives.[55]

The more than 30,000 active grantmaking foundations are usually referred to as *independent foundations* to distinguish them from *corporate foundations* through which most corporate giving is channeled. Independent foundations are usually designated as *general purpose* or *special purpose* and as suggested by these designations may have very broad or very narrow interests.[56] Foundations have established goals and objectives, and one of the "most important tasks is to identify and articulate the interests that a foundation and the institution share," a challenge somewhat akin to trying to arrange a marriage.[57] Most institutional advancement offices can provide useful information on how to identify foundations that are appropriate for a particular project, through access to one of the regional offices of the Foundation Center or through its *Foundation Directory*.[58] It is also useful to coordinate foundation requests through institutional advancement so that only one proposal at a time makes its way to the foundation.[59]

The key to success in soliciting individuals, corporations, or foundations is a strong proposal, which should include the clear definition of an issue or problem, the proposed solution to address that issue, the identification of all of the resources needed (including those you are contributing), and the means of evaluating success. It is also valuable to articulate the mutual rewards for the institution and the foundation.[60]

The important thing to remember about fundraising is that nobody gives money away. The term *charitable giving* may even be a misnomer for the process. Although altruistic individuals surely exist, the process of giving is a transaction between someone who needs money for a specific project and someone else who wishes to achieve particular goals through their financial support. The leader's role in expanding the resource pool is to move beyond the "we need" perspective of those at the institution to the grantmaker's view of a larger issue to be addressed.

Financial management involves looking at both sides of the ledger—revenue and expense. Leaders learn to see dollars everywhere, and they recognize that budgets must be wisely crafted and carefully controlled to ensure the financial viability of programs and services. Along with everything else, leaders are money managers.

MARY'S MENTOR

Mary's mentor wants her to remember these things about financial management:

- Leaders know how to read operational budgets and balance sheets.
- Accounting and auditing procedures are established by national bodies.
- Colleges and universities have several different fund accounts to manage educational and general expenses, sponsored programs, auxiliary enterprises, endowments, loans, and physical plant.
- Many components of budgets are planned well in advance of the fiscal year they serve.

- Leaders know when and how to enter into the budget planning cycle to negotiate their interests and influence decisions.

- Knowing where to look in the budget for uncommitted dollars is important, but so is cutting costs.

- Each budget system has its own set of assumptions about organizational behavior, motivation, and even human nature.

- A particular budget system will focus individuals on what the organization says is important.

- Leaders understand how budget systems foster or inhibit cooperation.

- The resource base can be enlarged by increasing enrollments, engaging in entrepreneurial activities, or seeking outside funding.

- An office of institutional advancement helps leaders locate funding sources and develop proposals for individual donors, corporations, and foundations.

- The lions will never believe they are well fed, even when they are.

NOTES

1. Richard J. Meisinger, Jr., *College and University Budgeting: An Introduction for Faculty and Administrators* (Washington, DC: National Association of College and University Business Officers, 1994). The story about the lions comes from the introduction.

2. Dierdre McDonald Greene, ed., *College and University Business Administration*, 5th ed., 3 vols. (Washington, DC: National Association of College and University Business Officers, 1992).

3. Meisinger, *College and University Budgeting*, p. 4.

4. Ibid., pp. 1–3.

5. Richard J. Meisinger, Jr. and Leroy W. Dubeck, "Fund Accounting," in David W. Breneman, Larry L. Leslie, and Richard Anderson, eds., *ASHE Reader on Finance in Higher Education* (Needham Heights, MA: Simon and Schuster Custom Publishing, 1996), p. 454.

6. Ibid., p. 456.

7. Abbot Wainwright "Overview of Financial Accounting and Reporting," in Greene, *College and University Business Administration*, p. 222.

8. Malvern Gross, Jr., Richard Laskin, and John H. McCarthy, *Financial and Accounting Guide for Not-For-Profit Organizations*, 6th ed. (New York: John Wiley & Sons, 2000), pp. 47–50.

9. Ibid., p. 225.

10. Meisinger and Dubeck, "Fund Accounting," p. 458.

11. Wainwright, "Overview of Financial Accounting and Reporting," p. 210.

12. Warren H. Spruill, "Auditing," in Greene, *College and University Business Administration*, p. 695.

13. Julie T. Norris, "Research and Sponsored Programs," in Greene, *College and University Business Administration*, p. 1083.

14. Ibid., p. 1087.

15. Ibid., p. 1088.

16. Donald B. Powell, et al., "Auxiliary Enterprises and Other Services," in Greene, *College and University Business Administration*, p. 1193.

17. Richard E. Anderson, "College and University Accounting: An Introduction," in Breneman, et al., *ASHE Reader on Finance in Higher Education*, p. 463.

18. Ibid., p. 465.

19. Ibid., p. 467.

20. Meisinger, *College and University Budgeting*, p. 3.

21. Ibid., pp. 11, 20.

22. Ibid., p. 62.

23. Ibid.

24. Nathan Dickmeyer, " Budgeting," in Greene, *College and University Business Administration*, p. 256.

25. Rhonda Martin Epper, "Applying Benchmarking to Higher Education," *Change* (November/December 1999), p. 26.

26. Meisinger, *College and University Budgeting*, pp. 20–21.

27. Kent John Chabotar, "How to Develop an Effective Budget Process," in *Roles and Responsibilities of the Chief Financial Officer* (New Directions for Higher Education, vol. 27, no. 3) (San Francisco: Jossey-Bass, 1999), p. 20.

28. Meisinger, *College and University Budgeting*, p. 3.

29. Chabotar, "How to Develop an Effective Budget Process," p. 22. The three questions are quoted directly.

30. Meisinger, *College and University Budgeting*, p. 76.

31. Dudley B. Woodward, Jr. and Mark von Destinon, "Budgeting and Fiscal Management," in Margaret J. Barr, Mary K. Desler, and Associates, *The Handbook of Student Affairs Administration* (San Francisco: Jossey-Bass, 2000), p. 336.

32. Meisinger, *College and University Budgeting*, p. 94.

33. Ibid.

34. Ibid., p. 169.

35. Ibid., p. 144.

36. Dickmeyer, " Budgeting," pp. 260–261.

37. Meisinger, *College and University Budgeting*, p. 169.

38. Ibid., p. 66.

39. Ibid., pp. 106–110.

40. Ibid., pp. 177–187.

41. Edward L. Whalen, *Responsibility Center Budgeting: An Approach to Decentralized Management for Institutions of Higher Education* (Bloomington: Indiana University Press, 1991).

42. Ibid., p. 2.

43. Ibid.

44. Ibid., pp. 5–6.

45. Ibid., pp. 10–13. Paraphrased with certain key phrases in quotes.

46. Michael J. Worth, "Defining Institutional Advancement, Development, and Fundraising," in Michael J. Worth, ed. *Educational Fundraising Principles and Practice* (Phoenix, AZ: American Council on Education and The Oryx Press, 1993), p. 5.

47. Ibid., p. 6

48. Kent Dove, *Conducting a Successful Fundraising Program* (San Francisco: Jossey-Bass, 2001), pp. 10–11.

49. Worth, "Defining Institutional Advancement, Development, and Fundraising," p. 3.

50. Frank H.T. Rhodes, ed., "Introduction," in Frank H.T. Rhodes, *Successful Fundraising for Higher Education: The Advancement of Learning* (Phoenix, AZ: American Council on Education and The Oryx Press, 1997), p. xviii.

51. Michael F. Adams, "How to Solicit a Major Gift," in Worth, *Educational Fundraising*, p. 131.

52. Ibid., pp. 132–40.

53. D. Chris Withers, "Obtaining Corporate Support," in Worth, *Educational Fundraising*, p. 181.

54. Ibid., pp. 183–184.

55. Ibid., p. 189.

56. Max G. Smith, "Obtaining Foundation Support," in Worth, *Educational Fundraising*, pp. 191–192.

57. Ibid., p. 195.

58. Ibid., p. 196.

59. Sarah Godfrey, "How to Write a Good Proposal," in Worth, *Educational Fundraising*, pp. 202–205. See also Dove, *Conducting a Successful Fundraising Program*, pp. 265–268.

60. Ibid., p. 202.

CHAPTER 8

Change:
Moving Forward Gracefully

Springtime everywhere! Dean Williams glances out of her office window and notices a flowering crabapple framed by two budding maples about to burst forth with new green leaves. She enjoys the change of seasons here.

Change? The whole world seems to be in turmoil but this place goes right on, business as usual. Does anything ever actually change here? No wonder they call it an ivory tower. Maybe its not supposed to change. Could that be true? Why does she feel so frustrated about her efforts to bring about change? Isn't that what a leader is supposed to do—change things?

When she talks to Fred, he compliments her on the small but important changes she has been able to nurture. Dolores, on the other hand, wants big, fast-paced changes; she's a born revolutionary. Who is right, Fred or Dolores? How much change is necessary? How much is prudent?

Dean Williams goes back to her desk chair and sits for a moment to try to think out answers to her own questions. Change is a problem in any organization—she knows that. But is it worse in academia? People don't care much about anything until some vital interest of their own is threatened. They show up for that particular meeting and then hibernate for months. One issue piles on top of another until the overbearing weight of it all crushes the change-makers. Some people are afraid of change; they even get nervous when the janitor comes to change a light bulb.

It would be valuable to know what the experts think about change. There must be studies and theories. What she needs is a good, solid change model—something she can follow step-by-step to make changes with more grace. What's the vision? Who will be her allies? Where will she begin? How can she get the changes to stick so that if she leaves, things won't just revert to the way they always were? So many difficult questions to ponder.

Dolores suggested a big meeting with no agenda. Just put everyone in one big room and get them talking. Stir the old place up. Light a few brush fires. Would that work or is that just a pyromaniac's fantasy?

Dean Williams remembers an old saying: "Only a wet baby wants change." Maybe that's the first step—to overcome complacency and establish a sense of urgency about something that truly needs to be changed.

C hange is broadly defined as an "act or process of substitution, alteration, or variation."[1] Change is something that organizations experience and respond to, but change is also something they initiate. Leaders are often referred to as change-agents, and some theories of leadership emphasize the leader's role in transforming organizations.

THE BROAD CONTEXT OF CHANGE

Two aspects of change have taken on new importance recently: the *extent* of change and the *rapidity* of change. Change is occurring in telecommunications, computer technology, the world market and capital system, organizational structures, demographics, bioengineering, and many other areas simultaneously so that changes in particular sectors of society have combined to produce a cumulative impact that can rightly be referred to as a *new era*. Futurists such as Alvin Toffler were able to see that the new era was coming and they knew that it was going to be upsetting. Toffler called the likely response to this new era *future shock*. Today, the future described by the futurists more than thirty years ago has arrived in full force.[2] Change is manifest nearly everywhere. Change in higher education takes place in this broad societal arena that forces all institutions to change.

The extent of change is matched by the remarkable rate of change, what Toffler referred to as the "accelerative thrust of change."[3] Years ago, the well-known theorist of adult learning, Malcolm Knowles, developed a schematic to describe the historical relationship of human longevity to the pace of social change. What he portrayed was an extending longevity—from thirty years in the Middle Ages to seventy today—accompanied by an ever-shrinking time span for social change.[4] Today many major social changes can occur in one lifetime. The anthropologist, Margaret Mead, observed that the relationship of elders and the young (teachers and learners) is quite different in a stable, traditional society when compared to modern societies characterized by rapid change. In stable societies, youth only learn from the elders; in fast-changing societies, the young learn both from the elders and their contemporaries, and the elders also learn from the young.[5] Change in higher education takes place in a context of rapid social change.

Peter Vaill has described the impact of extensive and rapid change on organizations in his book *Learning as a Way of Being: Strategies for Survival in a World of Permanent White Water*. He uses the metaphor of white water rafting—navigating a turbulent river—to describe what people must do today to cope with "events that are surprising, novel, messy, costly, and unpreventable."[6] Vaill believes that white water conditions in today's organization are permanent. Turbulence never ceases. "Permanent white water metaphorically defines the different conditions under which people exercise their will and judgment within society's macrosystems."[7]

REFLECTION

> How would you characterize the external environment with regard to change? Is "white water" a good metaphor? What aspects of your institution are affected by life in a new era? What is the appropriate role of postsecondary leaders in responding to changes in society? Can colleges and universities afford not to change?

In a society where change is said to be the only constant, leaders ponder how to respond to external forces that create a need for internal change. Leaders often serve as change-agents in a rapidly changing world.

RESISTANCE TO CHANGE

Colleges and universities appear to be highly resistant to change, so much so that professionals in other sectors of society sometimes joke about the glacial speed of change in higher education and the excessive time needed for decision making. In one sense, higher education is designed not to change. As Madeleine Green has observed in *Transforming Higher Education*, "its mission is to conserve, to embody the timeless values of scholarly inquiry and transmission of knowledge from one generation to the next."[8] As Clark Kerr once noted, universities are among a very small number of institutions still in existence today doing much the same as they did in the 1500s.[9] Green concludes, after collecting the observations of leaders from many foreign countries, however, that higher education does change, when seen in a global perspective, and has changed greatly in the last 25 years.[10]

Scholars have catalogued the reasons why institutions of higher education resist change. Adrianna Kezar provides a useful list of these explanations of resistance to change in her monograph *Understanding and Facilitating Change in the 21st Century*, several of which are summarized as follows:

- *Multiple power and authority structures*. Diffuse and complex governance structures (senates, committees, task forces) exist side-by-side with administrative structures so that sometimes it is difficult to tell who actually has the power to make changes. Because overt expression of power breaks a social norm, the true sources of power are often hidden.

- *Loosely coupled structure*. Connections and networks within the organization are weak favoring "opportunistic adaptation" rather than planned change.

- *Institutional status*. Colleges and universities, like hospitals, the judiciary, and schools have an "institutional status" and longstanding societal mission that makes change less likely.

- *Professional and administrative values*. Two sets of values exist in uneasy tension—the values of professionals (collegiality, autonomy, peer review) and the values of administrators (structure, rationality, control)—making cooperation to effect change difficult.[11]

Another, and perhaps more telling, description of factors that produce resistance to change can be found in the classic study of presidential leadership by Michael Cohen and James March, *Leadership and Ambiguity*. They refer to the governance system of higher education as *organized anarchy*. To put it bluntly, the system "does not know what it is doing. Its goals are either vague or in dispute. Its technology is familiar but not understood. Its major participants wander in and out of the organization." Each individual makes "autonomous decisions," and the so-called decisions of the system "are a consequence produced by the system but intended by no one and decisively controlled by no one."[12] Organized anarchies are characterized by:

- *Problematic goals*. A "variety of inconsistent and ill-defined preferences" substitute for clear unambiguous goals.

- *Unclear technology*. "Trial-and-error procedures, . . . imitation, and the inventions born of necessity" substitute for a clear understanding of its own procedures.

- *Fluid participation*. Variable time and effort by participants substitute for commitment and continuity.

Cohen and March characterize decision making as "a garbage can" into which various problems and solutions are dumped by participants. "The mix of garbage in a single can depends partly on the labels attached to the alternative cans; but it also depends on what garbage is being produced at the moment, on the mix of cans available, and on the speed with which garbage is collected and removed from the scene."[13] The authors also believe that the issues in the garbage cans tend to go around and around (like a merry-go-round) so that decision makers "feel like they are always working on the same problems in somewhat different contexts, mostly without results."[14] Participants wander in and out of the system, shaping decisions in the garbage cans that affect them the most.

If the descriptions by Kezar and by Cohen and March are at all accurate, change will be seriously circumscribed by a governance and decision-making process in higher education that inhibits rather than fosters change.

REFLECTION

> To what extent do factors that tend to inhibit change exist at the institution you serve? Which factors are more visible and important? How strongly do these factors inhibit change? Are they overwhelming or can they be managed? In your experience, are these factors unique to colleges and universities?

Leaders are aware of the forces that inhibit change in higher education generally and at their own institution in particular. They evaluate the strength of these forces and give consideration to what they must do to contend with them before embarking on proposed changes. Leaders are not, however, overwhelmed by forces that inhibit change.

TYPES OF CHANGE

Leaders can profit from a systematic examination of what type of change they are contemplating before they get involved in it. A useful set of categories for thinking about various types of change is provided in the volume by Adrianna Kezar cited earlier.[15] Her concepts have been reworked and reordered here as questions:

- *Is the change planned or unplanned?* Many changes simply occur. On the other hand, some changes are intentional and deliberate. Leaders are usually more directly associated with planned change and this is usually what they have in mind when they talk about change.

- *What are the forces and sources of change?* Are pressures coming from the external or internal environment? Are financial factors the source? Personnel matters? Quality standards?

- *Is the change proactive or reactive?* Is a response being contemplated to an important occurrence or crisis? Is the change preemptive or preventative? Is it an initiative simply to embark on something new?

- *What are the proposed outcomes of the change?* What targets are contemplated: new organizational structures, new personnel, new processes, different missions, changed behavior, or new services? What combination of outcomes is anticipated? Are unintended outcomes foreseeable?

- *What is the degree of change?* Is this a *first-order* change involving minor adjustments and improvements? Is this a *second order* change involving major multidimensional transformations?

- *What is the scale of change?* Is this change that takes place on a personal, interpersonal, or organizational level—or all of these levels?

- *What is the focus of the change?* Does the change focus on structures, processes, or attitudes—or all of these aspects?

- *What is the timing of the change?* Is this a change that will occur suddenly with drastic consequences or will this be a change that is well-planned and evolves over time?

- *Is this adaptive or generative change?* Is this a one-time response to a moment in time or is this part of an ongoing process of continuous improvement?

A useful model for categorizing types of change is provided by David Nadler in "Organizational Frame Bending: Types of Change in the Complex Organization."[16] Nadler creates a two-by-two configuration with dimensions for *scope of change* and *temporal position of change*. The result is displayed in Figure 8.1. The scope of change can be either *incremental*—focused on pieces or components of the organization—or *strategic*—focused on the organization as a whole. On the temporal dimension, change can be either *anticipatory*—in anticipation of events that may occur—or *reactive*—in response to events that have already occurred. The combination of dimensions produces an interesting array of types of changes that Nadler calls *tuning, adaptation, reorientation,* and *re-creation.* *Tuning* involves "incremental changes that are made in anticipation of future events." *Adaptation* is incremental change "made in reaction to external events." *Reorientation* is "strategic change made when and where the external events . . . were anticipated." *Re-creation* is strategic change

Figure 8.1
Nadler's Types of Organizational Change

Incremental		Strategic
Anticipatory	Tuning	Reorientation
Reactive	Adaptation	Re-creation

necessitated in response to external events, often a "radical departure" in reaction to a "life threatening" event. Some changes, therefore, are more intense than others, and Nadler ranks them from low to high: tuning, adaptation, reorientation, and re-creation. The nature of change is also influenced by the size and diversity of the organization. Nadler calls re-orientation in large complex institutions *frame-bending* changes. This is the type of change that will more than likely provide leaders with their biggest challenges.

REFLECTION

> Consider one or more changes that may occur or have occurred at your institution. What types of changes are they? Does it help to ana-lyze these changes using the questions and categories outlined above?

Before embarking on change, effective leaders ask what kind of change is contemplated. A leader's strategy for bringing about change will vary according to the type of change undertaken. Not all changes are the same and some may be much more difficult to achieve than others.

CHANGE THEORIES

Additional insights about the nature of change can be gained through the examination of change theories. Scholars who have studied the phenomena of change raise important questions about leadership in bringing about change. The role of the leader can shift dramatically de-pending on the operative change theory. As is the case with leadership theories, the theorists do not agree on what change is or how it takes place, but their insights are useful for those who wish to think more clearly and objectively about change. Each theory presents a different lens for viewing change. Fortunately, an excellent review of change theories can be found in the work of Adrianna Kezar mentioned ear-lier.[17] The theories presented in her work are summarized (in a slightly different order) and presented below.

Teleological Theories

The assumption behind these theories is that "organizations are purpose-ful and adaptive and that at the center of the change process one can find leaders who set goals and are influential in bringing about change. Teleological theories are often known by other names such as "planned change, scientific management, or rational models" and they employ such techniques as "strategic planning," "organizational development," or "continuous quality improvement." Teleological theories stress the importance of leaders, change agents, vision, and persistent pursuit of goals. These theories are criticized for stressing too much the idea of change as a rational and linear process and the importance of leaders in effecting change.[18]

Evolutionary Theories

These theories draw on "social evolutionary models and biological models, "and they stress organizational responses such as "adaptation," "self-organization," and "systems theory." According to these theories, change depends on situational variables and is greatly influenced by the environment." These models focus on the inability of organizations to plan for and respond to change, and their tendency to instead "manage" change as it occurs. "Evolutionary theories stress such ideas as *interactivity, openness*, and *homeostasis*. . . . These models de-emphasize action and focus on awareness of environmental influences and impacts." Evolutionary theories are criticized for their neglect of the "social element in change and for downplaying human initiative in affecting environmental trends."[19]

Life Cycle Theories

Drawing on models of human development and applying them to organizations, life cycle theories stress "organizational growth, maturity, and decline." Change occurs "as individuals within the organization adapt to its life cycle." Because the environment is ambiguous and threatening, people in organizations must fight off its decline through change processes that create new organizational purposes and identities. This model shifts the emphasis from leaders to people throughout the organization who play a key role in adjusting to its life cycle. These models have been criticized for lacking empirical grounds and for being overly deterministic.[20]

Dialectical Models

Drawing on the Hegelian-Marxist concept of the dialectical interaction of polar opposites, these theories view change as the outgrowth of conflicting forces. The "predominant change process" involves "bargaining," "persuasion," and "influence and power." Leaders moderate the conflict of interest groups and work with networks and coalitions. "Inherent conflict will create change." These models are criticized for their determinism and for their lack of emphasis on the external environment.[21]

Social Cognition Models

Based on a social-constructivist view of organizations, these models stress the importance of cognition and sense-making by the organization's participants. "People simply reach a point of cognitive dissonance at which values and actions clash or something seems outmoded, and they decide to change. . . . The outcome of the change is a new frame of mind or worldview." Leaders influence change through "framing, interpretation," and encouraging "learning." They help participants change "paradigms" and "conceptualize a different organizational reality." These models are criticized for their lack of attention to external environmental forces and for ignoring "values, feelings, and emotions" while overemphasizing "thinking, mental processes, and learning."[22]

Cultural Theories

Cultures are always changing, but "the change process tends to be long-term and slow." Change proceeds through the "alteration of values, beliefs, myths, and rituals" and the leader's role is to use "symbolic actions, language, and metaphors" to influence cultural change. Leaders become "change masters" by "creating new myths and rituals . . . performing symbolic actions, and communicating new values and beliefs." These theories have been criticized for their emphasis on the slowness of change and the doubtful ability of leaders to manage cultural symbols.[23]

REFLECTION

> Are the theories of change compatible or irreconcilable? What insights do they provide about the nature of change? Do they leave you more optimistic or pessimistic about change in organizations?

Change theories provide diverse perspectives on the nature of change. Although the theorists are by no means saying the same thing, their various insights may provide a richer understanding of change when used alternately or as multiple lenses for examining change in a particular context. Generalizing about change or reducing complex phenomena to one theory about change is probably dangerous.

CHANGE MODELS

The literature on change in organizations contains many models that suggest how to undertake change. The advocates of these models assume that change is possible, they stress one or more aspects of change, and they believe that leaders play an important role in change. A number of change models have been identified for brief description here, and although each one stresses a different aspect of change, they all provide useful ideas that have at least the potential for success in an appropriate context.

The Developmental Phase Model

The model presented by Ed Oakley and Doug Krug in *Enlightened Leadership* begins with an analysis of business development that provides a classic example of developmental change theory. All organizations go through a series of phases that the authors identify as *entrepreneurial, growth*, and *renewal* or *decline*.[24] The entrepreneurial phase represents a time of "infancy, invention, nurturing, formation and innovation." In this phase "most new businesses scramble to find a successful pattern, develop a better product, deliver exceptional service, and uncover the most effective marketing strategy."[25] This phase is characterized by excitement, energy and enthusiasm, and inevitable mistakes.[26] The growth phase is a time for putting into place systems, policies, and procedures, and for controlling growth in an attempt to hold on to what people in the organization have done that has worked.[27] "The danger is that late in the growth phase the very systems and procedures that have gotten a company successfully to where it is can become barriers to continued success."[28] People withdraw into the "boxes" of established policy and "work harder and harder to do more of what they have been doing all along."[29] Late in the growth phase, the organization will encounter a crisis and will face the choice between decline and renewal. An organization in decline continues to work harder at what it has done well, whereas an organization in the renewal phase begins to reexamine "systems, procedures, and processes."[30] It becomes revitalized, open, and flexible, and eventually it rekindles an entrepreneurial spirit.[31]

To make the needed changes and enter the renewal phase, an organization or a unit of an organization must face the "hard" issues posed by financial figures and quality data, as well as the "soft" issues of attitude and mindset. The model for change suggested by Oakley and Krug begins with *mindset*. Knowing that usually only 20 percent of the people will be open to change, the challenge is with the attitudes of the other 80 percent.[32] The technique for changing attitudes is to focus on the desired results, not on what has gone wrong.[33] Leaders generate this "forward energy" not by telling or giving directives but by asking effective questions so that people can learn through their own answering.[34] As they do so, a new entrepreneurial phase begins again and the cycle repeats.

The value in this model is in the analysis of business development phases. The model can be applied to a whole institution, but it is especially useful for thinking about colleges, schools, departments, and programs in need of renewal. Recognizing the importance of attitude change is valuable, as is the emphasis on future plans as opposed to past mistakes. On the other hand, are phases inevitable, and could the 80 to 20 ratio be reversed in an institution that becomes change-orientated?

The Right People Model

Charles Bishop, in his book *Making Change Happen One Person at a Time*, focuses on the importance of people in the change process. He describes four types of people: A-players, who "greet change as a friend not an enemy"; B-players, who "lack the perspective, enthusiasm and change leadership of A-players" but are willing to change; C-players, who are the silent majority willing to "try new methods and approaches in technical areas with which they're familiar but are not change leaders"; and D-players, who are "change resistors of the first rank," consistently "exhibiting antipathy" to "every new program."[35] Leaders of change begin by constructing profiles of the change response capabilities and versatility of the people who will be involved. The task is to assess who responds well to change and who is actually versatile enough to take on new responsibilities.[36] At this point it is possible to analyze the change capacity of particular weak links.[37] The overall plan for change includes a roadmap for identifying the ready and able players and the individuals who can profit from development, ongoing coaching and feedback, learning from others, or self-development.[38]

The strength of this model is its emphasis on the role of individuals in the change process. If people are the problem—as they often are in college or university settings—why not focus more deliberately on assessing capacity for change and developing versatility? This model focuses systematically on identifying people who are ready for change and those who need help in changing. On the other hand, perhaps organizations could have more A-players if they made consistent efforts to hire and develop people who welcome change.

The Democratic Engagement Model

Change driven by heroic leaders or parallel organizations (consultants or planning teams) produce unintended consequences and seldom work. This is the conclusion drawn by Richard Axelrod in *Terms of Engagement:*

Changing the Way We Change Organizations.[39] A process that "allows the few to decide for the many" is unlikely to develop sufficient organizational support for the needed changes, thus making the "change management process itself . . . the root of the problem." [40] The remedy is "widening the circle of involvement," by "expanding who gets to participate in the change process." This means "including new and different voices" and increasing the number in order to create a critical mass for change."[41] Axelrod describes what he calls the *engagement model,* a "series of connected conferences that are held every four or six weeks" and involve "a critical mass of the organization in planning for the future."[42] The challenge is "getting the whole system in the room" and involving as many as possible, not just the "best and the brightest."[43] Drawing on a theory called *complex adaptive systems,* the engagement model reflects the idea that change occurs in "systems where there are many different actions being carried out by many different people in a constantly changing environment."[44] "Bringing more people to the conversation is essential, but equally important is increasing the depth of the conversation."[45] The goal is to "move from a collection of individuals to a collaborative community of people who are willing to act."[46] The engagement model is based on old and familiar democratic principles: "equity and fairness, maximum sharing of information, open decision-making processes, and freedom and autonomy."[47]

In college and university settings where shared governance is already a strong value, broadening democratic participation will probably be well received. The value in this model is in its recognition of complexity in the organization as a system and the need to involve everyone in the change process who is affected by or who will be expected to implement the new directions. The weakness of the model is that democratic processes are often slow and cumbersome and may work against cultivating a sense of urgency.

The Four Levers Model

Change in organizations depends on leveraging four key elements: human factors, power, social process, and leadership. This is the thesis of Peter Brill and Richard Worth, the authors of *The Four Levers of Corporate Change.*[48] No one element in itself is sufficient. Understanding the natural human resistance to change is important: "human beings are not one-dimensional creatures who park their human nature at the door when they enter the workplace."[49] Just as important, however, is an awareness of different types of power and how these will be exerted by groups and individuals within the organization during the change process.[50] The "engine of change" is the social process, the series of activities that participants engage in to experience the dynamics of new forms of social relationships.[51] Change also requires leadership, not only from formal leaders who guide the change process through vision and alignment but informal leaders who support the change.[52] Effective change involves integrating and leveraging all four elements of the change process.

The value in this model is that it moves beyond one-dimensional views of change to identify four key elements, all of which must be leveraged to produce a successful change process. However, addressing all four process elements may cause a loss of focus on the purpose and desired outcomes of the change.

The Large-Scale Events Model

Drawing on the uses of large-scale events in organizational development, Steven Brigham has assembled a list of such events that can be used in colleges and universities. His article on large-scale events published in the magazine *Change* includes suggestions for holding retreats or a series of conferences for such activities as developing a vision, addressing problems, exploring a selected topic, or establishing plans for change. The agenda for town meetings or campus-wide events is either predetermined or left relatively open.[53] Brigham notes that large-scale events involve risk and are not for the faint-hearted, but when well designed can provide the right conditions for people to learn and collaborate.

Large-scale events bring the values of spontaneity and creativity into the change process. They also bring people into the process who otherwise might not be involved, thus affirming their potential for making important contributions. On the other hand, large-scale events may produce more frustration than progress, and participants may come away feeling that nothing happened.

The Campaign Model

One obstacle to change in today's overloaded institution is simply getting people's attention. Larry Hirschorn and Linda May suggest "The Campaign Approach to Change" in their article published in *Change*.[54] They recommend "listening in" to the institution to find prototype programs, emerging leaders, and points of tension in order to identify key themes around which change can be organized. Instead of trying to change the whole institution or even one of its subunits, the authors recommend focusing change on a promising theme and giving it a name, such as "student retention" or "students achieving." Then the task is to sweep people into the campaign who care about the outcome. As with a political campaign, an "architecture of participation" is needed—support systems, a communication system, even a "war room." Financial incentives and more permanent structures are needed to sustain the change, but the first task is to get people's attention.

The value in this model is the intense focus on a single issue and the use of a temporary architecture to structure participation. The point about getting attention is important, as is the recommendation for sweeping people in who care enough to get involved. On the other hand, academics generally dislike bandwagons, and a campaign could result in increased resistance or simply indifference.

The Epidemic Model

Malcolm Gladwell's fascinating best-seller, *The Tipping Point*, analyzes changes of a significant proportion, such as trends, waves, movements, and epidemics.[55] Although such changes are often regarded as "beyond control," they have their inner logic, as Gladwell points out, and can be encouraged by people who understand how they work. Change that is widespread in its popular embrace, although seemingly leaderless and sudden, can be nourished by factors that when taken together produce a tipping point—a moment when the change suddenly becomes sweeping and dramatic. Epidemics have their rules. Gladwell describes in detail three change principles that he calls the Law of the Few, the Stickiness Factor, and the Power of Context. The *Law of the Few* expresses the idea that epidemic change is usually carried by word of mouth and that the carriers are few in number. They talk a lot, however, and encounter a large number of people in their daily rounds—like Paul Revere on his famous ride. The *Stickiness Factor* captures the idea that the content of the epidemic is designed in such a way as to stick easily in people's minds, as an effective advertising slogan does. The content must be memorable and capable of motivating action. The *Power of Context* principle suggests that for epidemics "the conditions and circumstances of the times and places in which they occur must be favorable."[56] The message about change is found in Gladwell's conclusions. "Starting epidemics requires concentrating resources on a few key areas," relying on word-of-mouth publicity from a few well-connected players, and having a good concept well-tested for its "stickiness" that arrives in the right context at the right time.[57] Gladwell's final advice is: "Look at the world around you. It may seem like an immovable, implacable place. It is not. With the slightest push—in just the right place—it can be tipped."[58]

The epidemic model surely has appeal to leaders who envision dramatic change. The value of the model is in its identification of change carriers (the hyperactive, well-connected few) and the importance of a memorable message spread at the right time. The weakness of the model is that it appears to be a better description of how change happens than a prescription for how to make it happen.

A COMPREHENSIVE CHANGE MODEL

Most of the models described in the previous section focus on only narrow aspects of change or offer a particular change strategy. Good ideas appear in those models, but they lack comprehensiveness. They might better be called *mini-models* of change. One change model that has received high visibility and welcome response for its credibility and comprehensiveness is the eight-stage model developed by Harvard Business School professor John Kotter in his book, *Leading Change*.[59] Kotter's model consists of sequential stages, and he stresses the importance of taking the steps in order. Skipping stages or not doing the work of earlier stages threatens the success of the overall change process. Kotter believes that "successful transformation is 70 to 90 percent leadership and only 10 to 30 percent management."[60] His work represents the teleological change theorists who believe that change is possible, rational procedures are necessary, and leadership is indispensable. The eight stages are as follows:

1. *Establishing a Sense of Urgency*—With or without a crisis, the organization must be jolted out of its complacency and begin to seek higher standards of quality and new opportunities.

2. *Creating the Guiding Coalition*—To guide the change, a leader needs to establish a team composed of people with position, power, expertise, credibility, and proven leadership ability.

3. *Developing a Vision and Strategy*—The change process needs to be driven by a vision that is "imaginable, desirable, feasible, focused, flexible, and communicable," and a strategy must be established "to show how the vision can be accomplished."

4. *Communicating the Change Vision*—A simple message must be communicated frequently and in multiple forums through metaphors and examples, and behavior must be congruent with a consistent message.

5. *Empowering Broad-Based Action*—People within the organization must be empowered through new structures, effective training, well-aligned personnel systems, and supervisors who support change.

6. *Generating Short-Term Wins*—Targeted, unambiguous performance improvements must be demonstrated within six to eighteen months to provide evidence of success, reward those who support change, undermine cynics, and build momentum.

7. *Consolidating Change and Producing More Change*—After initial successes have been achieved, independent systems need to be aligned, and coordinated, and many new projects may need to be launched to bring about organization-wide transformation, sustain critical momentum, and avoid regression.

8. *Anchoring New Approaches in the Culture*—Efforts must be made to tie new practices to the old culture or, if necessary, to modify the norms of behavior and shared values to generate a new culture so that new practices can grow deep roots.[61]

Kotter points out that "the first four steps in the transformation process help defrost a hardened status quo. If change were easy, you wouldn't need all that effort. Phases five to seven then introduce many new practices. The last stage grounds the changes in corporate culture and makes them stick."[62]

REFLECTION

Identify a situation that you are involved in now in which change would be desirable, or visualize a situation that could profit from change. Do any of the mini-models provide useful ideas about how to proceed? Is the change you have in mind unidimensional or complex? Is a comprehensive change model needed? Why do you think some efforts at change fail?

WHY CHANGE FAILS

Veterans of change often look back and wonder why so many efforts at change end up in failure. Enormous amounts of time and effort are spent with little success. Kotter believes that change fails because leaders get in a rush and skip steps. His book opens with a discussion of eight reasons why change fails.[63] Not surprisingly, these errors correspond with his eight-step change model. Why does change fail? Because the organization is complacent and no one feels a sense of urgency. Because leaders don't take time to build a guiding coalition. Because no one put forth the effort to work out a vision or develop a strategy. And so forth. Kotter's positive change model grew out of his observations of *failed* change. The change process can break down at any one of the eight steps. That's Kotter's explanation.

Another explanation is set forth in Arthur Levine's book *Why Innovation Fails: The Institutionalization and Termination of Innovation in Higher Education.*[64] Levine's explanation is especially interesting because it grows out of a study of change in a higher education setting, the establishment of six specialized undergraduate colleges within an already existing university. Levine studied the change process from beginning to end and his conclusion is that the problem comes at the end. It is like the Cinderella story, he quips: Everyone gets caught up in the marvelous story of Cinderella, the prince, the slipper, and the search, but "the reader is left wondering whether the marriage was a good one. We assume it all worked out and are quite shocked when we hear differently from *People Magazine.*"[65] Levine's point is that institutionalization is the most important aspect of change and the point at which change is most likely to break down.

Levine develops useful concepts for describing what happens in the crucial period after an innovation has been established. *Boundary expansion* "involves the adoption of the innovation's personality traits by the host, or more simply an acceptance by the host of some or all of the innovation's differences."[66] The existing organization, as the host to something new, welcomes and absorbs the change to some degree. The acceptance can take two forms: *diffusion* or *enclaving*. "*Diffusion* is the process whereby innovation characteristics are allowed to spread through the host organization, and *enclaving* is the process whereby the innovation assumes an isolated position within the organization."[67] In other words, as the change becomes established, it begins to spread within the institution or it finds its niche in some corner of the institution. In either case, the innovation wins some acceptance. When the innovation fails, other forces are at work: *boundary contraction* through *resocialization* or *termination*. "*Boundary contraction* involves a constriction of organizational boundaries in such a manner as to exclude the innovation."[68] The innovation is held outside the boundaries and "is viewed as illegitimate and labeled *deviant*."[69] Even though the change has begun to be established, people don't actually accept it. They hold it at arm's length. Two things can happen: *resocialization* or *termination*. *Resocialization* "occurs when the innovation unit is made to renounce its past deviance and institute the acceptable norms, values, and goals it failed to incorporate previously."[70] In this case the change is watered down beyond recognition so that the innovative aspects of the change are stripped away and the change once again becomes acceptable because it is no longer a change. *Termination* "occurs when the innovation is eliminated."[71] Thus, any change can have four outcomes: *diffusion, enclaving, resocialization,* or *termination.* What makes the difference?

Levine introduces two more concepts to help explain an innovation's acceptance or rejection: *compatibility* and *profitability. Compatibility* "may be thought of as the degree to which the norms, values, and goals of an innovation are congruent with those of the host."[72] The issue has to do with the degree of difference posed by the innovation. *Profitability* can mean economic profitability but may also include "non-economic profits . . . such as security, prestige, peer approval, growth, efficiency, and improvement of quality of life." [73] The important thing is that the change is *perceived* as profitable, both in terms of the personal *self-interest* and *profitability* of individuals and the *general profitability* to the organization. Change apparently has a better chance of enduring when it is compatible with existing norms and is perceived as profitable.[74] If *innovation failure* is defined as "a premature decline in the planned level of impact or influence of an innovation on the host organization,"[75] then failure results from incompatibility, unprofitability, or both.[76]

REFLECTION

> Identify a change at your institution that failed. At what point and
> for what reasons did it fail? Do the explanations provided by Kotter
> or Levine provide useful concepts for analyzing the success or fail-
> ure of change?

Change can fail at any point in the process, but change that one hopes to institutionalize and sustain over time can fail because it was either incompatible, unprofitable, or both. To develop sustainable change, careful thought must be given initially to how the change will actually function in terms of compatibility with institutional norms and perceived profitability.

INCREMENTAL CHANGE, REENGINEERING, OR REVOLUTION?

Colleges and universities are now under close scrutiny (if not outright attack) by other sectors of society while facing new challenges from fierce competitors in the postsecondary marketplace. The issue facing leaders in postsecondary settings today is not whether change will occur but how radical it will be.

Many of the changes that have taken place in business organizations over the last decade can be called *radical.* In these organizations, the buzzword that emerged to describe radical change was *reengineering.* Whether reengineering was the mechanism that created change, or was the concept that arrived at the right time to describe what was already taking place, is open for debate; but there is little doubt that many organizations today have already experienced radical change.

The concept of *reengineering* comes from the best selling business book by Michael Hammer and James Champy entitled *Reengineering the Corporation: A Manifesto for Business Revolution.*[77] They define *reengineering* as "the fundamental rethinking and radical redesign of business processes to achieve dramatic improvements in critical contemporary measures of performance, such as cost, quality, service, and speed."[78] They single out selected keywords in that definition for further explanation and emphasis. *Fundamental* because "reengineering takes nothing for granted. It ignores what is and concentrates on what should be."[79] *Radical* because it means "getting to the root of things . . . *reinvention*—not business improvement, business enhancement, or business modification."[80] *Dramatic* because reengineering "demands blowing up the old place and replacing it with something new."[81] *Processes* because entire processes are changed, not just "tasks . . . jobs . . . people . . . or structures."[82] Reengineering in its many applications in diverse settings has come to be known for job restructuring that uses self-regulating work teams to increase quality while decreasing external checks and controls.[83]

Some would argue that reengineering is not actually radical change because it is related to process changes rather than fundamental shifts in mission, market, or services. For such changes, perhaps the best word is *revolutionary*. Noel Tichy and Stratford Sherman have documented Jack Welch's much-touted revolution at General Electric in a book with the interesting title, *Control Your Destiny or Someone Else Will.*[84] At the end of that book Noel Tichy provides a "Handbook for Revolutionaries" intended for leaders contemplating major organizational change.[85] Tichy points out that revolutions take a predictable path[86] and that they are structured like the three acts of a drama, which he names *Awakening* (kickstarting the revolution by creating a sense of urgency), *Envisioning* (creating a central vision backed by intellectually substantial ideas), and *Rearchitecting* (patiently rebuilding the social architecture of the organization from top to bottom).[87] The important thing to recognize about revolutions is that they usually cause serious displacements that affect people emotionally. During Act I people are learning to give up the way things have always been through processes that Tichy calls *disengagement, deidentification,* and *disenchantment* as they grapple with loss.[88] During Act II people are having to grow accustomed to a new vision and develop a commitment to a different future. In Act III people are replacing "old mastered routines with new ones" and are often coping with the sense of "frustration that accompanies failure."[89] Because revolutions produce actual pain for real people, Tichy suggests asking three serious questions before embarking on a revolution: "How much of a revolution do you need? Do you have the head, heart, and guts to lead a revolution? Are you ready for the revolution?"[90]

Although Tichy uses the rhetoric of revolution, his description of the drama is reminiscent of Kotter's change model. Aren't revolutions about a power struggle to overthrow the old regime and establish a new order? Where is the conflict, the coup, and the cabal?

REFLECTION

> Do colleges and universities today need a revolution? Is the re-engineering of processes too timid for the times? What are the risks of leading a revolution? Are leaders in institutions of higher education ever secure enough to lead revolutions? Are revolutions usually led by people in formal or informal leadership roles?

In his "Handbook for Revolutionaries" Tichy recounts the story of an old biological experiment—no doubt before the days of animal rights activists—that "demonstrates a frog's lack of attention to a changing environment."[91] A frog in a pan of water will never make efforts to jump out when the temperature is slowly raised from cold to boiling; it simply sits in the water until it is boiled to death. Will the changing environment of higher education one day reach a boiling point where revolutionary change is the only answer, or will the players—leaders and followers alike—simply submit to their doom?

Leaders in colleges and universities today are faced with an enormous dilemma. On the one hand, many processes cry out for radical change—revolution or at least the reengineering of whole systems. On the other hand, much of the literature on change—the descriptions of higher education settings, the change theories, the change models, even the explanations of why change fails—suggest that change is a slow process that takes careful planning and patient execution. Revolutions may not work, but proven methods may never bring radical change.

When leaders embark on change, they think carefully about what they are proposing. With a sound grounding in theory, they contemplate which change models to employ. They walk the fine line between taking on too much and attempting too little. Leaders are unashamedly calculating as they encourage change because they seek lasting transformations.

MARY'S MENTOR

Mary's mentor wants her to remember the following things about change:

- Societal change today is widespread and rapid.

- Colleges and universities are resistant to change due to their multiple power and authority structures, loosely coupled systems, institutional status, and clashing professional and administrative values.

- Institutions of higher education tend toward organized anarchy characterized by problematic goals, unclear technology, fluid participation, and a "garbage can" process of decision making.

- Change can be analyzed by type and may be planned or unplanned, emanating from diverse sources, proactive or reactive, varied in its outcomes, first-order or second-order in degree, of differing scales and foci, rapid or evolving, and adaptive or ongoing.

- Change can vary in difficulty from tuning and adaptation to reorientation and "frame-bending" recreation.

- Theories of change can be classified as teleological, evolutionary, dialectical, social cognitive, and cultural.

- Change models often focus on particular aspects of change such as developmental phases, people, or factors to be leveraged, as well as particular techniques for change, such as democratic engagement, large-scale events, campaigns, and epidemics.

- Kotter's sequential stage model focuses on urgency, guiding coalitions, vision and strategy, communication, broad-based action, short-term wins, consolidation, and anchoring in the culture.

- Change fails at any point when stages are poorly completed or skipped but also during institutionalization where innovation can be accepted or rejected based on its compatibility and perceived profitability.

- Extreme methods such as reengineering may not be effective in colleges and universities; but traditional methods may never produce badly needed radical change.

- There is no graceful way to leap a chasm.

NOTES

1. Victoria Newfeldt, ed., *Webster's New World College Dictionary*, 3rd ed. (New York: Macmillan, 1997).

2. Alvin Toffler, *Future Shock* (New York: Random House, 1970).

3. Ibid., pp. 20–34.

4. Malcolm Knowles, *The Modern Practice of Adult Education* (Chicago, IL: Follett Publishing Company, 1980), p. 41.

5. Margaret Mead, *Culture and Commitment* (New York: Columbia University Press, 1978).

6. Peter B.Vaill, *Learning as a Way of Being: Strategies for Survival in a World of Permanent White Water* (San Francisco: Jossey-Bass, 1996), p. 14.

7. Ibid., p. 6.

8. Madeleine F. Green, "Forces for Change," in Madeleine F. Green, ed., *Transforming Higher Education: Views from Leaders Around the World* (Phoenix, AZ: American Council on Education and The Oryx Press, 1997), p. 4.

9. Clark Kerr, *Higher Education Cannot Escape History: Issues for the Twenty-First Century* (Albany: State University of New York Press, 1994), pp. 45–46.

10. Green, "Forces for Change," p. 4.

11. Adrianna Kezar, *Understanding and Facilitating Organizational Change in the 21st Century: Recent Research and Conceptualizations* (San Francisco: Jossey-Bass, 2001), pp. 65–77.

12. Michael D. Cohen and James G. March, *Leadership and Ambiguity: The American College President,* 2nd ed. (Boston: Harvard Business School Press, 1974), pp. 3, 33.

13. Ibid., p. 81.

14. Ibid., p. 85.

15. Kezar, *Understanding and Facilitating Organizational Change in the 21st Century,* pp. 11–23.

16. David A. Nadler, "Organizational Frame Bending: Types of Change in the Complex Organization," in Ralph H. Kilmann, Teresa Joyce Covin, and Associates, *Corporate Transformation: Revitalizing Organizations for a Competitive World* (San Francisco: Jossey-Bass, 1990), pp. 70–73.

17. Kezar, *Understanding and Facilitating Organizational Change in the 21st Century,* pp. 25–57.

18. Ibid., pp. 32–36.

19. Ibid., pp. 28–32.

20. Ibid., pp. 36–40.

21. Ibid., pp. 40–44.

22. Ibid., pp. 44–49.

23. Ibid., pp. 49–53.

24. Ed Oakley and Doug Krug, *Enlightened Leadership* (Denver, CO: Stonetree Publishing, 1992).

25. Ibid., p. 13.

26. Ibid., p. 14.

27. Ibid.

28. Ibid., p. 15.

29. Ibid., p. 16.

30. Ibid.

31. Ibid., p. 20.

32. Ibid., p. 38.

33. Ibid., pp. 54–69.

34. Ibid., pp. 72–129.

35. Charles H. Bishop, Jr., *Making Change Happen One Person at a Time* (New York: AMACOM, 2001), pp. xv–xvii.

36. Ibid., pp. 46, 53.

37. Ibid., pp. 73–85, 86–102.

38. Ibid., pp. 162–168.

39. Richard H. Axelrod, *Terms of Engagement: Changing the Way We Change Organizations* (San Francisco: Berrett-Koehler, 2000), pp. 11–18.

40. Ibid., pp. 18, 32.

41. Ibid., p. 33.

42. Ibid., pp. 37–38.

43. Ibid., pp. 49–50.

44. Ibid., p. 56.

45. Ibid., p. 66.

46. Ibid., p. 105.

47. Ibid., p. 135.

48. Peter Brill and Richard Worth, *The Four Levers of Corporate Change* (New York: AMACOM, 1997).

49. Ibid., p. 56.

50. Ibid., pp. 68–86.

51. Ibid., pp. 87–106.

52. Ibid., pp. 107–126.

53. Steven E. Brigham, "Large-Scale Events: New Ways of Working Across the Organization," *Change* 28:6 (December 1996), pp. 28–37.

54. Larry Hirschorn and Linda May, "The Campaign Approach to Change," *Change* 32:3 (May/June 2000), pp. 30–37.

55. Malcolm Gladwell, *The Tipping Point* (New York: Little, Brown, and Company, 2000).

56. Ibid., p. 139.

57. Ibid., pp. 252–259.

58. Ibid., p. 259.

59. John P. Kotter, *Leading Change* (Boston: Harvard Business School Press, 1996).

60. Ibid., p. 26.

61. Ibid., p. 21. The descriptions of each of the eight stages are drawn from selected phrases that occur in the rest of the book, which contains a separate chapter on each stage.

62. Ibid., p. 22.

63. Ibid., pp. 3–16.

64. Arthur Levine, *Why Innovation Fails: The Institutionalization and Termination of Innovation in Higher Education* (Albany: State University of New York Press, 1980).

65. Ibid., p. 14.

66. Ibid.

67. Ibid.
68. Ibid., p. 15.
69. Ibid.
70. Ibid.
71. Ibid., p. 17.
72. Ibid., p. 18.
73. Ibid., p. 155.
74. Ibid., p. 156.
75. Ibid., p. 157.
76. Michael Hammer and James Champy, *Reengineering the Corporation: A Manifesto for Business Revolution* (New York: Harper Business, 1993).
77. Ibid., p. 32.
78. Ibid., p. 32.
79. Ibid., p. 33.
80. Ibid., p. 34.
81. Ibid., p. 35.
82. Ibid., pp. 50–64.
83. Ibid., pp. 65–82.
84. Noel M. Tichy and Stratford Sherman, *Control Your Destiny or Someone Else Will: How Jack Welch Is Making General Electric the World's Most Competitive Corporation* (New York: Currency Doubleday, 1993).
85. Ibid., pp. 303–374.
86. Ibid., p. 304.
87. Ibid., pp. 331–351.
88. Ibid., p. 306.
89. Ibid.
90. Ibid., pp. 311, 319, 329.
91. Ibid., p. 332.

CHAPTER 9

Positive Work Environments: Managing People and Encouraging Development

With the academic year drawing to a close, Dean Williams realizes that her trusted intern, Dolores Ortiz, will soon be leaving. Mary knows that this would be a good time to get some honest feedback from Dolores about her experience in the dean's office, as well as any observations she might have about the work environment more generally. They go to lunch off campus.

"Well, of course, it's been awesome for me," Dolores begins. "You know that. I've learned so much just watching you. You've been a great supervisor, and I've enjoyed our little informal chats as well as the monthly feedback sessions. I didn't like the idea of having to keep a log at first, but it's made me reflect on my experiences here."

"From which experiences did you learn the most?" Dean Williams asks.

"Just being able to sit in on different meetings. Serving as recorder for the two search committees was great. Attending the workplace law seminar was an eye-opener. I learned a lot from Fred even though we usually see things differently. And, of course, my little fact-finding projects to help you with some decisions."

"If you don't mind my asking so directly, how do you view the workplace for minorities here? Is it comfortable?"

"Well, yes, generally speaking. The legal environment sets the boundaries. There's not much overt stuff, but sometimes people say things and I have to ask myself if I really heard that; but in general, it's not a problem."

Dean Williams ponders that for a moment, then changes the subject. "Sometimes I wonder if we couldn't be doing a little more with leadership development here. What do you think?"

"It is a bit shocking, isn't it? I understand that we have a good faculty development program, but there's nothing for administrators, not even department chairs"

"In academia, you're not supposed to want to be an administrator, right? If you do, and you express it, it's the kiss of death," Dean Williams observes.

"Exactly. And then you suddenly land in it, after being a professor, and you have to learn on the job through trial and error."

"Yes, and administration is complicated. It's not like it used to be. I know that I could still use some help."

"But the atmosphere here doesn't seem to be right for people to share much about what they know. Do you ever talk to other administrators to get their advice or anything?" Dolores asks.

"Not really. Administrators are rather private around here. They don't share their thoughts and certainly not their feelings."

"And you never seem to call on faculty expertise much. The faculty in the higher education program—you know, where I'm working on my degree—they really know a lot about these things, but no one ever asks them. And faculty in marketing or finance—does anyone ever think they might provide valuable consultation?"

"You're right. Now that you mention it, everyone just works in their own little area without . . ."

"Parallel play. Like preschoolers. No one wants to share their toys. The Sandbox University. Wouldn't that make a great article?"

Mary laughs. "It's painfully true. We're not exactly a learning organization, are we?"

Dolores reaches into her big purse, pulls out a loose-leaf notebook, and presents it to Dean Williams. "Here's my contribution. I worked up this guide to being an intern for the person who comes after me, something to help them find key information, a summary of search committee procedures, and a few personal observations."

"How thoughtful," Dean Williams observes, genuinely pleased.

"The accumulated wisdom of a part-time intern."

"Maybe I should work up something like this for the next dean."

"You're not leaving, are you? You couldn't be leaving. You just got here."

Most social scientists know about the Hawthorne Effect as one of the classic threats to the validity of a research experiment: the impact of the conditions of the experiment and the activities of the researchers themselves on the results.[1] Not as many know the actual research project from which the Hawthorne Effect takes its name.

In 1924 efficiency experts at the Hawthorne, Illinois, plant of the Western Electric Company designed a research program to study the effects of illumination on productivity. In the initial experiment, worker productivity increased at the Hawthorne plant as the illumination was improved, but it was the "attention lavished" on the workers "by the experimenters," that made the difference.[2] Conducted over a decade by Elton Mayo of the Harvard Graduate School of Business Administration, the Hawthorne studies gave rise to what came to be known as the *human relations* movement in organizational development.[3]

Another classic set of experiments shed light on worker motivation. What is it that workers want from the work environment, and what motivates them to be more productive? Frederick Herzberg developed what came to be known as the *motivation-hygiene* theory, so-named for its analysis of preventive and environmental factors related to motivation. Based on studies of engineers and accountants in the late 1950s in the Pittsburgh, Pennsylvania, area (but subsequently replicated and fully established by many other researchers), the Herzberg theory identified two distinct categories of workplace factors that relate to employee performance. When people are dissatisfied with certain aspects of their job, it is usually with such things as "policies and administration, supervision, working conditions, interpersonal relations, money, status, and security."[4] Herzberg called these *maintenance* factors—the conditions under which a job is performed. The second category of factors consists of such things as "achievement, recognition for accomplishment, challenging work, increased responsibility, and growth and development." Herzberg called these *motivators*. He "found that when people felt dissatisfied about their jobs they were concerned about the environment in which they were working. On the other hand, when people felt good about their jobs, this had to do with the work itself."[5] Furthermore, productivity increases were found to be related to the job, that is, to the motivators, not to working conditions. Thus certain conditions in the work environment need to be maintained to prevent dissatisfaction, but other factors related to the job itself are the key to productivity.

Since the time of these two sets of classic studies, extensive research has been done on positive work environments and factors that influence productivity. Most organizations, including colleges and universities, are concerned about creating and sustaining positive work environments. **One aspect of the work of leaders involves maintaining a workplace where people enjoy coming to work and relish new challenges and opportunities for personal development.**

CHARACTERISTICS OF HEALTHY ENVIRONMENTS

In recent years, with greater emphasis being placed on workplace health and safety, and a general concern in the culture for wellness, emphasis has shifted to defining and describing *healthy* work environments. The characteristics of healthy work settings were explored in a collaborative, large-scale, international study conducted in 1987 by the Finnish Institute of Occupational Health (FIOH), University of Manchester (England) Institute for Science and Technology (UMIST), and the National Institute for Occupational Safety and Health (NIOSH). "Three rounds of bi-annual employee climate survey data were obtained from over 10,000 workers and 30 company locations . . . to empirically determine those characteristics associated with both worker well-being *and* organizational effectiveness."[6] The results yielded a list of seven organizational characteristics: "open two-way communication, worker growth and development (training), trust and mutual respect, strong commitment to core values, strategic planning to keep the organization competitive and adaptive, rewards for performance, and workers being aware of how their work contributes to the business objectives."[7] The study results are impressive because the characteristics describe not only a workplace conducive to health and satisfaction, but also one where people are actually more productive.

In a somewhat earlier (1991) qualitative interview study conducted in U.S. workplaces, R.H. Rosen found that healthy work environments grow out of a commitment to core values such as respect for all, lifelong learning, and celebrating diversity. Based on this research, Rosen developed a model of a healthy company containing the following dimensions:

- open communication
- employee involvement
- learning and renewal
- valued diversity
- institutional fairness
- equitable rewards and recognition
- economic security
- people-centered technology
- health enhancing environments
- meaningful work
- family/work/life balance
- community responsibility
- environmental protection.[8]

REFLECTION

Using relevant criteria from these studies as a scorecard, consider a college or university you know well and rate it on workplace health. What are the strong points and weak points? What can be done to improve the weak points?

Years of research have enhanced our understanding of workplace environments and have shown the importance of what was identified early in the process as *human relations*. The problem is not knowing what a positive environment is, but rather creating one.

WORKPLACE LAW

Positive workplace environments are not just an option; minimal standards are ensured by state and federal laws. Colleges and universities are not exempt from these laws, which cover all types of business, government, and not-for-profit organizations. Most colleges and universities, depending on size, have persons or offices responsible for assuring compliance with these laws, including required workshops or other methods of training as part of the demonstration of compliance. Any administrator in a supervisory capacity needs a basic understanding of these laws, and leaders will make efforts to move beyond minimal compliance to achieve the spirit of the intent behind the laws.

The most relevant of these laws are listed in Figure 9.1. Without going into detail about the provisions of any particular law, a quick analysis shows that the central themes of these laws are labor policy, nondiscrimination, and safety. Labor laws establish rules for classifying jobs as

Figure 9.1
Laws Affecting Workplace Policies and Practices

The Americans with Disabilities Act (ADA)
Civil Rights Act of 1964 as amended, Title VII
Age Discrimination in Employment Act of 1967 as amended (ADEA)
Drug-Free Workplace Act of 1988
Safe and Drug-Free Schools and Communities Act
Fair Labor Law
Family and Medical Leave Act of 1993 (FMLA)
Immigration Reform and Control Act of 1986 (IRCA)
Occupational Safety and Health Act (OSHA)
State Workers' Compensation Acts
Jeanne Clery Disclosure of Campus Security Policy and Campus Crime Statistics Act

professional or hourly (exempt or nonexempt) and spell out rules for over-time pay, job descriptions, hiring practices, equal pay requirements, and fringe benefits. Laws concerning discrimination prevent actions against individuals with respect to terms, conditions, privileges, or compensation for employment because of a person's race, color, religion, sex, national origin, or physical disability. These laws also prevent behaviors that create a hostile or offensive work environment, including sexual harassment. Laws that cover safety include not only safe and healthy working conditions but extend also (for colleges and universities) to general provisions for campus safety. In addition to these areas covered by federal law, certain state and local laws make provisions that extend to other areas or groups, for example, sexual orientation or weight discrimination.

Very few administrators know the details of all workplace laws, but they know how these laws translate into the institution's policies. They are aware that the institution has policies, and they are quick to recognize when they are operating in an area that may be or is covered by requirements of law. Effective leaders know when to confer with campus specialists in matters of workplace policy.

A positive workplace depends on more than minimal compliance to policy based on law. Leaders also seek to eliminate the subtle negative behaviors that express and nurture discrimination. A policy perspectives paper entitled "Gender Intelligence" that was produced by the Knight Higher Education Collaborative refers to this kind of discrimination as "death by a thousand paper cuts—an accumulation of small, incidental, behaviors, few very remarkable in themselves, which collectively denote that women in the profession are considered to be less than their male counterparts."[9] Although the essay is about gender discrimination, the same could be said for discrimination relating to race, ethnicity, age, social class, role, status, or any other form of behavior that treats people categorically as less than others.

Effective leaders try to eliminate the paper cuts of discrimination in the workplace and create environments that are positive, healthy, and celebrative of diversity.

REFLECTION

Do you know where to find out about workplace policies at your institution? How does your institution make positive efforts to comply with law and also move beyond compliance to create a positive environment? Can you provide examples of accumulated incidental "paper cut" behaviors that need to be eliminated?

MANAGING PEOPLE

Rudolph Weingartner provides the humorous reminder that "Academic administrators do not *manage* units composed of faculty or students however much they may at times dream of doing so."[10] Although this maxim carries an important message about the difficulty of managing faculty—who often see themselves as independent professionals—and students—who increasingly see themselves as the institution's customers—many other personnel of the institution require *management* in the more traditional sense of the word. Administrators often find themselves responsible for personnel functions such as *selection, supervision,* and *performance review.* Two valuable sources of information about traditional human resource management issues are *The ASTD Training and Development Handbook* published by the American Society for Training and Development, and *The Handbook of Human Performance Technology* published by the International Society for Performance Improvement.[11]

Selection

Hiring new people provides administrators with a great opportunity to build the organization but also the risk of serious error with long-term consequences. Although personnel selection is far from a science, certain procedures can be followed to increase the possibility of a positive outcome.[12] A sound selection process involves these four steps:

1. *Describing the job.* Develop a complete job description based on a careful job analysis. Ask the person currently in the job, superiors, subordinates, and colleagues to describe the job. Examine existing job descriptions. Consider what exemplary performers of this job or similar jobs do and set reasonable performance standards.[13]

2. *Identifying skills, knowledge, and personal characteristics.* Using the job description as a base, determine what qualities applicants will need to achieve desired performance.[14]

3. *Deciding on selection criteria.* Distinguish between required skills and personal characteristics such as "initiative, ability to handle difficult situations, self-confidence, a willingness to learn," and decide which are truly essential for job entry and which can be developed on the job.[15]

4. *Designing the assessment procedure.* Use common methods and information, such as "interviews, reference checks, testing, and . . . biographical data, academic records, and work samples." Be consistent and fair with all candidates in the use of these materials and processes.[16]

Developing a job description, statement of qualifications, and a job posting that is distributed widely, avoids the tendency to "build a job around a promising person" or to become attracted to people "close at hand." Not only are such practices risky from a legal standpoint, they do not serve the institution well in the long run in locating the very best talent.

Reference checks are sometimes suspect with regard to their usefulness because candidates often use friends, but asking for a frank assessment from an immediate supervisor—the person who does the annual performance review—can prove valuable. Although employers may resist disclosing negative information about an individual, recent case law suggests "employers can now find themselves in legal difficulty for not disclosing certain information."[17] Open-ended questions directly related to job performance work best.

Although interviews are popular, interviewees are becoming increasingly sophisticated about the process, making it somewhat unreliable. To make interviews more productive, a technique known as *behavioral interviewing* can be employed whereby questions are asked to elicit descriptions of specific things the candidate has done, such as, What was your role in this project? or What did you do when a crisis occurred? In this way, the candidates cannot hide behind vague generalities and must provide concrete examples. Although face-to-face interviews have definite advantages, videoconferencing or an amplified conference call may serve as useful interview screening devices.[18] Certain questions must be avoided in interviews, such as asking about the "candidate's age, children, country of birth, immigration status, disabilities, physical characteristics (such as height or weight), lawsuits a candidate may have filed, maiden name of female candidates, AIDS or HIV status, and passed injuries or accidents."[19] (The same questions should be avoided in reference checks.) Interviews may be supplemented with work sampling techniques such as asking the candidates to perform some aspect of the job—make a class presentation, interview a student, address a case, work with a team—as a simulation to observe how the candidate actually performs.[20]

Vigilant efforts need to be maintained to see that the process is fair, that discrimination is absent, and that adequate records of the process are kept. Most institutions have policies about these matters that apply to various types of hiring. Although consistency and fairness are important, so is maintaining high standards for matching the best possible candidate (available to this institution at this time) to a well-defined job. Weingartner offers another humorous "maxim" on this point: "'A' people hire (or retain) 'A' people, while 'B' people hire 'C' people."[21] If that is the case, efforts to be fair need to be coupled with strong efforts to set high standards.

Leaders recognize the importance of hiring, oversee and intervene in the process as appropriate, and help set standards of excellence in personnel selection. They know where and how to look for the best people.

Supervision

Even the best employees can profit from effective supervision. This varies widely in colleges and universities according to the job, but may include working with employees to plan for and control work flow, solve problems, manage time, improve oral and written communication, represent the unit or the organization more effectively, and plan for skill development and career advancement.[22] Effective supervision begins with collaborative goal setting and standard development. Employees and supervisors need to agree on what the job entails and what constitutes inadequate or outstanding performance. Only when clear standards have been agreed upon can useful feedback be provided. *Feedback* is information "fed" back to an employee with the hope of influencing future performance. Some feedback occurs naturally as a consequence of performance, but structured feedback, specific and well-defined, can be an important form of supervision.[23] Feedback needs to fit the employee's immediate needs and come in appropriate amounts in a vocabulary that can be understood.[24] Feedback can identify a need, suggest solutions, be structured around problem solving, or actually involve teaching new skills.[25] Naturally, the most useful feedback focuses on the behavior rather than the person, avoids mixed messages and overload, and is well-timed and specific.[26]

Although much has been said about the value of mixing positive comments with criticisms, experts suggest that to avoid sending mixed messages, different types of feedback should be clearly separated, not necessarily in different sessions, but for discussion. One clue for a mixed message is the word *but*: "you do this well, *but* you need to. . . ." Some will hear the reinforcement and miss the suggested correction, or hear only the correction and miss the reinforcement. Effective supervisors check for the receptivity of the feedback to see what has been understood, sometimes asking for feedback themselves on whether they have been clear.[27]

In today's workplace, certain kinds of supervision can take place without the supervisor's even being present in the form of *job aids* or *performance support systems*. Job aids, sometimes known as "cheat sheets," are used as reminders for complex, high-risk, or infrequently performed operations. There should be no embarrassment in using them—that's what an airline crew uses for the preflight routine check off.[28] Although job aids are used widely in manufacturing industries, there are many complex services provided in higher education—residence hall check-in or check-out procedures, financial aid assignments, study abroad applications—where even experienced employees may need this "remote" form of supervision. In some work settings computer assisted job aids, called *performance support systems* (PSS), are "bolted on" to complex computer tele-communications processes to provide easily accessible systems for complex operations. A low-end PSS is the Help button on a computer; more complex help may come in software "wizard" or "assistant" systems "to diffuse the knowledge and best practices that experts would otherwise carry in their heads."[29]

Supervision also involves addressing obstacles to getting the job done. An effective supervisor is perceived as being "on the employee's side" in making interventions when necessary to improve conditions under which work is performed. Although the emphasis in recent years has been on providing enough up-to-date computer systems and ergonomic seating, thought also is being given to the design and organization of social structure and physical space conducive to creative work. Because much of the so-called "work" in a college or university involves critical and creative thinking, alternately in collaboration and isolation, the space for doing this work needs to be appropriate. Unfortunately, in typical campus settings, the workspace is all wrong for higher education's most important work, so that increasingly people must work at home (not always an appropriate option either) or take a lot of work home at the end of the day. Studies in industry settings suggest that *body time*, being physically present, is not the same as *brain time*, being sufficiently free of interruptions and distractions to engage in creative work. In a university, where *nurture of students* and *availability* are strong values, it is not always easy to distinguish the actual work from distractions. A new term has emerged to describe the design of workspace conducive to thinking: *cognitive ergonomics*.[30] In an era when e-mail and cell phones create an atmosphere of 24/7 prompt, on-demand attention and response, supervisors may be spending more time conferring with employees to generate creative ideas about how to get the serious work of academia done, that is, if the supervisors can free themselves from distractions long enough to have such a conversation.

Leaders recognize that other employees need and often welcome supervision that can improve performance and the conditions under which work gets done effectively, accurately, and efficiently.

Performance Review

Some colleges and universities require formal performance appraisals known as *annual reviews*. In institutions where merit pay is based on performance, these annual reviews are often used to determine salary increases. Although this system may be necessary as a basis for documenting salary decisions, it is not very conducive to helping employees improve performance because it mixes the evaluative and developmental functions of performance review. If performance review is linked to pay increases, neither the employee (who wants to maximize the increase) nor the supervisor (who usually wants the employee to get the most of what is often a small raise anyway) is in a mood to be open an honest.

One approach is to uncouple performance review and evaluation from merit increase. In that way, performance review can become an ongoing process that occurs at several points throughout the year at moments well-timed for improvement, and done in an atmosphere that promotes genuine discussion focused on opportunities for betterment.

Peter Block, the author of *Stewardship: Choosing Service Over Self-Interest*, suggests that performance reviews by supervisors should be done away with entirely and instead replaced with opportunities for employees to conduct what he calls *self-directed appraisal*. Block's description of the typical annual review has a familiar ring:

> Performance appraisals are an instrument for social control. They are annual discussions, avoided more often than held, in which one adult identifies for another adult three improvement areas to work on over the next twelve months. You can soften them all you want, call them development discussions, have them on a regular basis, have the subordinate identify the improvement areas instead of the boss, and discuss values. None of this changes the basic transaction. Bosses evaluating subordinates, with the outcome determining pay treatment. As a boss you can conduct the appraisal in as loving way as possible. Most supervisors have been trained in listening skills, making good eye contact, asking open-ended questions, checking for agreement, making support statements, and identifying strength so we do not become obsessed with weaknesses. Although this helps, none of it heals. The transaction has an element of sovereignty to it in that will not go away. If the intent of the appraisal is learning, it is not going to happen when the context of the dialogue is evaluation and judgment.[31]

Block suggests that employees should be responsible for their own appraisal with choice about what they want to learn and from whom they want to learn it. They can profit from involving subordinates, peers, and those whom they serve—not just the boss. Block believes that self-directed appraisal should be unhinged from the pay system if either learning or improved performance are to take place. He argues "No learning can take place when we are being told by powerful people how much we are loved and how much we are going to get paid for that love."[32]

One system of appraisal that has become popular in business organizations is known as *360° feedback*.[33] This technique stresses the importance of gathering appraisal data from the boss, peers, and subordinates, that is, from the entire circle (360°) of associates who have a perspective on the employee's performance. In a college or university setting this might include gathering data from students and other colleagues in the unit, people whom this employee supervises, as well as the chair, director, or dean, to whom the employee reports. Although the system may be cumbersome and may produce conflicting or difficult-to evaluate-data, the technique has the virtue of broadening the sources of data to gain multiple perspectives on performance.

Effective hiring and supervision along with ongoing performance review should minimize the need for firing, but sometimes, even with appropriate personnel practices in place, termination becomes necessary. When that happens the process is clear, if not easy. It is necessary to provide unambiguous feedback on what the problem is and where performance needs to be improved. Then the employee must be given adequate time to improve. When these steps have been taken and documented in writing, the performance is then reviewed again at the agreed-upon time; if it is still inadequate, the employee may be terminated. Workplace laws establish the right to fair treatment for the employee, but they do not prevent termination when an appropriate process has been followed and documented.

Leaders know their institution's policies on performance reviews and how to carry them out. They may wish to work to change some of these policies. In any case, they know how to get beyond formal policies and procedures to establish a climate where frequent ongoing discussions of performance can be held based on the employee's self-directed appraisal or 360° evaluations. Effective hiring and supervision won't eliminate the need for termination, but should reduce it.

REFLECTION

Have you served on a search committee? What are your institution's policies on personnel selection? Do you supervise people? What role do you play in improving their performance? What are your views on performance appraisal? Has your own performance been reviewed?

What do you think of the method that was used? Have you ever had to terminate an employee?

DEVELOPING PEOPLE

Most colleges and universities provide training of one type or another for physical plant and support staff. This may be limited to compliance training on such topics as workplace law or training on new technologies or data management and accounting systems. Because academics often hold the stereotype of training as instruction on how to perform mindless repetitive tasks and may not be aware of increased sophistication of training strategies in business, government, and not-for-profit organizations in the last twenty-five years,[34] training in postsecondary institutions often survives in a less than friendly environment. The ideological gulf between training and education, unfounded as it is,[35] nevertheless creates an atmosphere on most campuses where training is preferably referred to as *development* and the process is called *facilitation*. For example, most training for faculty on instructional strategies or use of technology in teaching is referred to as *faculty development*; most training for administrators, if it exists at all, is referred to as *leadership development*. However designated, training is a matter of increasing importance in colleges and universities just as it is in other types of organizations. Leaders play an important role in ensuring its availability, relevance, and effectiveness.

The training and development function can be focused in two somewhat different ways: *performance improvement* or *enhancement of capacity*. The first stresses an immediate need; the second focuses on long-term development of ability.[36]

Performance Improvement

Not all performance problems require training. That is the conclusion of performance improvement specialists who work in business settings. They have developed techniques—almost a science—for analyzing performance problems in the workplace. Growing out of the field of behavioral psychology, drawing on general systems theory, and using the techniques of engineering science, human performance technology has emerged in the last twenty-five years as a sophisticated technique for analyzing workplace performance.[37] Although people who work in colleges and universities may be put off by the word *performance* (having their primary frame of reference for the word as music or theatre), *performance* simply refers to how efficiently and effectively a task or set of tasks gets done. What performance analysts have noted is that poor performance is usually affected by the following variables:

- *Deficient skill or knowledge.* The essential knowledge or skill is missing, so that even people who want to do the job can't do it because they don't know how.
- *Lack of motivation.* People have reservations about the value of the product or service being delivered and harbor doubts about their abilities to do the job.
- *Flawed incentives.* People experience few consequences for a job poorly done or few rewards for one well done.
- *Flawed environment.* People don't have the equipment, tools, systems, or space to get the work done.[38]

Using interviews, surveys, focus groups, and actual observations, performance technologists try to determine what the actual causes of the problem may be, how these causes work together, and what might be done to intervene.[39] Richard Swanson, the author of *Analysis for Improving Performance*, notes that performance improvement is "a problem-defining method" that produces "accurate definition and appropriate specification of intervention," and that it is hard work that "requires intellect, experience, and effort."[40] Its intent is to counter a trend in training that he characterizes as the "solution in search of a problem" method and "flavor-of-the-month approach to performance improvement, often based on management fads."[41]

Performance may require training if the issue is truly a deficiency in skill or knowledge, but many other interventions may also be necessary, with or without training. Attitudes may need to be addressed, the work may need to be redesigned, the place where the work is done may need to be modified, and so forth. If training is needed, it will be designed for the specific knowledge and skills needed to improve performance.

REFLECTION

Consider a situation—a process or service at your institution that does not work as well as it might—and try to design a plan for finding out what is actually taking place. What would you have to do and who would you need to talk to in order to diagnose the situation? Might you serve fairly well as an "amateur" performance analyst for this situation? How do you know when you need to call in expert help?

Enhancement of Capacity

Unlike performance improvement, some training is focused on general enhancement of capacity over a long-term period of months or years. The term *development* is often used to describe this kind of training. Some large companies, particularly those using the corporate university model, provide an array of opportunities for employee development, ranging from basic technology and communication skills to workshops and short courses on problem solving, time management, decision making, teamwork, and wellness. Their catalogs of available courses look like a college catalog in some respects. Which raises the question: What do colleges and universities, which presumably have college catalogs, do to enhance the general development of employees?

Most institutions make some arrangement for employees to take courses, sometimes at reduced or waived tuition, perhaps after the passage of a probationary period. For some employees this may mean pursuing an advanced degree; for others an occasional course from the adult or extension division fits their needs. In addition, some institutions provide an array of regular workshops on computer skills, technical writing, grantsmanship, and use of the library. In any given week, most colleges and universities have a full calendar of special lectures, colloquia, musical events, and exhibits, not to mention opportunities for recreation and wellness. In general, colleges and universities are overflowing with opportunities for personal and professional development.

For these options to function as actual opportunities for enhancement of capacity for employees, two things need to happen that often do not: *planning* and *encouragement to participate*. Many corporations are making efforts to recognize, stimulate, and encourage what has come to be called *informal learning*. Some even structure it into the performance review process where employees are urged to identify a specific number of hours that will be devoted to informal learning in the coming year.[42] Working with university employees to help them identify opportunities for personal and professional growth requires only a small amount of a supervisor's time, and in most institutional cultures would be perceived as genuine interest, not meddling. Employees may also need an occasional rearrangement of the work schedule, support for childcare, or modest funding for special events. In addition to these tangible arrangements, some employees may need encouragement to overcome their shyness or fears of failure or embarrassment.

REFLECTION

What opportunities are provided at your institution for long-term
employee development? Have you participated in these? Why or why
not? What do you do to encourage employees at your institution to
take advantage of the educational and cultural opportunities available to them? What is the appropriate balance of structure and encouragement needed for informal learning?

**Leaders learn how to engage in performance analysis that may point
to training focused on specific improvements, but they also know how
to encourage employees in formal and informal learning aimed at enhancing general capacity. Leaders nurture a healthy work environment
that supports employee development. Presumably, a culture that promotes development, attracts and retains people who are interested in
continuous learning.**

LEADERSHIP DEVELOPMENT

Administration of colleges and universities has never been a clearly identifiable profession. Surely it has never manifested the classic marks of a
profession—a consistent body of professional knowledge, a recognized
pathway of preparation, and control of entry—that give, for example, law,
medicine, social work, and clinical psychology the designation of *profession*. Although higher education as a formal field of study has grown since
its initiation by G. Stanley Hall at Clark University in 1893—having early
in the last century experienced extensive development in major universities at Ohio State, Teachers College (Columbia), Chicago, Pittsburgh,
Berkeley, and Michigan, and now having culminated in over 120 programs[43]—no administrator is required to hold such a degree or have mastered the subject represented by the degree. Although more administrators
have doctorates in higher education than one might guess—28 percent
overall—the percentage is highest in community colleges and lowest in
research universities and selective liberal arts colleges.[44]

For many reasons the typical and still-preferred path into administration in four-year colleges and universities is through the professorate with
a Ph.D. in a discipline or professional field. This means that many administrators stumble into administration with no formal preparation, the chief
virtue of their study and experience being a general awareness of the
values and mores of academia. This of course is important but not necessarily sufficient for success, given the rich array of courses that now define the formal study of higher education.[45] Add to this condition the view

held by many faculty that administration is at best a necessary evil (sometimes the modifier *necessary* is not even retained), and that no person of integrity would ever openly aspire to being an administrator, and one might conclude that postsecondary administration is almost the antithesis of a profession.

Because of this peculiar array of circumstances, a growing number of efforts are being made to provide leadership development for college administrators. These programs are described and catalogued by Madeleine Green and Sharon McDade in their useful book, *Investing in Higher Education: A Handbook of Leadership Development.*[46] A number of off-campus programs now exist, including those sponsored by national professional associations and selected universities. These national leadership development programs are usually in the form of summer workshops and may or may not include internships.[47] On-campus programs designed for producing "home-grown" leaders may include such experiences as rotating assignments, temporary experience in another job or place, specific programs to encourage women and members of minority groups, and ongoing general skill development programs. They may employ structured on-the-job development, seminars, a speaker series, workshops, retreats, or individualized opportunities for experience and reflection. They may be general programs or focused opportunities for particular groups of administrators, such as deans or department chairs.[48] As Green and McDade point out, these programs are "certainly not a frill." Rather, "leadership development is an investment both in the short-term effectiveness of an institution—increasing job performance and satisfaction—and in its long-range health—identifying and preparing people to assume greater responsibility and increase their contribution to the institution."[49]

REFLECTION

What on-campus leadership development opportunities exist at your institution? Have you had an opportunity to participate in these or off-campus programs? What should happen at your institution to make leadership development a more prominent opportunity and natural process?

Leaders recognize that widely available leadership development opportunities are a characteristic of positive work environments. They acknowledge that longstanding traditions tend to constrict the natural flow of new leadership talent in colleges and universities, and that special efforts need to be made to encourage women and members of minority groups to aspire to and prepare for leadership positions.

Leaders can be important role models in speaking of administration in a more positive and professional way, identifying and valuing its intellectual substance, and enabling talented people to feel more comfortable about expressing an interest in it.

CREATING LEARNING ORGANIZATIONS

Although colleges and universities exist to promote learning, they are not necessarily or automatically *learning organizations* in the sense that the term has been used recently to describe organizations that leverage knowledge for their own enhancement as an organization. The term is widely attributed to Peter Senge, who popularized its use in his book *The Fifth Discipline: The Art and Practice of the Learning Organization*.[50] Senge defines the learning organization "as an organization that is continually expanding its capacity to create its future."[51] It does so by acquiring and sharing knowledge important to its development. The essence of the concept is found somewhat earlier in a book by Warren Bennis and Burt Nanus is entitled *Leaders: The Strategies for Taking Charge*.

> Organizational learning is the process by which an organization obtains and uses new knowledge, tools, behaviors, and values. It happens at all levels of the organization—among individuals and groups as well as system wide. Individuals learn as part of their daily activities, particularly as they interact with each other and the outside world. Groups learn as their members cooperate to accomplish common goals. The entire system learns as it obtains feedback from the environment and anticipates further changes. At all levels, newly learned knowledge is translated into new goals, procedures, expectations, roll structures, and measures of success.[52]

A more current elaboration of the concept for business settings is found in Michael Marquardt's *Building the Learning Organization*: "A learning organization, systematically defined, is an organization which learns powerfully and collectively and is transforming itself to better collect, manage, and use knowledge for corporate success."[53]

An important distinction needs to be made between the role of a college or university in generating knowledge for society through its numerous contributions to the disciplines and professions, and its role in acquiring and sharing knowledge for its *own* use in its function *as an organization*. Most colleges and universities are very good at the former; they usually have room for significant improvement in the latter.

Why is the concept of the *learning organization* so important in the business world today? Does the idea have any relevance for postsecondary institutions? Is it more rhetoric, a clever buzzword, another passing fad; or is it a more substantial concept? Peter Drucker, the well-known author of management books, makes the argument in *Post-Capitalist Society* that knowledge is the key personal and economic resource. "In fact, knowledge is the only meaningful resource today. The traditional factors of production—land (i.e., natural resources), labor, and capital—have not disappeared, but they have become secondary. They can be obtained, and obtained easily, provided there is knowledge. And knowledge in this new sense means knowledge as a utility, knowledge as the means to obtain social and economic results."[54] What business organizations have done in response to this new awareness of the importance of knowledge is to learn how to manage knowledge. Marquardt calls this "managing know how."[55] He points out that "the survival of the fittest is quickly becoming the survival of the *fittest-to-learn*."[56] What an organization does, David Garvin points out in *Learning in Action: A Guide to Putting the Learning Organization to Work*, is to become "skilled at creating, acquiring, interpreting, transferring, and retaining knowledge, and at purposely modifying its behavior to reflect new knowledge and insights."[57]

Although many in the academic world are ambivalent about this new importance of knowledge—liking the new importance aspect but having reservations about the emphasis on utility—the organizations that academics inhabit, namely their colleges and universities, are not immune to this new importance of knowledge, for in their administration they must draw on knowledge just as other organizations do. They provide online registration, manage their financial aid commitments electronically, offer phone-in registration, provide printouts of academic progress, use highly sophisticated budget control software, manage residence hall occupancy, monitor investments, track their marketing efforts, and collect data on how frequently their faculty are mentioned in the press. All of these efforts require knowledge management.

Learning organizations develop self-awareness about knowledge management, they use certain techniques to manage knowledge, and they may even put people in charge of the process. Garvin outlines the basic building blocks for managing knowledge in his article in the *Harvard Business Review*, "Building a Learning Organization." They include systematic problem solving, experimentation through demonstration projects, learning from past experience by collecting lessons learned, learning from others through benchmarking and identifying best practices, and transferring knowledge internally.[58]

Sharing knowledge, though it sounds simple enough, often requires explicit attention. Nancy Dixon points out in her book, *Common*

Knowledge: How Companies Thrive by Sharing What They Know, that the word *share* "has two meanings; it means to give away a part, which is an act of generosity, and it means to hold in common, as in a 'shared belief system.' These seemingly different meanings emerge in the context of knowledge management. If I share my knowledge, that is, give it away, then we can both hold it in common—common knowledge that is known throughout the organization."[59] Because many organizations have a culture of turf protection and knowledge hoarding, special efforts sometimes need to be made to identify useful knowledge and then bring people into proximity to share it, either physical proximity or through groups that cut across functional line structures. Why don't people naturally share knowledge? Clara O'Dell and C. Jackson Grayson explore the reasons in their article "If Only We Knew What We Know." They point out that the most common excuses people give are "I did not know you needed this" and "I did not know that you had it."[60] Companies have learned that knowledge sharing goes well beyond putting information on a Web site (though this can help) to bringing people together so that they can discover that they actually have useful knowledge to share. Colleges and universities, with their "silo" structure of departments, divisions, and clearly defined areas of expertise, are not naturally well-equipped for knowledge sharing, and they often need to make special efforts to identify and share knowledge that is essential for effective administration.

REFLECTION

To what extent is the institution that you serve a *learning organization*? In what ways do its various units depend on knowledge for their success? Can you give examples of how sharing knowledge could be useful? What units have knowledge that would be useful to your unit? What needs to be done to enhance knowledge sharing?

Most colleges and universities "miss the mark" as learning organizations. Although generating and disseminating knowledge is their chief mission, ironically they are not always clever about identifying and sharing the knowledge most needed to improve their own effectiveness as an organization. They could resolve to gather knowledge more systematically and record what knowledge they already harbor in more useful formats. They tend to compartmentalize knowledge that is useful for administration just as they departmentalize academic knowledge, so that special efforts must be made to share knowledge across functional lines. Administrators might more often consider which professors on their own campus may have knowledge that would be useful to administration.

Positive work environments also display the characteristics of learning organizations. Leaders explore ways to create information-rich environments where people are conscious of the importance of knowledge to their work, where they are encouraged to experiment and learn from mistakes, and where they are brought together regularly to share knowledge that will improve the efficiency and effectiveness of administration. Effective leaders realize that part of their job is knowledge management.

Leaders play an important role in creating the environments within which they lead. They reflect on the characteristics of positive work environments and they ponder human motivation. They are aware of basic workplace laws and they go beyond minimum compliance to establish work settings that are fair and that celebrate diversity. They influence the hiring process in appropriate ways, and they play important roles as supervisors and in establishing favorable working conditions. They are advocates of training for performance improvement and for long-term development of employee capacity. They support leadership development and look for ways to promote organizational learning.

MARY'S MENTOR

Mary's mentor wants her to remember these things about healthy work environments:

- If people complain, it is usually about conditions under which the job is performed; increased motivation usually comes from factors associated with the job itself.
- Healthy work environments are associated with such factors as employee involvement, learning and renewal, valued diversity, and balanced work and family life.
- Federal and state laws provide the foundation for many workplace policies and practices.
- Leaders play an important role in establishing procedures and setting standards for hiring.
- Effective supervisors provide timely feedback and job support, sometimes intervening to help establish conditions that enable people to get their work done.
- Leaders strive to broaden and improve performance review procedures.
- Performance improvement depends on many factors, and training may or may not be the remedy.
- Training is undertaken for performance improvement; long-term development helps build capacity.

- Leadership development is often neglected at colleges and universities because it runs counter to the culture.

- Learning organizations know how to acquire, interpret, share, and retain knowledge for the enhancement of the organization as a whole.

- "I didn't know you needed it" and "I didn't know you had it" are the most frequently given reasons for forgetting to share information in organizations.

- Leaders play important roles in creating and maintaining positive work environments.

NOTES

1. Walter R. Borg and Meredith Damien Gall, *Educational Research: An Introduction*, 5th ed. (New York: Longman, 1989), pp. 189–190.

2. Paul Heresy and Kenneth H. Blanchard, *Management of Organizational Behavior: Utilizing Human Resources* (Englewood Cliffs, NJ: Prentice-Hall, 1988), p. 51. The Hawthorne studies are reported in Elton Mayo, *The Human Problems of an Industrial Civilization* (New York: Macmillan, 1933).

3. Ibid., p. 52.

4. Ibid., p. 64.

5. Ibid.

6. Lawrence R. Murphy and Carly L. Cooper, "Models of Healthy Work Organizations," in Lawrence R. Murphy and Carly L. Cooper, *Healthy and Productive Work: An International Perspective* (New York: Taylor and Francis, 2000), p. 7. The study referred to is G.J. Pfiffer, "Corporate Health Can Improve If Firms Take Organizational Approach," in *Occupational Health and Safety* (October 1987), pp. 96–99.

7. Ibid.

8. Ibid., p. 4. The study and list are reported in R.H. Rosen, *The Healthy Company: Eight Strategies to Develop People, Productivity, and Profits* (Los Angeles: Jeremy P. Tarcher, 1991). The list was compiled by the University of Denver Human Resources Department and distributed through its Workplace Law Workshops for Managers.

9. The Knight Higher Education Collaborative, "Gender Intelligence," in *Policy Perspectives*10:2 (September 2001), p. 2. The essay grows out of a roundtable on opportunities for women in higher education, jointly convened in January 2001 by the American Association of University Women and the Knight Collaborative.

10. Rudolph H. Weingartner, *Fitting Form to Function* (Phoenix, AZ: American Council on Education and The Oryx Press, 1996), p. xvi.

11. Robert L. Craig, ed., *The ASTD Training and Development Handbook: A Guide to Human Resource Development*, 4th ed. (New York: McGraw Hill,

1996), and Harold D. Stolovich and Ericka J. Keeps, eds., *The Handbook of Human Performance Technology: Improving Individual and Organizational Performance Worldwide*, 2nd ed. (San Francisco: Jossey-Bass/Pfeiffer, 1999).

12. Seth N. Leiber and Ann W. Parkman, "Human Resources Selection," in Stolovich and Keeps, *Handbook of Human Performance Technology*, pp. 351–352.

13. Ibid., pp. 353–357.

14. Ibid., pp. 357–358.

15. Ibid., pp. 358–360.

16. Ibid., pp. 360–366.

17. Ibid., p. 363.

18. Ibid.

19. Ibid., p. 367.

20. Ibid., p. 365.

21. Weingartner, *Fitting Form to Function*, p. 74.

22. Lester R. Bittel and John W. Newstrom, "Supervisor Development," in Craig, *The ASTD Training and Development Handbook*, p. 657.

23. Donald Tosti and Stephanie Jackson, "Feedback," in Stolovich and Keeps, *The Handbook of Human Performance Technology*, p. 395.

24. Ibid., p. 400.

25. Ibid., p. 401.

26. Ibid., pp. 401–402.

27. Ibid., p. 402.

28. Paul H Elliot, "Job Aids," in Stolovich and Keeps, *The Handbook of Human Performance Technology*, pp. 430–435.

29. Steven W. Villachia and Deborah L. Stone, "Performance Support System," in Stolovich and Keeps, *The Handbook of Human Performance Technology*, p. 447.

30. Lynn Kearny and Phyl Smith, "Workplace Design for Creative Thinking," in Stolovich and Keeps, *The Handbook of Human Performance Technology*, pp. 469–472.

31. Peter Block, *Stewardship: Choosing Service Over Self-Interest* (San Francisco: Berrett-Koehler, 1993), p. 152.

32. Ibid., p. 153.

33. J.E. Jones and W.L. Bearly, *360° Feedback: Strategies, Tactics, and Techniques for Developing Leaders* (Amherst, MA: Human Resource Development Press, 1996).

34. James R. Davis and Adelaide B. Davis, *Effective Training Strategies: A Comprehensive Guide to Maximizing Learning in Organizations* (San Francisco: Berrett-Koehler, 1998). Examples of training from more than sixty organizations in the United States and twelve foreign countries are provided.

35. Ibid., pp. 50–52.

36. Ibid., pp. 46–47.

37. Harold D. Stolovich and Ericka J. Keeps, "What Is Human Performance

Technology?" in Stolovich and Keeps, *The Handbook of Human Performance Technology*, pp. 3–20.

38. Allison Rossett, "Analysis for Human Performance Technology," in Stolovich and Keeps, *The Handbook of Human Performance Technology*, pp. 145–147.

39. Ibid., pp. 151–154.

40. Richard A. Swanson, *Analysis for Improving Performance: Tools for Diagnosing Organizations & Documenting Workplace Expertise* (San Francisco: Berrett-Koehler, 1994), p. 38.

41. Ibid.

42. Davis and Davis, *Effective Training Strategies*, pp. 49–50. The example described is the Eastman Kodak Company.

43. Lester F. Goodchild, "Higher Education as a Field of Study: Its Origins, Programs, and Purposes, 1893–1960," in Jonathan D. Fife and Lester F. Goodchild, eds., *Administration as a Profession* (New Directions in Higher Education, 76) (San Francisco: Jossey-Bass, 1991), pp. 15–28.

44. Barbara K. Townsend and Michael D. Wiese, "The Higher Education Doctorate as a Passport to Higher Education Administration," in Fife and Goodchild, *Higher Education as a Field of Study*, p. 6.

45. Jonathan D. Fife, "Course Offerings in Higher Education Doctoral Programs," in Fife and Goodchild, *Higher Education as a Field of Study*, pp. 80–85.

46. Madeleine F. Green and Sharon A. McDade, *Investing in Higher Education: A Handbook of Leadership Development* (Washington, DC: American Council on Education, 1991).

47. Ibid., pp. 205–212.

48. Ibid., pp. 213–234.

49. Ibid., p. 13.

50. Peter M. Senge, *The Fifth Discipline: The Art and Practice of the Learning Organization* (New York: Doubleday, 1990).

51. Ibid., p. 14.

52. Warren Bennis and Burt Nanus, *Leaders: The Strategies for Taking Charge* (New York: Harper & Row, 1985), p. 191.

53. Michael Marquardt, *Building the Learning Organization* (New York: McGraw Hill and American Society for Training and Development, 1996), p. 19.

54. Peter F. Drucker, *Post-Capitalist Society* (New York: HarperBusiness, 1993), p. 42.

55. Marquardt, *Building the Learning Organization*, p. 7.

56. Ibid., p. 1.

57. David A. Garvin, *Learning in Action: A Guide to Putting the Learning Organization to Work* (Boston: Harvard Business School Press, 2000), p. 11.

58. David A. Garvin, "Building a Learning Organization," *Harvard Business Review* (July–August 1993), pp. 81–89.

59. Nancy M. Dixon, *Common Knowledge: How Companies Thrive by Sharing What They Know* (Boston: Harvard Business School Press, 2000), p. 9.

60. Carla O'Dell and C. Jackson Grayson, "If Only We Knew What We Know: Identification and Transfer of Internal Best Practices," *California Management Review* 40:3 (Spring 1998), p. 155.

PART III

Continuing to Learn about Leadership

The chapter in this section and the Appendix are designed to provide guidance for continuing development as a leader. The stressful nature of leadership and the continually changing environment within which leadership is practiced require perpetual learning and nurture of certain essential personal qualities. Leaders know how to manage their work, to look within for strength, and to keep learning.

CHAPTER 10

Perpetual Learning and Personal Renewal: Shaping the Leader Within

Commencement is over. Dean Williams picks up a few leftover cookies from the graduation reception to take back to the office. When she arrives everyone is gone except Fred, who is staring at the wall, as if in a trance. "We survived, Fred, didn't we?" She offers him a cookie.

"Barely," he replies, reaching out mechanically with an open hand.

"How many years did you say you've worked in this office?" she asks. "I should know, but I don't remember."

"Seven, " he replies, munching on his cookie.

"And all you get is a leftover cookie?" she jokes.

"It has its other rewards," he replies.

"True. But it is exhausting isn't it?" Dean Williams flops down in the chair that Fred usually reserves for students. "I knew it would be challenging, but I had no idea it would be this challenging."

"No one much appreciates what goes on in an office like this," Fred observes.

"How do you go on year after year? What do you do for renewal?"

"I'm not sure I'm the one to ask. I think I'm right on the edge of burnout most of the time."

"You don't act like it."

"Well, I'm fairly organized, and I guess that helps. And over the years I've learned to cope with the stress."

"I've been asking myself recently" Mary ventures in a candid moment, "whether it's all worth it."

Fred looks at her with a look of puzzlement creeping across his usually expressionless face.

"Not that I would leave after one year," she continues. "I'm just wondering how I will sustain it over, say, seven years like you have. The first year you enter an unlit room and you stumble around a lot. But now, at least, I know where the furniture is and to what extent it can or cannot be rearranged. Knowing what I know, I have to ask myself why I would do this year after year."

"They say that a second marriage is the triumph of hope over experience," Fred says, without further explanation.

"I don't get it," Mary frowns.

"In some ways, wouldn't you say, continuing in a leadership role year after year is a triumph of hope over experience."

"You've got a point," Mary nods thoughtfully, never having thought of Fred as someone so philosophical. "So how do you rekindle your hope?"

"I try to learn from experience. Never make the same mistake twice. I read. I go to one conference a year. I try to get a better handle on my emotions. And I seek some larger purpose in all of the details."

"And what is that larger purpose?" Mary asks, now genuinely intrigued by the shy, retiring old man, so full of wisdom, seated across from her.

"It's different for everybody, I would guess, but for me, the university is the one institution left in society with the explicit charge of eradicating ignorance."

The work of leaders is demanding, stressful, and often discouraging. The sheer amount of work is daunting. Leaders frequently see a side of the institution—appeals, lawsuits, manipulation of resources, and manifestations of egocentrism—that is far from pretty. And how is one to keep up with new developments? Potentially interesting information arrives, but there is little time to study it; new books come out, but there is little time to read them. What do leaders do to avoid burnout and foster perpetual learning and personal renewal?

Because administrators have demonstrated high intelligence and unflagging persistence in pursuing advanced degrees, they usually believe that they already know or can quickly figure out how to lead. They often view with skepticism professional development opportunities focused on time and information management, stress control, or general leadership skills; and they don't especially enjoy national professional meetings on higher education although they may still attend meetings in their discipline. The tendency is to "go it alone," believing that whatever problems one faces are personal or situation-specific, so that any general advice received from others will be irrelevant. This is a formula for stagnation, isolation, and eventual decline in performance, not to mention pervasive unhappiness. Administration ought to be a fulfilling profession, and leadership ought to be fun, at least some of the time.

GETTING ORGANIZED

Although most administrators take a stab at developing systems for organizing their work (or rely heavily on skilled assistants to do so for them), certain tricks of the trade do exist, and like other skills that leaders need to have, these also can be learned. It may at first appear to be demeaning to take a workshop on "Remedial Time Management 101" or even to read a book chapter on the topic, but the alternative is to flounder in one's chaos, while unwittingly causing chaos for others.

Chaos is the name given to disorganization by Harriet Schecter, well-known organizational consultant and author of *Conquering Chaos at Work: Strategies for Managing Disorganization and the People Who Cause It*.[1] Schecter argues that most people at work are either chaos creators or victims of someone who is. Chaos creators are people who for example regularly violate procedures, neglect correspondence and phone messages or e-mail, show up unprepared and late to meetings, forget details, don't meet deadlines, lose things, blame others, and refuse to take responsibility for their chaos-creating behavior.[2] Usually chaos creators are also messy, although Schecter distinguishes between them and *mess mavens*, who are underneath it all well-organized.[3] Unfortunately, disorganization has somehow come to be identified with creativity, a myth that Schecter refuses to buy.[4] Instead, Schecter labels chaos creators as simply *inconsiderate*.[5]

Schecter identifies five categories of chaos symptoms: time-related, memory-related, communication-related, information-related, and project-related. To deal with time-related chaos, Schecter recommends distinguishing between Project Time—setting up systems, developing new ideas, products, or services—and Maintenance Time—doing the tasks that need to be done over and over, such as calls, correspondence, and managing accounts. Maintenance Time needs to be scheduled, but limited, Schecter argues, or there won't be time for projects, which also need to be scheduled, but in larger blocks of time. Because activity will naturally fill the time allotted, Schecter recommends setting strict limits for maintenance activities, perhaps even using a timer (a kitchen timer or watch alarm) to control time spent on them. For people who are consistently late or "running behind," Schecter recommends scheduling what she calls *gap time*, a period right before or right after a meeting or appointment to allow for catching up.[6] "Running late yourself is one thing; causing others to run late is another," Schecter points out.[7]

Memory-related chaos can be addressed by developing systems for recording important information, such as (obviously) writing things down in the right place; verbalizing out loud names, numbers, or information to be remembered; bookmarking files; tabbing books; and carrying around memory notebooks or small tape recorders.[8]

Communication-related chaos can be addressed by asking others what medium to use and letting others know how and when it is best to communicate with you. Schecter recommends preparing an agenda for appointments as well as meetings; clarifying, mirroring (repeating back), and recapping main points, both as speaker or listener; and setting aside specific times for phone and e-mail communication. In the age of e-mail and voicemail, it is important to learn how to leave focused and effective messages and to encourage others to do so. For written communication, the Journalist's Rule of the Five W's still makes sense—who, what, when, where, and why—as a set of questions to ask about any communication.[9]

Information-related chaos can be addressed through systems that control the flow of paper, including effective file systems. Schecter recommends asking five simple questions about every piece of paper:

1. What is this?
2. Why should I want to keep it?
3. When would I need it?
4. Where would I look for it?
5. Who else might have it?[10]

The answers to these questions provide the guidelines not only for dealing with each piece of paper at the moment, but also for generating the appropriate system for filing and retrieving important information. Schecter recommends setting up a simple file system with a small number of basic categories and in setting aside regular blocks of time for what she calls *speed weeding*.[11]

Project-related chaos can be addressed by using project maps that identify goals and steps and commitment calendars that tie the *what*, *who* and *when* of the project to specific deadlines. These guides can be used for team projects but also for anyone working on a project alone. The key to avoiding chaos with projects is careful planning and effective follow-through.[12]

Schecter's book provides a good overview of how to become more organized, but two other works give additional guidance for zeroing in on time and information management. One of the these useful resources is the classic work by Alan Lakein entitled, *How to Get Control of Your Time and Your Life*.[13] (Subsequent works cite Lakein as the source of key ideas.) Lakein stresses the importance of recovering the ability to make choices about the use of one's time. Nobody can actually do all there is to do and "everyone wants some of your time," so the responses Lakein suggests, are to "drift, drown, or decide."[14] Choices imply control, control starts with planning, and planning involves setting priorities.[15] People who know what they value and what they are trying to achieve can look at the tasks that make demands on their time, Lakein says, and use an ABC priority system to label them as high, medium, and low priority.[16] Lakein recommends planning each day (in the morning or the night before) and then blocking out prime time (the time when one's thinking is clearest and one is likely to be the most productive) for A-priority projects.[17] Unfortunately, people often spend prime time "unnecessarily on secondary matters and let many important ones go undone."[18]

Lakein also recommends using a To Do List every day "as a guide to action as you go through the day."[19] When the items on the list are arranged according to the value they really have, one soon discovers that 80 percent of the value comes from 20 percent of the items. Out of ten items on the To Do List, Lakein suggests that two will produce most of the value, so the challenge is to identify these items and be sure to do them.[20] Low priority items can be delegated, deferred to another day, or left "to die a natural death."[21] Lakein also suggests keeping in mind and asking at several points throughout the day what he calls Lakein's Question: "What is the best use of my time right now?"[22] A person who has trouble getting started on a big A-priority item because it is too complex and overwhelming can use what Lakein calls the Swiss Cheese Method to punch holes in the project, that is to get started on some smaller aspects of the project called *instant tasks* (even when time is limited) in order to avoid procrastination.[23] As Jack D. Ferner points out in *Successful Time Management: A Self-Teaching Guide*, "time is the only resource we all have equally. Once used, it's gone forever."[24]

An impressive system for managing information is found in a book by G. Lynne Snead and Joyce Wycoff entitled *To Do . . . Doing . . . Done! A Creative Approach to Managing Projects and Effectively Finishing What Matters Most.*[25] They suggest the use of a Monthly Calendar for an overview, a Day Planner that includes not only an hourly appointment schedule, but also a To Do List (including a place to check off items done), and a Daily Record of Events for notes and important information. The key advice of Snead and Wycoff is to get rid of all the little slips of paper with names, addresses, phone numbers, e-mail addresses, and other pieces of crucial information (so easily lost or misplaced) and to write down everything of importance in one place: the Day Planner. To supplement the Day Planner, one also needs two file systems: storage files for records and activity files for the projects one is working on currently. To keep the desk clean and

know where everything is, one simply codes everything into the Day Planner. As papers are filed into activity files (handy to one's desk) they are
identified in the Daily Record of Events.[26] In effect, one leaves a "paper
trail" of all the paper recorded in one place. Does the system take a modest
investment of time? Yes, but the system offsets the amount of time spent
looking for things or coping with costly losses of vital information.

REFLECTION

> Are you a chaos creator? Do you work with someone who is? Do you
> have systems for managing your time and paperwork? Do you need
> to create them? Renew them? Do electronic devices, software sys-
> tems, and other commercial time and information management aids
> help?

Getting organized is, of course, not something one learns to do once
and for all. It is a matter of development, and, therefore, needs constant
attention and renewal. Nurturing one's systems for getting and staying
organized is an important aspect of sustaining effectiveness. Selecting the
right system is a personal matter, but obviously, having some system and
renewing it regularly, is very important.

**Leaders who are disorganized pay a price, both in what they are able
to achieve and in how they are perceived. Disorganized leaders turn into
discouraged followers of someone else's agenda. Organizational systems
need frequent renewal.**

COPING WITH STRESS

Getting organized should help to reduce stress, and no doubt will to some
extent; but stress grows out of many factors in the workplace and within
the individual and cannot be avoided or managed simply by becoming
better organized. The serious study of stress began with the work of Walter
Cannon, who labeled it an *emergency reaction*,[27] and Hans Selye, who
linked it to the release of adrenal gland hormones.[28] Stress research has
now become a major activity within medicine and the social sciences, and
it has produced and established several useful theories about what stress
is and how it functions in people's lives. Fortunately, these theories are
summarized and explained in separate chapters in a valuable volume edited by Cary L. Cooper, entitled *Theories of Organizational Stress*.[29] Three
major theories selected from this collection are described here along with
interpretations of their significance for leaders.

The first theory, "An Organizational Psychology Meta-Model of Occupational Stress," is described by Terry Behr. Within the meta-model

"*stressors* are stress-producing events or conditions . . . *strains* are the individuals' responses to stressor stimuli that are deemed harmful to themselves . . . and *stress* is a more general term describing situations in which stressors or strains are present."[30] Employees put forth effort through performance to achieve some specific valued outcomes. Unfortunately, a disconnect often arises between effort, performance, and outcomes, so that "the employee has no idea what level of effort makes sense."[31] Perhaps the goals (outcomes) are unclear or ambiguous, the performance falls short in some unidentifiable way, or the effort is too great or small. The chain of causation becomes upset. The goals are not being achieved, but the reasons are not clear. Frustration sets in. "It is, in a sense, a hopeless situation in which the proactive person has goals (desired outcomes), but has no clear way of knowing how to obtain them. This type of uncertainty is the crux of job stress for many people."[32]

As Behr points out, the job may be too simple or too difficult, the role of the employee may be ambiguous, or the outcomes may be uncertain over an extended duration.[33] As symptoms of stress arise, the natural inclination is to treat the person, although "individually targeted treatments for occupational stress seem to be mildly effective at best," when in fact "a main cause (of the stress) is the nature of the work environment."[34] What the employee needs is social support to "reduce the stressors directly, reduce the strains directly, or reduce the strength of the effect of the stressors on the strains."[35]

This theory is especially useful as a lens for examining the stress of administrators in leadership roles. Surely the outcomes of one's efforts are not always clear, nor are the established goals necessarily realistic. The knowledge and skill one brings to the job are usually one's "personal best," but may not be adequate for what is required, and the effort—even though it appears to be more than enough (sometimes bordering on superhuman)—fails to produce what one had hoped to achieve. The discrepancy between effort and outcome and the uncertainty of one's achievement are internalized—probably not consciously—as stress.

What is the appropriate response to stress based on this model? Although biofeedback, meditation, or stress reduction workshops may be useful for dealing with symptoms of stress, the key response is to identify and address the causes of stress. The first step is to become consciously aware of how the work of leadership is inherently stressful. One may be able to reduce some of the stress by developing realistic and measurable goals, by being clearer about the elements of effective performance, and by gaining an accurate perception of the effort required. In doing this, one needs various forms of social support, such as agreement with colleagues and superiors about outcomes, insights from friends and colleagues about the knowledge and skill needed, and encouragement in establishing appropriate levels of effort. Effort, performance, and outcomes need to be realigned.

A second theory of stress called "Person-Environment Fit Theory" is described in a chapter by Jeffrey R. Edwards, Robert D. Caplan and R. Van Harrison.[36] The "core premise of P-E theory is that stress arises not from the person or environment separately, rather by their fit or congruence with one another."[37] Actually, "stress arises from the misfit between the person and environment."[38] The authors distinguish between the objective environment and person, on the one hand, and the subjective or perceived environment and person.[39] In other words, there can be an actual misfit between the person and environment, but the misfit may also occur because of the way the person perceives the environment or the self. The lack of fit may come about through both the demands of the environment and the abilities of the person. *"Demands* include quantitative and qualitative job requirements, role expectations, and group and organizational norms, whereas *abilities* include the aptitudes, skills, training, time, and energy the person may muster to meet demands."[40] The concept of *needs* is used to characterize the "innate biological and psychological requirements" of the individual, and the term *supplies* to describe the "resources and rewards that may fulfill the person's needs such as food, shelter, money, social involvement, and the opportunity to achieve."[41] When a "bad fit" between the person and the job exists, two responses may occur—*defense* or *coping.* Defense, the less healthy response, usually involves some distortion of the environment or self (e.g., through "repression, projection, or denial); whereas coping entails changing the environment (e.g., by negotiating a reduced workload) or changing the person (e.g., through training to enhance abilities).[42] Thus, coping may include changing certain actual elements of the environment or one's perceptions of it, or changing something about the self, developing one's actual skills and abilities, modifying one's needs, adjusting preferences, or decreasing the importance of certain rewards. The goal is not necessarily to find the "perfect P-E fit" but "an interval"[43] "signifying a range of tolerance" because "small amounts of misfit may create challenge and provide opportunities to utilize valued skills, thereby reducing strain."[44]

Leaders will find this theory useful as a lens for examining the fit between their abilities and the demands of the job as well as their needs and what the job supplies to fulfill these needs. Contingency theory, one aspect of leadership theory that emphasizes the importance of situational variables in a leader's success, reinforces the idea of leader-organization fit. Leaders who suffer high levels of stress may wish to ask if they are actually in the right setting or job. The solution is not necessarily to leave the job—though that may eventually be necessary—but to ask what aspects of the job are a bad fit and then to adjust these, either by changing certain elements of the job or modifying one's perception of what is most important. Leaders need to identify their defensive reactions to a bad fit and to develop instead productive coping skills, asking themselves whether they need to change certain things about the job or whether they need some new skills or "attitude adjustment" about their needs and satisfactions.

The third theory about stress called, "A Multidimensional Theory of Burnout," is described by Christina Maslach.[45] She defines *job burnout* as "a prolonged response to chronic interpersonal stressors on the job," that includes "an overwhelming exhaustion, feelings of cynicism and detachment from the job, and a sense of ineffectiveness and failure."[46] Burnout is most likely to occur in "people-oriented professions, such as human services, education, and health-care" where the "prevailing norms are to be selfless and put others' needs first," and where one "works long hours" in environments that are "low in resources."[47] The three key characteristics of burnout are:

- *Emotional exhaustion*—feeling drained and used up (the stress dimension)
- *Depersonalization*—feeling negative, cynical, and detached (the interpersonal dimension)
- *Reduced personal accomplishments*—decline in feelings of competence and productivity (the self-evaluation dimension).[48]

Recent research, Maslach notes, has put exhaustion, cynicism, and ineffectiveness on the opposite end of a continuum that "stands in contrast to the energetic, involved, and effective state of engagement with work."[49] "Engagement consists of high *energy* (rather than exhaustion), strong *involvement* (rather than cynicism), and sense of *efficacy* (rather than reduced sense of accomplishment)."[50] What produces burnout rather than engagement? Maslach identifies these five factors:

- *Work overload*—job demands that exceed human limits
- *Insufficient reward*—low pay and benefits coupled with lack of recognition
- *Breakdown of community*—chronic unresolved conflict
- *Absence of fairness*—inequity of workload or pay, cheating, lack of voice
- *Value conflict*—incompatible job demands and personal principles.[51]

The implication of placing burnout at the opposite end of a continuum with engagement, Maslach notes, "is that strategies to promote engagement may be just as important for burnout prevention as strategies to reduce the risk of burnout." The goal of reducing burnout may be best met by focusing on the "development of the three core qualities of energy, involvement, and effectiveness." In any case, the challenge is to find ways "to change the job situation as opposed to focus on reducing stress, which leads to strategies of changing the person."[52]

Leaders will find this theory useful as a lens for examining high levels of stress. The symptoms of exhaustion, depersonalization, and reduced sense of accomplishment are clearly warning signs. Although one can treat the symptoms (perhaps through a stress-reduction program or restorative vacation), addressing root causes of stress related to workload, rewards, and conflict is of primary importance. One way to cope with stress is to focus on its opposite—how to create high energy, strong involvement, and a sense of efficacy.

REFLECTION

> What stressors produce strain for you in your work? Do you sense a lack of connection between effort, performance, and outcomes? Is the fit between your job and your talents tolerable, or is it a bad fit that produces stress? Where would you describe yourself on the continuum of burnout and engagement? What root causes of stress may you need to address in order to bring about personal renewal? Does taking a vacation help?

Leaders recognize that leadership can be stressful, and they know that the causes, not just the symptoms of stress must be addressed. Effective leaders are aware of job stressors, they analyze the goodness of fit between their needs and the job's rewards, and they recognize the signs of burnout. Leaders seek renewal by regularly analyzing which aspects of the job are stress-producing and they take steps to eliminate or mitigate these factors while cultivating involvement.

MAINTAINING EMOTIONAL BALANCE

The field of abnormal psychology, reaching all the way back to Freud, has identified two general classes of emotional disorders: neuroses and psychoses. *Neuroses* include the functional disorders characterized by anxiety, such as compulsions, phobias, depression, and so forth. *Psychoses* involve serious disorders of the personality where contact with reality is impaired. Leaders are subject to both, although only occasionally do leaders go "over the top" to manifest truly dysfunctional behavior. The two concepts are still useful today—perhaps more as metaphors than as diagnostic categories—for thinking about the challenges to emotional balance that most leaders face.

Leaders are prone to expressed criticism, if not outright attack, from many quarters. People in organizations seldom agree on a course of action, so that whatever path a leader chooses, there are those who will say it is the wrong one. The ranks of the critical and uncooperative are legion, and pleasing everyone is seldom possible. Peter Block, the author of *Stewardship: Choosing Service Over Self-Interest*, reminds us that every organization has its "cynics, victims, and bystanders":[53]

- *Cynics* doubt that anything will work. They know that "the organization has been down this path before." They especially doubt the sincerity of leaders. They "demand a promise to cure their lack of faith, and the promise they want is certainty." They are often "partially right" and they "put into words the doubts we all have." Unfortunately, "one verbal cynic in a room of fifty can set the tone and carry the day."[54]

- *Victims* are paralyzed from "learned powerlessness." They can't get the job done because they don't have enough resources. Victims believe that leaders "have all the marbles." Victims "are strong believers in patriarchy, they are just angry they are not the patriarchs." Victims "do not want a change in the governance system, they just want a change in who governs."[55]

- *Bystanders* want proof before they will act. They want to know where an idea has been tried before and how it worked out. Bystanders are unwilling to commit to or invest in a uncertain outcome.[56]

Cynics, victims, and bystanders make leaders nervous. They know how to create self-doubt in leaders. One might add to the list *controllers*. These are the people who must have a disproportionate voice in every decision, who need to control the leader (because they believe leaders are dangerous), and who will obstruct the path of progress if decisions don't go their way. When leaders are the objects of outspoken or underhanded criticism and scorn, particularly from those whose opinions they once valued highly, this can eventually affect self-esteem. Leaders begin to feel inadequate in precisely the ways their critics charge. Anxiety mounts. What a recipe for neurosis!

On the other hand, organizations are not filled only with cynics, victims, bystanders, and controllers. Some people in the organization actually like and respect leaders. They admire their leaders, sometimes putting them on a pedestal, while others pretend to. Leaders who are looked up to and admired begin to enjoy this admiration especially when others in the organization are attacking them. They may take this admiration too seriously. Some leaders, therefore, may suffer from *delusions of grandeur*. This is a common problem for movie stars, politicians, and professional athletes— people in the public eye. Robert Millman, a professor of psychiatry at Cornell University Medical School has described this condition as *acquired situational narcissism*. One may smile at the formal diagnostic category for something more commonly referred to as *arrogance*, but Millman points out that this kind of narcissism has its onset long after childhood or adolescence and comes from a situation that involves fame, money, or power (or all three) hence the modifiers *acquired* and *situational*.[57]

Leaders in high positions sometimes grow so accustomed to followers looking up to them that they forget to look back. They not only lose eye contact but also their capacity for empathy and caring. They lose touch with their constituencies and begin to withdraw into their own self-constructed worlds. They are encouraged by those around them to believe they are superhuman, and they develop a distorted view of their accomplishments and their place in the organization. Their associates only tell them what they want to hear, and soon they believe that their imaginary world is real. What a recipe for psychosis!

In addition to the forces that push leaders to distort reality, certain realities in themselves have inescapable emotional impact. Sometimes leaders are faced with heart-rending choices between what is good for an individual faculty or staff member and what is best for the unit. A conscientious decision often brings inescapable pain. Similarly, leaders are often faced with situations that produce anger, guilt, frustration and a sense of failure. These are natural feelings growing out of real circumstances. How do leaders cope with such feelings?

Perhaps the challenging work of leaders and the public roles they assume make them especially vulnerable in their emotional life. One might at least hypothesize that leadership requires a special level of emotional stability. Daniel Goleman, in his best-selling book, *Emotional Intelligence*, suggests that the ability to manage one's emotional life may be more important than the natural endowments traditionally measured as I.Q. He argues that in essence "we have two brains, two minds—and two different kinds of intelligence: rational and emotional. How we do in life is determined by both—it is not just I.Q., but *emotional* intelligence that matters. Indeed, intellect cannot work at its best without emotional intelligence."[58]

Goleman describes *emotional intelligence* as including "abilities such as being able to motivate oneself and persist in the face of frustrations; to control impulse and delay gratification; to regulate one's moods and keep distress from swamping the ability to think; to empathize and to hope."[59] More specifically, Goleman spells out five components of emotional intelligence:

1. Knowing one's emotions.
2. Managing emotions.
3. Motivating oneself.
4. Recognizing emotions in others.
5. Handling relations.[60]

In a second book entitled *Working with Emotional Intelligence*, Goleman spells out how these five aspects of emotional intelligence are used in the workplace. He gives each of the five components a corresponding name: self-awareness, self-regulation, motivation, empathy, and social skills.[61] Goleman then elaborates these five areas by developing subcomponents for each one, and he operationalizes them by listing what people with this competence have. For example, *self-awareness* is broken into *emotional awareness, accurate self-assessment,* and *self-confidence.* People who have *emotional awareness,* for example, have competence to "know which emotions they are feeling and why," and to "recognize how their feelings affect performance."[62] People who have *accurate self-assessment,* for example, are "aware of their strengths and weaknesses," and are "able to show a sense of human perspective about themselves."[63] People with *self-confidence,* for example, "present themselves with self assurance" and "can voice views that are unpopular and go out on a limb for what is right."[64]

Goleman's elaboration of the various emotional intelligences in *Working with Emotional Intelligence* provides a valuable list for leaders to consider as they seek to develop the emotional competencies that will enhance and maintain their emotional balance as leaders. The key word here is *develop.* As with getting organized and coping with stress, maintaining balance is a matter of developing and using certain techniques and abilities that have been proven to be successful over time.

REFLECTION

How would you assess your emotional intelligence? In what areas are you strong? What areas are candidates for development? Why is emotional intelligence so important for leaders?

Emotional intelligence is not something that one has or lacks; it is a set of competencies to be developed to progressively higher levels. Effective leaders monitor their emotional balance, recognizing that they are vulnerable to the particular neuroses and psychoses that derive from

a public leadership role. They continue to develop and renew their capacities for various types of emotional intelligence.

MANAGING PERPETUAL LEARNING

Administrators in colleges and universities face the same challenge as professionals in other fields: managing their continuing learning. Patients want their doctors to be up-to-date on the newest methods of diagnosis and treatment and clients want their accountants to know the latest tax laws. For certain professionals, a clearly identifiable body of new knowledge must be watched closely and absorbed, and some professional associations provide regular access to the knowledge needed for continuing education. But what exactly does a college administrator need to know to remain current? If the body of knowledge and skills for entry into an administrative position are not clearly defined, let alone required, how is one to know what might be profitable for continuing learning?

Because the pathways into administration are so varied and the background of leaders so diverse, no general arrangements for continuing learning exist. Instead, each leader must craft his or her own individualized plan for perpetual learning. As responsibilities accumulate, the need for learning increases as the time available diminishes. Without a plan, leaders probably won't learn much even though their intentions are good.

This simple approach to planning called *gap analysis* may help:[65]

- *Establish a baseline.* Describe previous learning by thinking about what was studied in college and graduate school. What are the "proficiencies, conversancies, and specialties" of one's education?[66] Proficiencies include such things as reading, writing, speaking, and listening skills; interpersonal, group, or cross-cultural communication skills; critical and creative thinking skills; quantitative skills in math, statistics, computer science, or accounting; foreign language skills; or professional performance skills. *Conversancies* are fields where one has a familiarity with basic information and ways of thinking, areas where an informed conversation within a subject area or professional field can be carried on with ease. *Specialties* include one or more academic or professional areas where study was in-depth, as in an undergraduate major, minor, or program of graduate studies. Baseline learning can also include *informal* learning that may have been acquired through work settings or areas of avocational interest. The baseline is the foundation on which further learning can be built.

- *Assess strengths and weaknesses.* What learning does one take pride in and what regrets are harbored about omissions or underdeveloped areas? What reaction does one have to this snapshot of previous learning?

- *Determine learning needs.* A detailed analysis of the job will identify a list of things to be learned. These include not only *job-specific* knowledge and skills but also *related* learning that could have an impact on performance. What does the job call for now or what might it require in the future? What future responsibility might one prepare for now?

- *Analyze the gap.* What gap exists between the baseline of learning and the present or future requirements of the job? Be specific about the kind of learning needed to fill the gap. Of the many things that could be learned, which are most pressing? Can priorities be established?

- *Develop an action plan.* How can the desired learning be obtained? Is further formal study needed? Can this learning be obtained through a conference or short-term workshop? Would a self-paced, self-directed project work best? Can this learning be done alone or online, or is human interaction important? What will it cost and how much time will it take?

REFLECTION

Using the steps provided above, conduct a gap analysis of your own need for learning. What learning is most desirable? What will be the best approach for attaining this learning? Does it help to identify priorities and formats? Can you find the time? Can you afford not to find the time?

Continuing learning, for leaders, needs to be focused on specific needs and should be carefully planned to remedy deficiencies in prior education and expand knowledge and skills needed for improved performance. A plan defines what learning is most needed and establishes how to go about it. Planning converts good intentions into action.

The chapters of this book have been carefully crafted to address the generic skills needed by leaders. Because leadership is always to a certain extent situational, leaders also need to continue to learn about the specific issues that arise in the setting in which they lead—for example, academic administration, student affairs, financial operations, or institutional advancement—and the various professional subspecialties within these domains. The best resources for further learning in these specific areas are found in the professional associations that have grown up around the functional areas of college and university administration. The appendix contains a comprehensive list of such associations. These associations sponsor annual conferences, provide publications, and maintain Web sites about their activities. Most administrators belong to one or more of these associations relevant to their specific work, and in some cases colleges and universities hold institutional membership in these associations. In addition, the appendix contains a short list of key journals, magazines, newspapers, and Web sites devoted to some aspect of higher education administration. Many of the associations also publish journals or newsletters about administration in their functional areas.

REFLECTION

To what professional associations do you belong? Which associations address issues in the area where you work? What periodicals do you read regularly? When you examine the appendix are you surprised to find so many professional organizations devoted to college and university administration?

One important part of the continuing education of leaders is the perpetual development of the general knowledge and skills needed for leadership; but learning about the latest issues and developments in one's particular functional area of administration is also important.

At one level, then, the continuing education of leaders is cognitive, involving the continuous gathering of information, ideas, concepts, and theories that enhance leadership. At another level, however, the continuing education of leaders is affective and personal and is more likely to grow out of the experience of the day-to-day challenges that all leaders face.

An old adage states "everyone learns from experience," but side-by-side with it another adage suggests that "some people never learn from experience." What is the difference? Under what conditions does learning derive from experience? Colleges and universities sponsor many forms of experience-based learning for students—study abroad, service learning, cooperative education, internships, field placements, and outdoor education—and much has been learned about this kind of learning through these programs. Besides matching students to the right experience and orienting them well for it, the key to learning from experience appears to be in providing appropriate mechanisms for reflection. Experience comes alive through writing and talking about it.

REFLECTION

Leaders are not perfect and sometimes make mistakes. They hire the wrong person, fail to get input from important constituencies, forget to project the consequences of a decision, ignore senior faculty, neglect the valuable ideas of students, tolerate the lazy, overwork the committed, stretch the truth, and get into e-mail wars with critics. Have you ever done any of these things? What did you learn from the experience? What opportunities do you have for reflecting on experience?

Donald A. Schön, in his book *The Reflective Practitioner*, suggests that professionals learn best through what he calls *reflection-in-action*. Although the basic model for professional education has been to give students a mix of hard science and practical courses and then send them out for an internship, Schön suggests that much of the most important learning for professionals bubbles up from experience. Often taken by surprise, they "turn thought back on action and on the knowing which is implicit in action. . . .There is some puzzling, troubling, or interesting phenomena with which the individual is trying to deal."[67] This is how the reflective practitioner is developed—through reflection on professional experience. What leaders need most for this kind of learning, is someone to talk to, openly and frankly, about the experiences they are having.

Unfortunately, the highly competitive, politically charged environment in which leaders often find themselves in colleges and universities is not always conducive to frank and earnest sharing. After all who wants to lay bare one's soul in front of so-called colleagues who may one day use that spontaneous confession of bewilderment to their own advantage. Although some natural groupings of "designated" leaders—the president's cabinet, the provost's staff, the student life team—may develop a rapport that enables honest sharing about leadership, such an achievement is probably rare. What is the solution? Two well-established opportunities for reflection hold forth at least some promise when adapted to the special needs of leaders: mentoring and personal growth groups.

Chip Bell provides this humorous history of the concept of mentoring in his book *Managers as Mentors*:

> The word "mentor" comes from *The Odyssey*, written by the Greek poet Homer. As Odysseus ("Ulysses," in the Latin translation) is preparing to go fight the Trojan War, he realizes he is leaving behind his one and only heir, Telemachus. Since "Telie" (as he was known to his buddies) is only in junior high, and since wars tend to drag on for years (the Trojan War lasted ten), Odysseus recognizes that Telie needs to be coached on how to "king" while Daddy is off fighting. He hires a trusted family friend named Mentor to be Telie's tutor. Mentor is both wise and sensitive—two important ingredients of world-class mentoring.[68]

A mentor, then, is usually someone older and wiser who has a special talent for providing a "safe context for growth."[69] As Bell notes, "mentors practice their skills with a never ending compassion, crystal-clear communication, and a sincere joy in the role of being a helper along a journey toward mastery."[70]

Laurent Daloz, notes in *Mentors: Guiding the Journey of Adult Learners*, that "if mentors did not exist, we would have to invent them."[71] They have existed, of course, since ancient times and have become popular recently in the business world as guides to success in organizations. The recent literature on mentors is extensive [72] and suggests that "mentors are especially important at the beginning of people's careers or at crucial turning points in their professional lives."[73] What do mentors do and why are they still important? Daloz describes their work as follows:

> Clearly, the mentor is concerned with transmission of wisdom. How, then, do mentors transmit wisdom? Most often, it seems, they take us on a journey. In this aspect of their work, mentors are guides. They lead us along the journey of our lives. We trust them because they have been there before. They embody our hopes, cast light on the way ahead, interpret arcane signs, warn us of lurking dangers, and point out unexpected delights along the way.[74]

Daloz also concludes, "mentors, it seems, have something to do with growing up, with developing identity."[75] Sometimes mentors also help raise aspirations by helping leaders follow paths that they might never have considered.

Mentors can be especially important for leaders, then, not just to share ideas and skills, but to provide the safe context where leaders can grow during the journey of becoming a leader. Mentors are useful for providing guidance on managing time, coping with frustration, and making meaning of one's work, but the more important function of the mentor may be in helping to nurture the professional qualities essential for effective leadership, through the old-fashioned concept of *character development*. A mentor should be someone to whom a leader can ask such questions as: Why am I so indecisive? What do I do that turns people off? What is the right thing to do? What can I do with my discouragement? What should be the next step in my career? Effective mentors don't necessarily have the answers to these questions, but they know how to help leaders discover their own answers by providing support, insight, and inspiration.

A second opportunity for reflection is the use of personal renewal groups, voluntary associations of leaders that cut across operational lines and internal institutional boundaries or that reach out across institutions. Summer workshops and seminars constitute such groups nationally, and on many campuses women administrators have formed such groups. The composition of the group is not as important as its purpose: to talk to other leaders about what they are struggling with as leaders.

Early in his career at the University of Chicago, Carl Rogers began to experiment with group processes designed to facilitate personal growth. Unlike formal group therapy, yet drawing on some of the same principles, personal growth groups, as they developed over the years in both religious and secular settings, have been used as a medium for deep learning related to the self. Although much has been learned through the years about the dynamics of such groups, including the perils of unbridled encounter, the original purpose of such groups was to provide an opportunity for deep learning related to the self. Rogers described the purposes of these groups as follows:

> In such a group the individual comes to know himself and each of the others more completely than is possible in the usual social or working relationships. He becomes deeply acquainted with the other members and with his own inner self, the self that otherwise tends to be hidden behind his façade. Hence he relates better to others, both in the group and later in the everyday life situation.[76]

A personal growth group for leaders needs only a few ground rules to be effective: honest sharing, real issues, and confidentiality. Intellectualizing, one-upmanship, and defensiveness are out of bounds. There's only one topic: What are you struggling with as a leader right now?

REFLECTION

To what extent have you learned leadership through the experience of leading? What opportunities do you have for serious reflection on the nature of leadership? Do you have a mentor or do you belong to a group where you can reflect on leadership? Do you need to create such opportunities for yourself or others?

Another important aspect of the continuing education of leaders is the development of the self as a reflective practitioner. Effective leaders have mentors, use groups, or devise other opportunities for reflection on their experience of being a leader.

MAKING MEANING

Administrative work is often broken into hour-by-hour and minute-by-minute fragments, individual and group meetings, phone calls, e-mail and voicemail responses to requests for information and advice, as well as the various written communications prompted by an unending flow of paper in a supposedly paperless workplace. A leader can get lost in the forest after dealing with so many trees; indeed, one's job may seem more like manufacturing toothpicks than cultivating a forest. What do leaders do to maintain perspective and bring a larger purpose and meaning to the minutiae that fill the workday? During the 1990s, several new books appeared on a theme that might be called *spirituality in the workplace*.[77] Exactly why so many books should be published on this hitherto taboo topic is difficult to explain, but these publications apparently addressed a need to bridge what C. Michael Thompson calls the Great Divorce: the perceived "split between work and the rest of life."[78] Although some writers address the topic in an explicitly religious way, as Thompson often does, others offer a more humanistic discussion of work within the context of the broader meaning of life. Although *spirituality* may be a welcome topic at certain church-related colleges and universities, the subject is at least awkward today at the large, public, secular university; but the concern behind the topic, namely the place of work in the context of the meaning of life, is worth discussion and thoughtful contemplation by leaders. Leaders who find little meaning in their own work, and whose lives lack congruence and integrity, are likely to be unable to sustain their effectiveness as leaders over an extended period of time.

C. Michael Thompson, in his book *The Congruent Life: Following the Inward Path to Fulfilling Work and Inspired Leadership*, traces how the Great Divorce came to be, pointing out how work evolved from Luther's concept of vocation (sacred calling) to the secularized, post-Enlightenment view of work as the "individual advancement and material success of the person"; that is, "as a means to fulfill narrowly personal ends."[79] Both Adam Smith and Karl Marx saw the "alienating nature of work," but Smith, unlike Marx, viewed it as worth the price.[80] As Thompson notes, "work lost its human dignity in exchange for its usefulness."[81] One might say in the extreme, the modern worker sells his or her soul five days a week in order to buy it back on the weekend.

Although Thompson recognizes that certain types of work have "greater *potential* than others for personal meaningfulness"[82]—"larger hooks than others on which to hang our deepest values"[83]—he believes that it is essentially the *individual's* challenge to give work meaning and purpose. Some of these meanings, Thompson points out, can be found by seeing work as the opportunity for personal growth, as the "raw material for our own self-construction"[84] or as what Maslow called *self-actualization*.[85] Meaning also comes from seeing work as service, the pursuit of higher principles captured in words such as "*humanity, justice, society, higher good,* or *ultimate values*."[86] Meaning also derives, at least for some, in the distinction between *career* and *vocation*—linking one's work to some ultimate or larger community.[87] The process of finding this meaning, Thompson argues, is "personal and internal. It is unique and subjective to each meaning-maker and relies more on the workings of the inner world than on the logic and influence of the external order. Meaningfulness is in the eye—or more accurately the heart—of the beholder."[88] For Thompson, then, *human spirituality* is defined as "the way in which people connect the activities of their daily lives with their wellsprings of deepest meaning."[89]

The meaning in one's work comes both from the satisfaction in the concrete achievements of organizational accomplishment and from orchestrating the process of collaborative interaction in an effective and aesthetically pleasing way. The meaning found in or brought to one's work, needs to be balanced, of course, with the other sources of meaning in one's life. Striking the right balance is not always easy, especially when work itself is not just demanding but also meaningful.

REFLECTION

Is your work intrinsically meaningful? If not, is it possible to see your work in a larger context that helps it to become more meaningful? What wellsprings of meaning give purpose to your work? What other sources of meaning enrich your life? Does the balance feel right?

Leadership is probably not sustainable over a long period of time without at least some positive sense of transcendent purpose. Perhaps the most important source of self-renewal for leaders is the habit of the heart that finds in one's work a larger purpose and persistent satisfaction.

What is the larger purpose of higher education? Some would call it *pushing back the frontiers of knowledge*. Others would say it is *promoting student development* or *facilitating inquiry*. Perhaps one might describe it simply as *eradicating ignorance*. Those who provide leadership for colleges and universities have a tough job, but who would deny the value of such an elevating mission? Perhaps the activity actually justifies all the effort that goes into getting organized, coping with stress, maintaining emotional balance, and keeping up to date. Is it not an enterprise worth learning to lead?

MARY'S MENTOR

Mary's mentor wants her to remember these things about perpetual learning and personal renewal:

- Some people are victims of chaos; others create it.
- Chaos can be related to time, memory, communication, information, or projects, and methods exist for dealing with each type.

- Disorganized leaders pay a price in what they can achieve and how they are perceived.

- Stressors create strains that accumulate over time and produce generalized stress, often because the chain of causation from effort to outcome has been upset.

- Some stress arises from a misalignment between the person and the job.

- Burnout is the opposite of engagement, and its warning signs are emotional exhaustion, depersonalization, and a reduced sense of accomplishment.

- Intense and prolonged criticism can make leaders anxious, but excessive adulation can produce acquired narcissism.

- Leaders cultivate emotional intelligence.

- Busy administrators develop a plan for continuing their education by focusing their learning on specific needs.

- Leaders identify and participate in professional associations.

- Reflective-practitioners engage in dialogue with mentors or peers.

- The work of leaders is best sustained over time through some broader purpose or sense of meaning.

- There is more to life than work.

NOTES

1. Harriet Schecter, *Conquering Chaos at Work: Strategies for Managing Disorganization and the People Who Cause It* (New York: Simon & Schuster, 2000).

2. Ibid., p. 30.

3. Ibid., pp. 57–58.

4. Ibid., p. 54.

5. Ibid., p. 60.

6. Ibid., pp. 70–73.

7. Ibid., pp. 71–72.

8. Ibid., pp. 79–90.

9. Ibid., pp. 91–109.

10. Ibid., p. 114.

11. Ibid., p. 134.

12. Ibid., p. 140–151.

13. Alan Lakein, *How to Get Control of Your Time and Your Life* (New York: New American Library, 1973).

14. Ibid., pp.18–20.

15. Ibid., pp. 25–28.

16. Ibid., p. 28.

17. Ibid., pp. 48–49.

18. Ibid., p. 52.

19. Ibid., p. 64.

20. Ibid., p. 71.

21. Ibid., pp. 73–74.

22. Ibid., p. 96.

23. Ibid., pp. 100–103.

24. Jack D. Ferner, *Successful Time Management: A Self-Teaching Guide*, 2nd ed. (New York: John Wiley & Sons, 1995), p. 11.

25. G. Lynne Snead and Joyce Wycoff, *To Do . . . Doing . . . Done! A Creative Approach to Managing Projects and Effectively Finishing What Matters Most* (New York: Simon & Schuster, 1997).

26. Ibid., pp. 92–110.

27. Walter B. Cannon, *Bodily Changes in Pain, Hunger, Fear and Rage* (New York: D. Appleton Century, 1929).

28. Hans Selye, *Stress in Health and Disease* (Boston: Butterworth, 1976).

29. Cary L. Cooper, ed., *Theories of Organizational Stress* (New York: Oxford University Press, 1998).

30. Terry Behr, "An Organizational Psychology Meta-Model of Occupational Stress," in Cooper, *Theories of Organizational Stress*, p. 6.

31. Ibid., p. 10.

32. Ibid.

33. Ibid., p. 11.

34. Ibid., p. 20.

35. Ibid., p. 22.

36. Jeffrey R. Edwards, Robert D. Caplan, and R. Van Harrison, "Person-Environment Fit Theory: Conceptual Foundations, Empirical Evidence, and Directions for Future Research," in Cooper, *Theories of Organizational Stress*.

37. Ibid., p. 28.

38. Ibid., p. 29.

39. Ibid., p. 30.

40. Ibid.

41. Ibid., pp. 30–31.

42. Ibid., p. 32.

43. Ibid., p. 53.

44. Ibid., p. 51.

45. Christina Maslach, "A Multidimensional Theory of Burnout," in Cooper, *Theories of Organizational Stress*.

46. Ibid., p. 68.

47. Ibid.

48. Ibid., p. 69.

49. Ibid., p. 73.

50. Ibid.

51. Ibid., pp. 75–76.

52. Ibid., p. 81.

53. Peter Block, *Stewardship: Choosing Service Over Self-Interest* (San Francisco: Berrett-Koehler, 1993), p. 221.

54. Ibid., pp. 222–223.

55. Ibid., pp. 224–225.

56. Ibid., p. 226.

57. Robert Millman's concept of *acquired, situational narcissism* was described and cited in "The Year in Ideas," *New York Times Magazine*, December 9, 2001, Section 6, p. 50.

58. Daniel Goleman, *Emotional Intelligence* (New York: Bantam Books, 1995), p. 28.

59. Ibid., p. 34.

60. Ibid., p. 43.

61. Daniel Goleman, *Working with Emotional Intelligence* (New York: Bantam Books, 2000), pp. 26–27.

62. Ibid., p. 54.

63. Ibid., pp. 61–62.

64. Ibid., p. 68.

65. James R. Davis and Adelaide B. Davis, *Managing Your Own Learning* (San Francisco: Berrett-Koehler, 2000), pp. 11–21.

66. Rudolph H. Weingartner *Undergraduate Education: Goals and Means* (Phoenix, AZ: American Council on Education and The Oryx Press, 1993). The concept of *proficiencies*, *conversancies*, and *specialties* is taken from this work and is used in the schema developed here called *gap analysis* by Davis and Davis.

67. Donald A. Schön, *The Reflective Practitioner* (New York: Basic Books, 1983), p. 50.

68. Chip Bell, *Managers as Mentors: Building Partnerships for Learning* (San Francisco: Berrett-Koehler, 1996), p. 7.

69. Ibid.

70. Ibid., p. 8.

71. Laurent Daloz, *Mentors: Guiding the Journey of Adult Learners* (San Francisco: Jossey-Bass, 1999), p. 17.

72. G. Roche, "Much Ado About Mentors," *Harvard Business Review* 20 (1979), pp. 14–28; A. K. Missirian, *The Corporate Connection: Why Executive Women Need Mentors to Reach the Top* (Upper Saddle River, NJ: Prentice-Hall, 1982); L. Phillips-Jones, *Mentors and Protégés* (New York: Arbor House, 1982); M. Murray, *Beyond the Myths and Magic of Mentoring* (San Francisco: Jossey-Bass, 1991); F. G. Shea, *Mentoring: Helping Employees Reach Their Full Potential* (New York: AMACOM, 1994); M. N. Maack and J. Passet, *Aspirations and Mentoring in an Academic Environment* (Westport, CT: Greenwood Press, 1994); and M. A. Wunsch, *Mentoring Revisited: Making an Impact on Individuals and Institutions* (San Francisco: Jossey-Bass, 1994). Cited in Daloz, *Mentors*.

73. Daloz, *Mentors*, p. 21.

74. Ibid., p. 18.

75. Ibid., p. 20.

76. Carl Rogers, *On Encounter Groups* (New York: Harper & Row, 1970), p. 9.

77. See the chapter notes and "further readings" in C. Michael Thompson, *The Congruent Life: Following the Inward Path to Fulfilling Work and Inspired Leadership* (San Francisco: Jossey-Bass, 2000) for more than twenty such works published in the 1990s. Exemplary books listed there include: L. Ryken, *Redeeming the Time: A Christian Approach to Work and Leisure* (Grand Rapids, MI: Baker Books, 1995); M. Fox, *The Reinvention of Work: A New Vision of Livelihood for Our Time* (San Francisco: Harper, 1995); R.W. Gillett, *The Human Enterprise: A Christian Perspective on Work* (Kansas City: Sheed and Ward, 1985); J.C. Haughey, *Converting Nine to Five: A Spirituality of Daily Work* (New York: Crossroad, 1989); G.F. Pierce, ed., *Of Human Hands: A Reader in the Spirituality of Work* (Chicago: ACTA Publications, 1991); M. Volf, *Work in the Spirit: Toward a Theology of Work* (New York: Oxford University Press, 1991); P. Block, *Stewardship: Choosing Service over Self-Interest* (San Francisco: Berrett-Koehler, 1993); G. Fairholm, *Capturing the Heart of Leadership: Spirituality and Community in the New American Workplace* (Westport, CT: Praeger, 1997).

78. Ibid., p. 15.

79. Ibid., p. 20.

80. Ibid., p. 21.

81. Ibid.

82. Ibid., p. 31.

83. Ibid., p. 32.

84. Ibid., p. 36.

85. Ibid., p. 37.

86. Ibid., p. 39.

87. Ibid., p. 40.

88. Ibid., p. 51.

89. Ibid., p. 52.

APPENDIX
Directory of Resources

T his concise directory has been developed to provide busy administrators with a selected list of organizations, journals, magazines, and newspapers that will be useful to support continuing learning. The goal has been to be selective, rather than all-inclusive, with the hope that the lists assembled here provide the most important resources needed. International associations or publications are not included. The huge number and variety of existing organizations makes the selection process difficult, and unintentional omissions may have occurred.

ASSOCIATIONS

The associations listed here are those related to the administration of colleges and universities generally or to a particular aspect of administration. Academic disciplinary or professional associations have intentionally been excluded. The purpose of the organization is usually self-evident from its name, but in cases where this is not so, a brief description has been included in brackets directly below the name of the organization. Please note that addresses, phone numbers, and Web sites change frequently; entries that were correct at the time of publication may no longer be so.

American Association for Adult
and Continuing Education
(AAACE)
4380 Forbes Boulevard
Lanham, MD 20706
301.918.1913
301.918.1846 (fax)
www.aaace.org

American Association for Higher
Education (AAHE)
One Dupont Circle, Suite 360
Washington, DC 20036
202.293.6440
202.293.0073 (fax)
www.aahe.org

American Association of Collegiate
Registrars and Admissions
Officers (AACRAO)
One Dupont Circle, NW, Suite 520
Washington, DC 20036
202.293.9161
202.872.8857 (fax)
www.aacrao.org

American Association of Community Colleges (AACC)
One Dupont Circle, NW, Suite 410
Washington, DC 20036
202.728.0200
202.833.2467 (fax)
www.aacc.nche.edu

American Association of State
Colleges and Universities
(AASCU)
1307 New York Avenue, NW, 5th
Floor
Washington, DC 20005
202.293.7070
202.296.5819 (fax)
www.aascu.org

American Association of University
Administrators (AAUA)
2602 Rutford Avenue
Richardson, TX 75080
972.248.3957
972.713.8209 (fax)
www.aaua.org

American Association of University
Professors (AAUP)
1012 Fourteenth Street, NW, Suite
500
Washington, DC 20005
202.737.5900
202.737.5526 (fax)
www.aaup.org

American Association of University
Women (AAUW)
1111 Sixteenth Street, NW
Washington, DC 20036
800.326.AAUW
202.872.1425 (fax)
www.aauw.org

American College Health Association (ACHA)
PO Box 28937
Baltimore, MD 21240
410.859.1500
410.859.1510 (fax)
www.acha.org

American College Personnel
Association (ACPA)
One Dupont Circle, NW, Suite 300
Washington, DC 20036
202.835.2272
202.296.3286 (fax)
www.acpa.nche.edu

American Conference of Academic
  Deans (ACAD)
1818 R Street, NW
Washington, DC 20009
202.387.3760
202.265.9532 (fax)
www.acad-edu.org

American Council on Education
  (ACE)
One Dupont Circle, NW
Washington, DC 20036
202.939.9300
202.833.4760 (fax)
www.acenet.edu

American Educational Research
  Association (AERA)
1230 Seventeenth Street, NW
Washington, DC 20036
202.223.9485
202.775.1825 (fax)
www.aera.net

American Indian Higher Education
  Consortium (AIHEC)
121 Oronoco Street
Alexandria, VA 22314
703.838.0400
703.838.0388 (fax)
www.aihec.org

American Library Association
  (ALA)
50 East Huron
Chicago, IL 60611
800.545.2433
312.440.9374 (fax)
www.ala.org

American Society for Training and
  Development (ASTD)
1640 King Street, Box 1443
Alexandria, VA 22313
800.628.2783
703.683.1523 (fax)
www.astd.org

Association for Higher Education
  and Disability (AHEAD)
University of Massachusetts, Boston
100 Morrissey Boulevard
Boston, MA 02125
617.287.3880
617.287.3881 (fax)
617.287.3882 (hearing impaired)
www.ahead.org

Association for Institutional
  Research (AIR)
114 Stone Building, Florida State
  University
Tallahassee, FL 32306
850.644.4470
850.644.8824 (fax)
airweb.org

Association for the Study of Higher
  Education (ASHE)
202 Hill Hall
Columbia, MO 65211
573.882.9645
573.884.2197 (fax)
www.ashe.missouri.edu

Association of American Colleges
  and Universities (AAC&U)
1818 R Street, NW
Washington, DC 20009
202.387.3760
202.265.9532 (fax)
www.aacu-edu.org

Association of American Universities
  (AAU)
1200 New York Avenue, NW, Suite
  550
Washington, DC 20005
202.408.7500
202.408.8184 (fax)
www.aau.edu

Association of College and University
  Housing Officers—International
  (ACUHO-I)
941 Chatham Lane, Suite 318
Columbus, OH 43221
614.292.0099
614.292.3205 (fax)
www.acuho-i.org

Association of College Unions
  International (ACUI)
One City Centre, Suite 200
120 West Seventh Street
Bloomington, IN 47404
812.855.8550
812.855.0162 (fax)
acuiweb.org

Association of Governing Boards of
  Universities and Colleges (AGB)
One Dupont Circle, Suite 400
Washington, DC 20036
202.296.8400
202.223.7053 (fax)
www.agb.org

Association of Research Libraries
  (ARL)
21 Dupont Circle
Washington, DC 20036
202.296.2296
202.872.0884 (fax)
www.arl.org

Campus Compact [association for
  community service in higher
  education]
Brown University, Box 1975
Providence, RI 02912
401.863.1119
401.863.3779 (fax)
www.compact.org

College and University Professional
  Association for Human Resources
  (CUPA-HR)
1233 20th Street, NW, Suite 301
Washington, DC 20036
202.429.0311
202.429.0149 (fax)
www.cupahr.org

Council for Adult and Experiential
  Learning (CAEL)
55 East Monroe Street, Suite 1930
Chicago, IL 60603
312.499.2600
312.499.2601 (fax)
www.cael.org

Council for Advancement and
  Support of Education (CASE)
  [association for alumni relations,
  communications, and develop-
  ment]
1307 New York Avenue, NW, Suite
  1000
Washington, DC 20005
202.328.2273
202.387.4973 (fax)
www.case.org

Council of Colleges of Arts and
  Sciences (CCAS)
PO Box 873108
Tempe, AZ 85287
480.727.6064
480.727.6078 (fax)
www.ccas.net

Council of Graduate Schools (CGS)
One Dupont Circle, NW, Suite 430
Washington, DC 20036
202.223.3791
202.331.7157 (fax)
www.cgsnet.org

Council of Independent Colleges
(CIC)
One Dupont Circle, NW, Suite 320
Washington, DC 20036
202.466.7230
202.466.7238 (fax)
www.cic.org

Council on Governmental Relations
(COGR)
1200 New York Avenue, NW, Suite
320
Washington, DC 20005
202.289.6655
202.289.6698 (fax)
www.cogr.edu

EDUCAUSE [association for the
support of information technology in higher education]
4772 Walnut Street, Suite 206
Boulder, CO 80301
303.449.4430
303.440.0461 (fax)
www.educause.edu

Hispanic Association of Colleges
and Universities (HACU)
8415 Datapoint Drive, Suite 400
San Antonio, TX 78229
210.692.3805
210.692.0823 (fax)
www.hacu.net

Institute of International Education
(IIE)
809 United Nations Plaza
New York, NY 10017
212.984.5375
212.984.5358 (fax)
www.iie.org

International Association of
Campus Law Enforcement
Administrators (IACLEA)
342 North Main Street
West Hartford, CT 06117
860.586.7517
860.586.7550 (fax)
www.iaclea.org

NAFSA: Association of International Educators
1307 New York Avenue, NW, 8th
Floor
Washington, DC 20005
202.737.3699
202.737.3657 (fax)
www.nafsa.org

National Academic Advising
Association (NACADA)
Kansas State University
2323 Anderson Avenue, Suite 225
Manhattan, KS 66502
785.532.5717
785.532.7732 (fax)
www.nacada.ksu.edu

National Association for Equal
Opportunity in Higher Education
(NAFEO)
8701 Georgia Avenue, Suite 200
Silver Spring, MD 20910
301.650.2440
301.495.3306 (fax)
www.nafeo.org

National Association of College
and University Attorneys
(NACUA)
One Dupont Circle, Suite 620
Washington, DC 20036
202.833.8390
202.296.8379 (fax)
www.nacua.org

National Association of College
and University Business Officers
(NACUBO)
2501 M Street, NW, Suite 400
Washington, DC 20037
202.861.2500
202.861.2583 (fax)
www.nacubo.org

National Association of College
and University Food Services
(NACUFS)
1405 South Harrison Road, Suite 305
Manly Miles Building, MSU
East Lansing, MI 48824
517.332.2494
517.332.8144 (fax)
www.nacufs.org

National Association of Colleges
and Employers (NACE) [associa-
tion for career services and
placement]
62 Highland Avenue
Bethlehem, PA 18017
800.544.5272
610.868.0208 (fax)
www.naceweb.org

National Association of Educational
Buyers, Inc. (NAEB)
450 Wireless Boulevard
Hauppauge, NY 11788
631.273.2600
631.952.3660 (fax)
www.naeb.org

National Association of Independent
Colleges and Universities (NAICU)
1025 Connecticut Avenue, NW,
Suite 700
Washington, DC 20036
202.785.8866
202.835.0003 (fax)
www.naicu.edu

National Association of Inter-
collegiate Athletics (NAIA)
23500 West 105th Street
PO Box 1325
Olathe, KS 66051
913.791.0044
913.791.9555 (fax)
www.naia.org

National Association of State
Universities and Land-Grant
Colleges (NASULGC)
1307 New York Avenue, NW, Suite
400
Washington, DC 20005
202.478.6040
202.478.6046 (fax)
www.nasulgc.org

National Association of Student
Financial Aid Administrators
(NASFAA)
1129 20th Street, NW, Suite 400
Washington, DC 20036
202.785.0453
202.785.1487 (fax)
www.nasfaa.org

National Association of Student
Personnel Administrators
(NASPA)
1875 Connecticut Avenue, NW,
Suite 418
Washington, DC 20009
202.265.7500
202.797.1157 (fax)
www.naspa.org

National Association of System Heads
(NASH) [association for chief executive officers for state systems]
1725 K Street, NW, Suite 200
Washington, DC 20006
202.887.0614
202.293.2605 (fax)
www.nashonline.org

National Collegiate Athletic
Association (NCAA)
PO Box 6222
Indianapolis, IN 46206
317.917.6222
317.917.6888 (fax)
www.ncaa.org

National Collegiate Honors
Council (NCHC)
Radford University, Box 7017
Radford, VA 24142
540.831.6100
540.831.5004 (fax)
www.runet.edu/~nchc/

National Commission for Cooperative Education
360 Huntington Avenue, 384CP
Boston, MA 02115-5096
617.373.3770
617.373.3463 (fax)
www.co-op.edu

National Council of University
Research Administrators
(NCURA)
One Dupont Circle, NW, Suite 220
Washington, DC 20036
202.466.3894
202.223.5573 (fax)
www.ncura.edu

National Orientation Directors
Association (NODA)
Washington State University,
Office of New Student Programs
PO Box 641070
Pullman, WA 99164
509.335.6459
509.335.2078 (fax)
www.nodaweb.org

North American Association of
Summer Sessions (NAASS)
43 Belanger Drive
Dover, NH 03820
603.740.9880
www.naass.org

Society for College and University
Planning (SCUP)
311 Maynard Street
Ann Arbor, MI 48104
734.998.7832
734.998.6532 (fax)
www.scup.org

State Higher Education Executive
Officers (SHEEO)
700 Broadway, Suite 1200
Denver, CO 80203
303.299.3685
303.296.9016 (fax)
www.sheeo.org

United Negro College Fund (UNCF)
8260 Willow Oaks
Corporate Drive
Fairfax, VA 22031
703.205.3400
703.205.3550 (fax)
www.uncf.org

United States Distance Learning
Association (USDLA)
140 Gould Street, Suite 200B
Needham, MA 02494
800.275.5162
781.453.2389 (fax)
www.usdla.org

University Continuing Education
Association (UCEA)
One Dupont Circle, NW, Suite 615
Washington, DC 20036
202.659.3130
202.785.0374 (fax)
www.ucea.edu

Washington Higher Education
  Secretariat (WHES) [forum for
  higher education associations]
One Dupont Circle, NW, Suite 800
Washington, DC 20036
202.939.9410
202.833.4760 (fax)
www.whes.org

Women's College Coalition
125 Michigan Avenue, NE
Washington, DC 20017
202.234.0443
202.234.0445 (fax)
www.womenscolleges.org

JOURNALS

More than forty journals in the field of higher education are currently
available, including several published outside of the United States. Many
of these journals contain articles on specialized aspects of higher education. Because administrators have limited time for continuing study,
eleven journals have been selected from the longer list that are likely to
be of most immediate use to leaders for keeping well-informed generally
about research on current issues and major trends in higher education.

ASHE-ERIC Report Series
Jossey-Bass
989 Market Street
San Francisco, CA 94103
800.956.7739
800.605.2665 (fax)
www.eriche.org/publications/
  asheeric.html

College and University
AACRAO Distribution Center
PO Box 231
Annapolis Junction, MD 20701
301.490.7651 (to order)
202.293.9161 (for questions)
301.206.9789 (fax)
www.aacrao.org/publications/candu/
  index.htm

Higher Education Policy [Interna-
  tional Association of Universities
  journal]
Elsevier Science
Customer Service Department
PO Box 945
New York, NY 10159
888.437.4636
212.633.3680 (fax)
www.unesco.org/iau/hep.html

Journal of College Student Development
ACPA
One Dupont Circle, NW, Suite 300
Washington, DC 20036
202.835.2272
202.296.3286 (fax)
www.jcsd.appstate.edu

Journal of General Education
USB-1, Suite C
820 North University Drive
University Park, PA 16802
814.865.1327
814.863.1408 (fax)
www.psupress.org/journals/jnls_jge.html

Journal of Higher Education
Ohio State University Press
Chicago Distribution Center
11030 South Langley Avenue
Chicago, IL 60628
773.568.1550
800.621.8476 (fax)
www.ohiostatepress.org/journals/
  jhemain.htm

Journal of Higher Education Policy
  and Management
Taylor & Francis
325 Chestnut Street, Suite 800
Philadelphia, PA 19106
800.354.1420
215.625.8914 (fax)
www.tandf.co.uk/journals/carfax/
  1360080X.html

Liberal Education
AAC&U
1818 R Street, NW
Washington, DC 20009
800.297.3775
202.265.9532 (fax)
www.aacu-edu.org/liberaleducation/
  index.cfm

NASPA Journal
NASPA Publications Department
PO Box 753
Waldorf, MD 20604
301.638.1749
301.843.0159 (fax)
www.naspa.org/publications/journal/
  index.cfm

Research in Higher Education
Kluwer Academic Publishers
Journals Department
101 Philip Drive, Assinippi Park
Norwell, MA 02061
781.871.6600
781.681.9045 (fax)
airweb.org/publications/rhe.htm

Review of Higher Education [ASHE
  journal]
The Johns Hopkins University Press
PO Box 19966
Baltimore, MD 21211
800.548.1784
410.516.6968 (fax)
www.press.jhu.edu/press/journals/
  rhe/rhe.html

MAGAZINES AND NEWSPAPERS

In addition to the more formal outlets for scholarly research found in journals, several periodicals take the form of magazines or newspapers. Eight have been selected as especially important for leaders.

About Campus: Enriching the Student
  Learning Experience
ACPA
One Dupont Circle, NW, Suite 300
Washington, DC 20036
202.835.2272
202.296.3286 (fax)
www.acpa.nche.edu/pubs/public.htm

Academe [AAUP's bimonthly
  magazine about news affecting
  professors]
1012 Fourteenth Street, NW, Suite
  500
Washington, DC 20005
800.424.2973 x3012
202.737.5526
www.aaup.org/publications/Academe/
  index.htm

*American Association for Higher
   Education Bulletin*
AAHE Publications
PO Box 1932
Merrifield, VA 22116
202.293.6440
202.293.0073 (fax)
www.aahe.org/bulletin

Change
AAHE Publications
PO Box 1932
Merrifield, VA 22116
202.293.6440 x778
202.293.0073 (fax)
www.aahe.org/change

Chronicle of Higher Education
1255 Twenty-Third Street, NW
Washington, DC 20037
800.728.2803
202.223.6292 (fax)
chronicle.com

Chronicle of Philanthropy
1255 Twenty-Third Street, NW
Washington, DC 20037
800.842.7817
202.223.6292 (fax)
philanthropy.com

Education Week.
6935 Arlington Road, Suite 100
Bethesda, MD 20814
800.728.2790
740.389.6720 (fax)
www.edweek.org

Higher Education and National Affairs
ACE
One Dupont Circle, NW
Washington DC, 20036
202.939.9300
202.833.4760 (fax)
www.acenet.edu/hena

The Presidency
ACE
One Dupont Circle, NW
Washington DC, 20036
202.939.9300
202.833.4760 (fax)
www.acenet.edu

WEB SITES

Certain Web sites are particularly useful to leaders as they continue to learn about postsecondary education. Several of these are listed here, among a growing number now available. Government agencies or independent organizations and compacts usually maintain these sites. Web sites change and may take on different interests, purposes, or even names over time. These are current Web sites at the time of printing.

American Educational Research Association
www.aera.org
   Encourages scholarly inquiry related to education and promotes dissemination and practical application of research results.

College Board
www.collegeboard.com

The College Board is an association of schools, colleges, universities, and other educational organizations in the United States and abroad. Facilitates access to higher education and promotes high academic standards through programs and services in college admissions, guidance, financial aid, assessment, and teaching and learning.

Education Commission of the States
www.ecs.org

Helps state leaders shape education policy. Provides policy makers with up-to-date information and results of studies on key policy issues. Maintains a comprehensive list of links to federal agencies and other national and regional research centers and organizations.

Educational Resources Information Center (ERIC)
www.eric.ed.gov

A federally funded national information system that provides a variety of services and products on a broad range of education-related issues. Especially useful for unpublished as well as published articles on higher education. Requires library access.

National Center for Education Statistics (NCES)
www.nces.ed.gov

A U.S. Department of Education agency that maintains a comprehensive statistical database providing detailed information on all levels of education. Note especially the Integrated Postsecondary Education Data System (IPEDS) resources on enrollment, faculty and staff, libraries, institutional characteristics, and state profiles.

National Center for Higher Education Management Systems (NCHEMS)
www.nchems.org

A private not-for-profit organization whose mission is to assist colleges and universities as they improve their management capability.

National Center for Postsecondary Improvement
www.stanford.edu/group/ncpi

A collaborative research venture of Stanford University, the University of Pennsylvania, and the University of Michigan whose quest is to link research with policy and practice in American higher education.

National Postsecondary Education Cooperative
www.nces.ed.gov/npec

Established in 1994 by the National Center for Education Statistics to identify and communicate emerging issues and to support comparability and utility of data in policy development. Composed of many participating organizations representing various aspects of postsecondary education.

Pew Forum on Undergraduate Learning
www.pewundergradforum.org

Supported by the Pew Charitable Trusts, the Pew Forum aims to encourage and enable colleges and universities to take responsibility for helping their undergraduates attain demonstrable learning outcomes and to strengthen the incentives for doing so by making what colleges contribute to undergraduate learning an important factor in the decisions of the marketplace, the policies of the state and federal governments, and the processes of academic peer review.

State Higher Education Executive Officers
www.sheeo.org

A not-for-profit, nationwide association of the chief executive officers serving state coordinating and governing boards for postsecondary education.

U.S. Department of Education
www.ed.gov

Provides information about the federal government activities affecting education, including postsecondary issues and services. Includes a link to *www.students.gov*, a guide for students and parents on college selection and financial aid, career development, community service, military service, travel, and study abroad. Also maintains Education Resource Organizations Directory (EROD) of more than 2,700 national regional, and state education organizations.

Western Interstate Commission for Higher Education
www.wiche.edu

One of four regional compacts of states that work collaboratively to serve the interests of intuitions in various regions of the country. Provides useful data, studies, and links to other organizations. The other regional compacts are:

Midwestern Higher Education Commission
www.mhec.org

New England Board of Higher Education
www.nebhe.org

Southern Regional Education Board
www.sreb.org

INDEX

About the Author

JAMES R. DAVIS, Ph.D., is Dean of University College, University of Denver. He was formerly Professor of Higher Education and Adult Studies at the University of Denver. He has also held various administrative posts at the university, including assistant to the provost, director of the School of Education, and associate vice chancellor for academic affairs. Early in his career he served as academic dean at Wilberforce University. He holds degrees from Oberlin College and Yale University, and a Ph.D. in Higher Education Administration from Michigan State University. Dr. Davis is the author of two other books in the ACE/Praeger Series on Higher Education: *Better Teaching, More Learning* (1993) and *Interdisciplinary Courses and Team Teaching* (1995). As time permits, he also leads workshops and provides consulting and facilitation.